INTERNATIONAL CODE OF SIGNALS

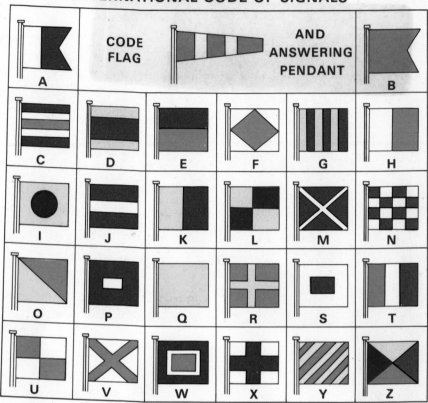

CODE FLAG

AND ANSWERING PENDANT

NUMERAL PENDANTS

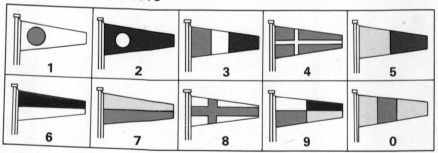

SUBSTITUTES

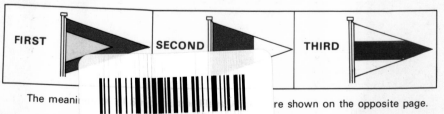

FIRST SECOND THIRD

The meani[...] re shown on the opposite page.

MODERN SMALL BOAT SAILING

MODERN
SMALL BOAT
SAILING

John Hart

LONDON
G. BELL & SONS, LTD.
1973

© 1973 John M. Hart

Published by G. Bell and Sons Ltd.
York House, Portugal Street, London, WC2A 2HL

ISBN 0 7135 1754 9

Printed in Great Britain by
Fletcher & Son Ltd, Norwich

Contents

List of Illustrations

Preface

My primary aim throughout this book has been to give advice based on sound seamanship. As a secondary aim I have tried to be up-to-date, covering subjects which other books have sometimes neglected: including for example, a chapter on 'Survival'.

This book is for beginners to sailing; for those requiring a 'refresher' course which will bring them up-to-date with current techniques and information; and also perhaps for more experienced sailors whose knowledge of certain aspects of sailing may be sketchy.

Part I is intended to be read by the novice before going afloat for the first time; Part II will be largely for reference when specific information is required at the intermediate stage; and Part III is to be read whenever the intermediate helmsman feels that he or she is ready to progress to another level of sailing experience.

I do not believe that anyone can learn to sail entirely from a book. Some practical instruction, however informal, is essential. It should be as thorough as possible and preferably based on a formal syllabus to ensure that no gaps in knowledge are left. In January 1972 a new National Proficiency Scheme was introduced by the Royal Yachting Association and the National Schools Sailing Association. The contents of this book are tied quite closely to the syllabus of that scheme and will therefore also serve as a handbook for those wishing to qualify for any of the R.Y.A. certificates.

Full details of the National Proficiency Scheme, the International Regulations for Prevention of Collision at Sea and the Single Letter Signals of the International Code are all included, together with a Glossary of Sailing Terms and a comprehensive Index. I hope, therefore, that this book will serve as a complete manual for all who seek enjoyment in small sailing boats.

I have included some information about racing and cruising in

Chapter Twelve, but I have not set out to cover these subjects in any detail; my purpose has been simply to introduce the newcomer to these aspects of the sport at an elementary level.

Because sailing covers such a wide sphere, I have limited myself throughout the book to dinghies and dayboat types up to about eighteen feet in length, although references to larger craft have sometimes been made where it seemed desirable, particularly in the final chapter.

JOHN HART

ONE

Boats for sailing

Historic

Sailing boats have been used as a means of transport for many centuries and it is somewhat surprising that, in Europe at least, they took so long to develop their present efficient rig. The old square-riggers with their sails set across the boat were very inefficient by present-day standards, unable to sail even at right angles to the wind. Also they made leeway (slipped sideways) at such a rate that a captain would normally prefer to spend weeks waiting for a favourable wind. It was not until quite recent times that sails were rigged 'fore-and-aft' along the boat, and keels deepened to prevent excessive leeway. This was a great breakthrough: fore-and-aft rig enabled boats to sail with the wind coming from ahead of the beam, and triangular sails improved still further the windward performance of a vessel.

Once the efficiency of the fore-and-aft rig had been appreciated, refinements began to appear, and almost all modifications in recent years have been towards producing boats which would sail closer to the wind, and faster. These refinements are dealt with in some detail in Chapter Twelve.

In the Western world we have reached the point in the history of sailing where square sails, rigged across the boat, have almost disappeared. There are still some special situations where a square rig can be seen, such as in sail training ships. Generally, though, the change to fore-and-aft rig and triangular sails is almost complete, certainly in the pleasure sailing world. In referring to 'square' sails I am thinking of sails which set across the boat. These must not be confused with four-sided sails which set fore and aft, such as a gunter mainsail, as used on a Mirror dinghy.

Types

While I shall sometimes refer to larger boats, this book, particularly Part I, will mainly consider dinghies; that is the group of smaller sailing boats up to about eighteen feet. Let us look at some of the popular types or 'classes'.

Those with most prestige are the International classes. These are classes which have flourished under the auspices of the International Yacht Racing Union, the I.Y.R.U. for short, largely resulting from Olympic competition and development on an international scale.

The International Classes are:

The Twelve Metre	Fourteen-Foot Dinghy
Eight-Metre Cruiser Racer	Cadet
Six Metre	Finn
Five Point Five Metre	Five-O-Five
Dragon	Flying Dutchman
Soling	Lightning
Tempest	International Moth
Contender	Snipe
Four Seventy	Star
Enterprise	Twelve Square Metre Sharpie
Fireball	Vaurien
Flying Junior	2-man Dinghy
Four Twenty	
Optimist	

and three catamaran classes:

C Class	Australis
Tornado	

Of these the following are raced in the Olympic Games:

470	Soling
Tornado catamaran	Flying Dutchman
Tempest	Finn

Of these international classes, the ones which are liked most in the United Kingdom are the Dragon, the popularity of which is probably waning as they are a rather expensive boat; the Soling, a recent selection for the Olympics, a modern boat produced in G.R.P. (glass reinforced plastic); the Enterprise, with over twenty thousand sail numbers, almost exclusively British, certainly one of Britain's most popular classes; the Fireball, very fast and 'hairy' and deservedly a favourite of the younger helmsman; the Fourteen-Foot Dinghy, the Cadet, the Five-O-Five and the Flying Dutchman. These last four have a special place in sailing in this country. In some ways the International Fourteen is the purest traditional dinghy, being an open boat and requiring a lot of expertise. One of the premier events of the sailing year is the National Championship of this class when top helmsmen compete for the Prince of Wales Trophy.

The Cadet has a large following of young folk; it is an ideal trainer for the not-so-large and many of our top racing helmsmen started their days in a Cadet. The Five-O-Five and the Flying Dutchman are old rivals and while the F.D. is at present in the Olympics the 'Five-O' is constantly pressing its claims for selection. The F.D. is 'queen' of the dinghy racing scene. At just under twenty feet length, it is almost out of the dinghy class. Nevertheless, it can correctly be described as a dinghy.

Of the catamarans, the 'C' class is too expensive to ever be popular, but the Tornado is growing in numbers and should have a great future now that it has been selected as the sixth Olympic class.

Next we come to the National classes. These are the boats which have been given National status by the governing body of sailing in the U.K., the Royal Yachting Association, which also administers these classes.

The National Classes are:

Albacore	Redwing
Eighteen Footer	Scorpion
Firefly	Shearwater Catamaran
Flying Fifteen	Solo
Graduate	Swallow
Hornet	Swordfish
Merlin Rocket	Twelve Foot Dinghy
Osprey	Squib

Of these the most popular are the Albacore, Firefly, Flying Fifteen, Graduate, Hornet, Merlin Rocket, Shearwater Catamaran, Solo and Twelve Foot Dinghy, all of which are sailed throughout the country.

There are many other classes with large numbers of boats. Although they do not have the prestige of the international or national classes, they often have more to recommend them to the average man, particularly their price. In this group are the Cherub, the G.P. Fourteen, the Lark, the Mirror, the British Moth, the O.K., the Unicorn Catamaran, the Wayfarer and the Yachting World Fourteen-Foot Day boat. The G.P. Fourteen and Wayfarer are widely used for instruction and general purpose sailing, and the Mirror, with over twenty-five thousand sail numbers, is possibly the most popular British dinghy; it is also one of the cheapest.

The newcomer to sailing will begin now to realize what a large choice of boats he has. I will help with choosing a boat later in this chapter by a process involving elimination and common sense.

The history of the development of all these classes within the last century would make fascinating reading; it would also run into several volumes. It will suffice to summarize in the following form.

Craft have tended to fall into one of three categories:

1   The stolid, day-cruising type of boat with fairly heavy construction and metal centre-plates or fixed keels: e.g. the Yachting World Fourteen-Foot Day boat. This is one 'extreme'.

2   At the other end of the scale is the out-and-out racing machine such as the Flying Dutchman. Some of these are very sophisticated boats.

3   Somewhere in the middle is the boat which allows its owner to have the best of both worlds – fast and lively enough to race but also safe enough to 'potter' in. The G.P. Fourteen and the Wayfarer come into this category.

One cannot really compartmentalize but this is a general guide. All designers have a specific set of aims in mind when they set out to design a sailing boat. Many boats have developed to suit a particular area. These types are found especially around the coasts and in estuaries. Some notable localized classes are the 'X' class, the Norfolk Punt, the Yare & Bure One Design, the Thames Estuary One Design, the Loch Long One Design, the Shannon One Design and the Liverpool Bay Falcon. Most of these boats were designed pre-war. They are really 'tailored' to suit local weather and tidal conditions.

A recent type of 'fun boat' to appear on the sailing scene is the surf boat – little more than a surf-board with a sail on. Of more than a dozen classes, the Minisail is probably the most popular. They are very buoyant and most exhilarating to sail. They do have limitations and should only be used in sheltered areas or inland. I would not recommend sailing surfboards to anyone about to take up sailing as they are potentially unseaworthy. Nevertheless, in the right conditions and location they can be very good fun for an experienced helmsman.

Although not exclusively a sailing boat, I should not exclude the motor-sailer from this general look at types of boat. People have limited time for sailing, often only weekends. Winds can be fickle, and blow the wrong way or not at all when they are most needed. So the sailing boat with an auxiliary motor is becoming increasingly popular. In cruisers the motor will normally be inboard. Providing that these are fitted professionally, that they are marine engines and not marinized car engines, they are usually reliable if well looked after. Diesel is much more reliable than petrol; it is also safer.

There are many dinghy people who, for the same reasons, consider it advisable to carry an outboard engine in their day-boat. This is sound common sense and in a boat like a National Eighteen or a Y.W. Dayboat there should be few problems; just an additional pad on the transom to take the outboard bracket, and use of the outboard should be fairly painless.

You may be tempted to mount an outboard on a racing dinghy and this is where I would like to offer a word of warning. Most racing dinghies are built as lightly as possible and the transom will not be intended to take the extra weight and forces of an outboard motor. Neither is the shape of the 'racing machine' conducive to seaworthiness when the sails are not in use. So if you are going day cruising and intend using an engine to get you back on time, make sure that you have a fairly heavy, stable and seaworthy type of boat which can easily take an outboard and which is strong enough to stand up to fairly rough conditions while motoring. Do bear in mind that sailing dinghies are basically designed for sailing and only some of them are suitable for motoring. One or two craft are designed to do both, for example the Drascombe lugger.

Rigs

The well-known 'Kon-Tiki' represents about the simplest rig for a sailing boat. When small boys begin experimenting with rafts, they usually come up with this basic rig. The concept is simple: a platform, a mast and a square sail spread across the boat, so that the wind, blowing from *behind*, pushes the craft along. Add a steering oar and a sailing craft is born.

As the 'Kon-Tiki' proved, it is possible to sail many thousands of miles successfully with a craft having this simple rig, but only sailing in the direction that the wind is blowing!

Quite obviously this rig was very limiting and it gradually became recognized that, by attaching one side of the square sail to the mast, the boat could be made to sail with the wind blowing from either side as well as from behind. And so the lug-sail and the gaff-sail were developed. These sails are very efficient when the wind is coming from astern or on the quarters and, even today, when three-sided sails are used extensively the gaff rig is still preferred by many for this reason.

Once sails were rigged 'fore and aft', (that is to say when one side of a sail was attached to a mast or stay), then the problem of sideways drift had to be dealt with; otherwise, when boats were sailing with the wind coming from the side, they would drift crabwise across the water. The shape of boats, therefore, began to change. Instead of the ship with a rounded bottom, there developed a deeper-keeled craft which would get some 'grip' on the water from its keel and would not be pushed sideways so much when the wind was abeam. When dinghies came to be used for sailing, this lateral resistance was obtained by giving it a daggerplate or, later, a pivoting centreplate.

At the end of the nineteenth century a few rich people were able to use boats for pleasure purposes and very soon they took up racing. It was then that windward performance, the ability of a craft to sail to between ninety and fifty degrees or even forty-five degrees of the wind's direction, became top priority. The need to compete on world trade routes also meant that ships like the tea clippers had to be very fast to windward, and so the triangular sail arrived. This shape of sail gives a much better performance when sailing close to the wind than does a four-sided sail.

Although the gaff-rig was still faster with the wind behind, the all-round performance of a boat with triangular sails, called a 'bermudan rig', was much better. For reasons that I will deal with more fully in a later chapter, the triangular sail meant that a vessel could sometimes sail as close as forty-five degrees to the direction of the true wind.

Nowadays one sees very few boats with four-sided sails, although there is a certain old-fashioned charm about the 'old-gaffers' and some people feel that they have much to offer as a cruising boat where windward performance is unimportant. Certainly to see a gaff-rigged boat under full sail in a good breeze is a sight which will stir the heart

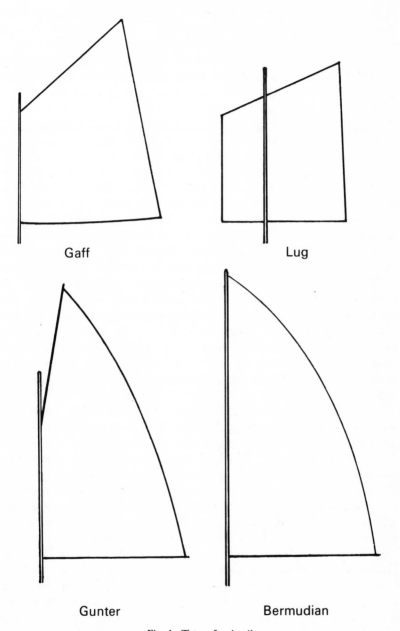

Gaff

Lug

Gunter

Bermudian

Fig. 1. Types of mainsail

of all who love sailing ships, but the attraction is emotional rather than utilitarian. There are Old Gaffer Races around the coasts of Britain and on any summer weekend one can see these superb old craft at Cowes or any of a dozen or so harbours around our coasts.

As well as in the shape of sails, boats vary as to the number of sails. The basic rig is that of a single sail set on a single mast, known as a 'una' or 'cat rig'. By adding a sail in front (ahead) of the mast we get a much more efficient rig (see Chapter Three). This is a 'sloop', i.e. a mainsail and a headsail. Or, if more than one headsail is carried, then the boat becomes a 'cutter'. The cutter can be the most efficient rig of all but it requires a certain degree of expertise in sail setting. The skill is all to do with the shape and size of the gap or 'slot' between the different sails and we will look at this in detail later.

Most dinghies are either una- or sloop-rigged, many having one additional sail called a 'spinnaker' which does not affect its classification. Larger yachts which have to be handled by a smaller number of crew, such as a family, have the sail area divided up into smaller sections. They might be cutters or, more likely, ketches or yawls.

Both ketches and yawls have two masts: a main and a mizzen, the latter being the one at the back (stern) of the boat. In the case of a ketch, the mizzen mast is forward of the steering post and is usually quite large, but a yawl has the mizzen right aft and the mizzen sail is usually much smaller, acting only as a steadying sail. Often fishing boats have a mizzen in this position and hoist it to prevent the boat rolling.

The advantages of ketch- and yawl-rigs over other types is in balance and ease of handling. Sails can all be in reasonable sizes and when reefed (i.e. when sail area is reduced in heavy weather) the boat can easily be balanced; that is to say a sail right aft (mizzen) will balance a sail right forward (jib) and the boat will remain 'light' on the helm. This makes her safe, and she can be more easily steered.

A few large yachts have a schooner rig. In this case the main mast will be aft and there will be one or more masts in front of it. Again this makes it much easier to handle the sails because they have been split into roughly equal sections. A few quite small boats have a schooner rig; they are mainly used for single-handed sailing.

At the beginning of this century, when wealthy owners could afford large racing yachts with big professional crews, there was no need to limit the size of sails and so a few very large racing yachts were built with a bermudan sloop or cutter-rig, as these are the most

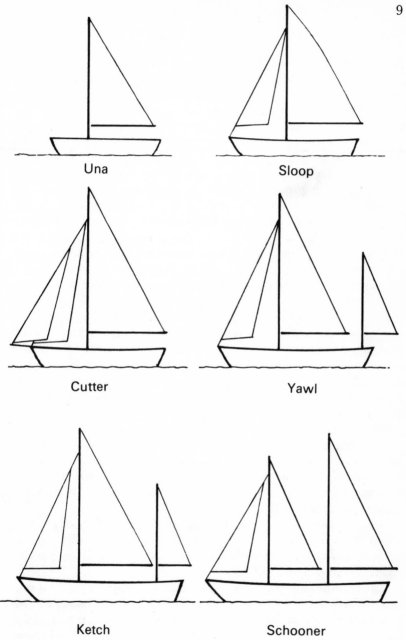

Fig. 2. *Types of rig*

efficient to windward. The 'J' class belonged to that era and one can still find pictures of these magnificent giants competing in the Solent for all the honours of the day.

Nowadays most people cannot afford large crews even if they can afford large yachts, so we see more ketches, yawls and schooners, particularly among cruising boats. A few large racing sloops and cutters are built, mainly Twelve-Metre yachts which compete for the America's Cup. In a few cases, large crews can still be found to haul the enormous mainsails aloft, but there are many and varied efficient mechanical devices to take the sweat out of sail hoisting and sheeting: winches, 'coffee-grinders' and the like. Some are hand operated but many are power operated.

Modern developments in rigs have come mainly from racing boats. The tendency now is to have a tall mainsail with large headsails overlapping it. As the front third of a mainsail is the most useful part of the sail when a boat is closehauled, i.e. as close to the wind direction as she can get, the modern mainsail has become increasingly tall with a very short foot. This is called 'high aspect ratio'.

Headsails have grown bigger as mainsails have become smaller and modern racing yachts will probably have a 'genoa' which is about one-and-a-half times the size of the mainsail. Because of this shift in sail area many masts are now further aft than they used to be; in some cases they are about half way along the boat, whereas some old sloops had their masts only about one-third way along from the stem. This is because the boat must balance around a central pivot point in order to be safe and easily steered.

Modern headsails include foresails, staysails, genoas and yankees. Sometimes it is very difficult to tell what sort of a headsail one is looking at merely from its shape as designers may go to extremes to gain maximum advantage from a set of rules. Roughly they are categorized as shown in Fig. 3.

Now let us examine a typical dinghy-rig because this book is mainly about dinghies. More than 90 per cent of modern dinghies are bermudan-sloop-rig. Most of the rest are gunter lug-sail sloops or unarigged sloops (single handers).

The bermudan sloop is the most useful and efficient rig for a small boat. It will go well to windward, is easy to rig and hoist sails, and can conveniently be handled by two people. The sail plan is simple and this leaves the crew free to practise all the other skills of balance, tactics (if racing) and pilotage. Some modern dinghies are in fact

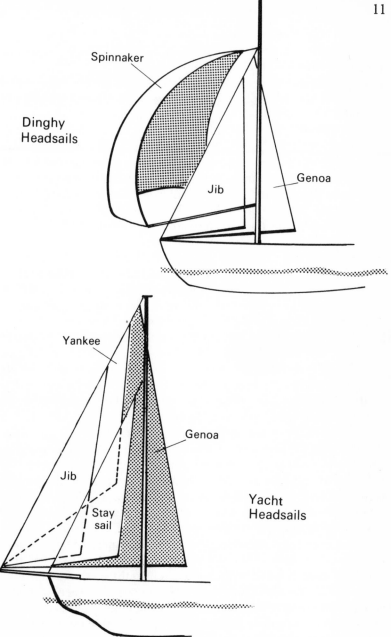

Dinghy
Headsails

Spinnaker

Jib

Genoa

Yankee

Genoa

Jib

Stay
sail

Yacht
Headsails

Fig. 3. Types of headsails

extremely complicated even though they are bermudan sloops, but as a basic non-racing boat they are easily handled and sail well and this is why most people choose them.

Although there are other types of rig, I shall for reasons of simplicity and clarity be referring to the bermudan-sloop-rigged-dinghy throughout this book when describing techniques of handling, unless I state otherwise. So let us be sure that we know what a bermudan sloop really is: a boat with one mast, a triangular mainsail controlled by a rope called a mainsheet, a single triangular foresail which is usually called the jib, similarly attached by its forward edge to a wire forestay and controlled from its clew by two ropes called jib-sheets, each leading to one side of the boat. This type of boat is the one in which most beginners will learn to sail.

Choice of boat

When buying a first boat it is quite a good idea to consider a second-hand one. If it is a class boat, remember that the price will be affected by the sail number and whether or not it has a current measurement certificate, as well as the general condition and how many 'extras' it has. If it has an early sail number then, no matter how good its condition, the price should be fairly low. If it does not have a current measurement certificate, then it cannot take part in racing. Extras may make a big difference to the price. For instance, a second-hand road-trailer for an Enterprise would probably be worth £15. A spare suit of sails might add £10 to £15 and so on.

The boats for sale columns of yachting magazines will give a good price guide if studied over a few weeks. Remember end of season and winter prices will be much lower than spring and summer ones.

If possible take a knowledgeable friend along when buying a first boat. A G.R.P. boat will be a better buy than a wooden one as it will require less maintenance. On the other hand faults in G.R.P. will be more difficult to spot for the inexperienced eye.

There are many considerations when buying a boat. If it is not your first boat, you will have a better idea of what to look for. If you are a beginner, however, the choice can be quite mesmerizing.

First of all, decide whether you wish to cruise or race, or both. If you intend sailing mainly inland – a very sensible thing to do for your first season – you will probably want to join in some racing when you have learnt to helm your boat. There is not much else to do on small stretches of inland water and racing will give some purpose to your sailing. It will also help to improve your boat handling much quicker than if you just potter, and it gives some excitement.

If you do decide just to potter, then almost any boat will suffice providing it suits the locality that you sail in. If, on the other hand, you go for a boat in which you can race, it will be well worth finding out what classes local clubs race. There is little fun in open handicap racing where you may be the only one of your class and have no idea about whether you are doing well or not until after the race. Class racing is much more fun and 'one-design' classes give the most evenly matched racing. This is when boats are all exactly the same in hull shape, sail area, centreboard, etc. 'Restricted classes' do allow some variety in shape and sail area and are not usually such fun for beginners as the differences are somewhat sophisticated.

Boats which many clubs race are: the G.P. Fourteen, Enterprise, Mirror, Fireball, Merlin-Rocket, Firefly, National Twelve, O.K., Hornet and Cadet. The R.Y.A. produce a booklet listing all clubs and the classes that they race. It is coded G. 14, priced $17\frac{1}{2}$p. and is free to members. It is obtainable from:

> The Royal Yachting Association,
> 5, Buckingham Gate,
> Westminster,
> LONDON, S.W.1 E 6JT

A dinghy from one of the well-known racing dinghy classes is a good investment as they tend to hold their value.

The size and weight of a dinghy are important considerations. If it is to be kept ashore, will you and your crew be able to load it on to a launching trolley and manhandle it to the dinghy park without getting a slipped disc? Is it light enough to be lifted by two people? An Enterprise or a Mirror can easily be managed by two, but a G.P. Fourteen is quite a struggle, particularly for youngsters, whereas a Y.W. Fourteen-Foot Dayboat or a Wayfarer needs four people to lift it on and off a trailer.

Will your boat be used exclusively inland or sometimes on the sea? A boat quite safe for inland racing might be completely unsuited to day cruising in the Solent. There are many factors to consider. Perhaps most important of all is the amount of time that you will be able to spend on it for maintenance purposes. A fibreglass boat needs little or no maintenance. A plywood boat will require some annual work on repainting or re-varnishing, but a solid wood boat in either clinker or carvel construction (see Chapter Two) will need a great deal of 'fiddling' work.

If you decide to buy a new boat you would be well advised to go to an established boat builder, preferably a member of the S.B.B.N.F., the Ship and Boat Builders National Federation. This organization lays down minimum standards for construction in a similar way that Lloyds lay down standards for larger craft. There is quite a lot of healthy competition among boat builders so don't be afraid to shop around for the best quote.

TWO

Getting to know the boat

Boat construction

As with a simple rig, a boat hull is a perfectly logical thing. A hollowed-out log was probably the first boat, or perhaps several logs lashed together to make a raft. These two types of boat construction have been followed with varying degrees of sophistication in different parts of the world. Either you get into it or you sit on it. In the Pacific Ocean the raft type of sailboat has been used and developed over thousands of years, whereas in the Western world, perhaps because there is more need for protection from the elements of weather and sea, we have always built craft around a framework and enclosed ourselves as much as possible inside the boat.

In recent times these two ideas have merged. We now have dinghies, surfboats in particular, which are little more than floating buoyancy tanks; the need to fill the interior of a hull with buoyant materials has been realized and in this sense we have gone back towards the solid log idea. On the other hand there are many cruising catamarans and trimarans, built partly on the 'raft' principle, which the crew get into; the hulls actually have accommodation within them.

So a combination of the need for floatation (buoyancy) and protection for the crew are the basics of design in a modern dinghy. Add to this the requirement for speed and it is easy to see how modern racing dinghies developed. Whether it be a Five-O-Five or a Tornado cat, these principles are apparent. In cruising dinghies, seaworthiness is also important and this includes stability, so shape too plays a part in hull design. A beamy flat-bottomed boat is stable, whereas a long, narrow sleek hull will more easily be driven fast but will be less stable.

The shape of a hull in cross section has been greatly influenced recently by the development of boats which can be built at home in plywood. This material was used extensively between the Second World War and the advent of glass fibre in the 1960s. As it is difficult to bend plywood, shapes of hulls became flat with 'corners' or chines at the junction of pieces of ply. Boats constructed in this way were the G.P. 14, with a single chine, called hard chine: the Enterprise, with two chines, called double chine: the Wayfarer (double chine): and the O.K. (hard chine). These are some of the best known; there are many more.

These shapes, particularly hard chine, are not the best for sea-worthiness and speed, although they do have some small advantages over rounded hulls. The beginner may wonder why they have endured now that glassfibre is in general use, as this can be moulded into a smooth rounded shape. The reason is to do with class rules. As 'one-design' classes these boats must be identical in hull shape so it would have been quite unfair to the hundreds of owners who had wooden boats to change the shape in any way as the older half of the class would have become obsolete. No class association would want that.

There are five main types of dinghy construction to be seen today in Britain. Starting with the oldest first, we have carvel (see Fig. 4). In this method a framework of ribs and stringers is built up and then the planks are attached to this framework, lengthways, along the boat. The edges of the planks lay alongside each other and small gaps between each plank are filled with caulking (lengths of cotton strands) and filler, giving an appearance on the outside of one uniformly smooth surface. Most large yachts were of carvel construction before the use of glass-fibre. They are easy to maintain on the outside but inside the ribs make repainting a rather slow job.

A cheaper, mainly pre-war method of building, was clinker con-struction. The clinker method is similar to carvel except that the planks slightly overlap each other and this gives extra strength. This shape gives a very characteristic 'slopping' noise when water is hit-ting the side of the boat and some people who have sailed in clinker boats for a long time become very attached to this sound. A clinker boat seems to epitomize for them all that is best in sailing. So, al-though they are very fiddling to maintain, people still buy them. The newcomer to sailing, however, would be well advised to steer clear of a second-hand clinker-built boat as they often leak, and replacing planks is usually a job for a professional boat builder.

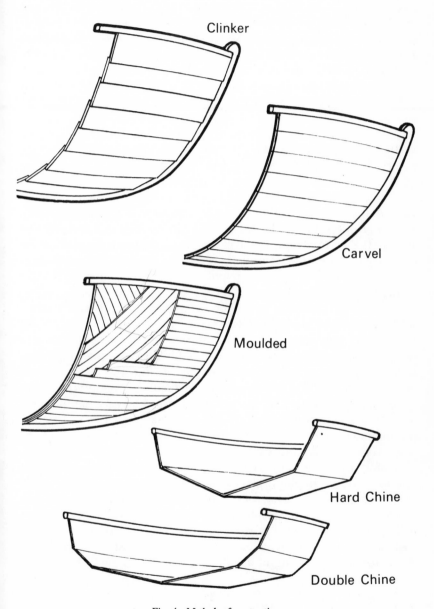

Clinker

Carvel

Moulded

Hard Chine

Double Chine

Fig. 4. Methods of construction

The third method evolved largely during the last war. A need for a strong but light method of construction for craft such as MTBs and MGBs and an improvement in glue-technology led to the development of hot and cold moulding techniques and nowadays dinghies like the Albacore are built in this way.

A layer of strips of thin wood is fixed onto a mould, followed by a second and third layer which are each glued to the layer beneath and go in different directions, giving a good strength-to-weight ratio. This is a very good, though somewhat expensive, method of construction. Repairs almost always have to be done professionally and can be costly. A boat built by this method should last a long time as the layers of glue prevent any seepage of moisture beyond the outer skins of the boat.

I have already mentioned the fourth method: plywood construction. A framework or former is built, and pieces of plywood, which should be of marine grade and to B.S.S. 1088, are glued and screwed to this. It is certainly one of the easiest methods and well suited to the do-it-yourself builder. Maintenance of this type of boat is straightforward and it is, therefore, popular with many sailors who have limited cash and limited time.

A recent development in plywood construction has been the stitch and glue method. This was pioneered by the designers of the Mirror dinghy and is easier and cheaper than the normal way of building in ply. No framework is used, the sheets of ply being simply stitched together with bits of copper wire (see Fig. 5) and the seams covered with a resin glue and glassfibre tape. A further development of this method has been used on boats like the Unicorn catamaran where very thin sheets of wood which will bend have been fixed together by the stitch and glue method to build the dart-like shape of the hulls of this fast 'A' class cat.

Finally we come to the type of construction which is now used for the majority of dinghies: glass reinforced plastic. Made in a mould rather as a jelly is, layers of glass-fibre mat are impregnated with resin and when dry the resulting hull is simply lifted out in one piece. All that is then needed is some stiffening in the form of wood or G.R.P. bulkheads, buoyancy tanks or thwarts (most boats have all of these items), the fitting of a 'lid' (a deck section), and the boat is complete.

The great strength and minimum maintenance required has made G.R.P. the popular material that it is today. Initially in the 1960s there were some poor hulls produced but in the 1970s a G.R.P. boat from a reputable builder should be a sound buy.

The aesthetic appeal of wood will continue to be important to many people so it is unlikely that wood will ever completely die out, but there can be no doubt that the coming of glass-fibre has revolutionized the boating industry. While it is expensive to make a mould

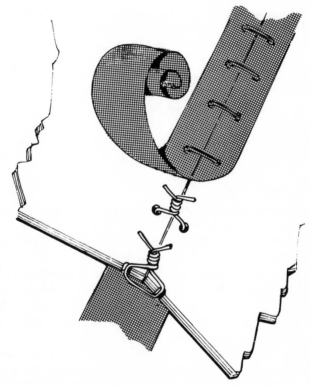

Fig. 5. Stitch and glue method of construction

for one hull only, when boats are produced in hundreds the cost can be even less than the cost of a wooden boat. I should add that wood still has a few advantages over G.R.P. In particular it floats!

Some large yachts are built in steel and some in ferro-cement. While these methods may well develop, it is unlikely that dinghies will be built in them in the near future. They lend themselves to large yacht construction, where blue water seagoing strength is of paramount importance.

Home building

If you can use a plane, pliers, screwdriver and a paint brush and have some spare time it might well be worth considering building your own dinghy. The Mirror, for instance, can be built for well under £100 and this represents a saving of about 40 per cent on the new price. You will also have an absorbing hobby for a number of weeks and will understand your boat better when you eventually sail it.

The D.I.Y. man can choose either to build from scratch, if he is a fairly competent woodworker, or buy a kit of parts which will be already cut to size and only need assembling. Or it is possible to save quite a lot of money by simply finishing the boat, i.e. screwing on the fittings and painting and varnishing. Some boats which can be home built are the G.P. 14, the Enterprise, the Mirror, the Fireball and the Unicorn cat. There are many others. Most home building kits will be supplied in marine plywood, but in a few cases G.R.P. hulls can be bought and all the finishing carried out at home.

Parts of a boat

Let us now find out about this special sailing language that is the subject of so many cartoons and jokes! A simple sailing dinghy is composed of a hull with all its fittings; the steering equipment which is a rudder and tiller attached to the hull by 'hinges' called pintles and gudgeons; spars, which is the name given to the mast and boom; two types of rigging, the standing rigging which holds the mast up, and the running rigging by which the sails are controlled; and finally, the sails. Figs. 6 and 7 will help novices to become familiar with all these names.

Some further explanation is necessary as one or two of the items mentioned have certain specific functions which might not be obvious to sailing newcomers.

The standing rigging supports the mast. In a typical bermudan-rigged dinghy this comprises a port and starboard shroud and a fore-stay. Very often the work of the forestay is taken over (when the sail is hoisted) by a wire running up the luff (front edge) of the foresail or jib. This assures that the jib is right when hoisted. Most standing rigging nowadays is stainless steel wire, although galvanized wire will suffice but will not last as long. To tension the shrouds, bottlescrews are used. These are expensive, and pre-stretched terylene lanyards are just as good until you get into top competition and even then it is

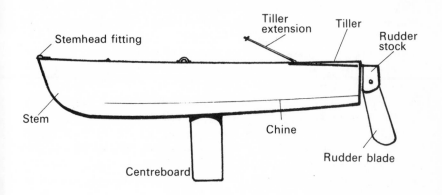

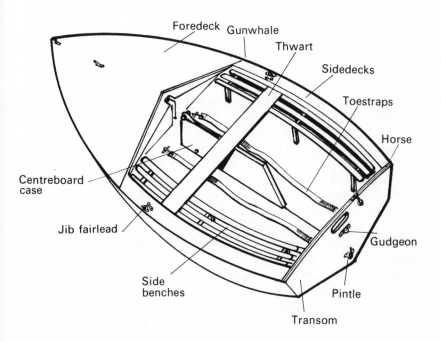

Fig. 6. Parts of the Hull

only necessary to have a bottlescrew on the forestay; the shrouds can be adjusted with adjustable plates, having a row of holes about one-eighth inch apart through which fits a clevis pin. A disadvantage of bottlescrews is that they fracture easily if bent and then have to be discarded. If 'used they must be prevented from unscrewing by threading stiff wire through the centre hole and around the top and bottom. It is also a sensible precaution to cover the wire with tape to prevent sails or sheets catching on it. Altogether bottlescrews are rather a nuisance.

Running rigging consists of mainsail and jib halliards, mainsheet and two jib sheets and a kicking strap. The function of a halliard is to hoist sails; a sheet enables crew to tighten a sail to the required setting. The kicking strap has a rather specialized job: as the mainsail is let out from the centre of the boat, the weight of wind in the sail tends to make the boom lift. If it lifts, the area of the mainsail will be reduced and the boat will slow down. It will also become rather dangerous to handle. The kicking strap prevents the boom from lifting, and on racing dinghies it also helps to control sail shape and mast bend – but more about that later.

In some ways a centre-mainsheet does the job of the kicking strap. It exerts a more even pull on the boom and not just a pull on the outer end as does a transom mainsheet. I will have more to say about these in Chapter Ten.

The purpose of decking is often not fully understood. A typical dinghy like the Enterprise has a foredeck with a coaming at its aft end, to prevent water getting into the cockpit. It also has a side deck about seven inches wide. This provides somewhere for the two crew to sit; they only sit in the boat if the wind is light or if sailing 'off the wind'. In addition, when the boat heels over, the side deck prevents water coming into the cockpit until the whole of the width of the side deck is under water. This is the real reason why boats have decking. Logically if a boat is completely decked in it will be watertight and less likely to sink or get rolled over in really bad weather. Some extreme boats are built in this way, such as 'Endeavour' which recently tackled the appalling conditions of Canada's North-West Passage.

The centreboard, also, is commonly misused by the novice. In heavy old boats which had metal centreplates there was a certain self-righting effect resulting from the suspension of this heavy piece of metal low down under the boat. This, however, is not now the main purpose of a wooden centreboard. Its function is to prevent the boat

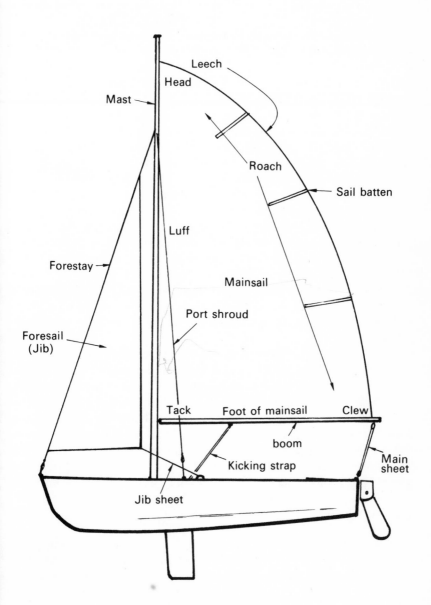

Fig. 7. Parts of spars and rigging

making leeway, or slipping sideways, when sailing with the wind coming from the side of the boat, particularly when sailing close-hauled. A secondary function is that of providing a quick and easy means of 'balancing' a boat, i.e. making it easy to steer with not too much weight on the tiller.

As boats became more racy, certain additional items of gear were added, which enabled crews to lean out over the side to balance the boat and keep it upright. Examples are the toe straps and tiller extensions. Toe straps should always be adjustable so that a small crew does not have to suffer the discomfort of being only half out over the side. Tiller extensions, or jiggers, must be functional and not have sharp corners which the mainsheet will catch on.

In addition to the standard equipment shown in Diagrams 6 and 7, most dinghies will carry a jib stick, spinnaker pole, flag halliard, oars or paddles, anchor and painter.

A jib stick helps to hold the jib out from the mast when the wind is blowing from behind or nearly behind. One end attaches to the clew of the sail and the other to an eye plate on the mast. It is usually stored in special clips when not in use, as is the spinnaker pole. Use of the spinnaker will be dealt with in Part III as it is not a beginner's sail, but stowage of the pole can be a problem in any boat. The Cherub dinghy class has solved this by stowing it along the underside of the boom.

Whether to carry oars or paddles really depends on the type of boat and where it will be used. Oars are much more efficient, but if a boat is sailed inland and mainly used for racing, paddles should be sufficient to get you back to base when the wind drops. I would like to put in a strong plea that all dinghy sailors should be able to use a pair of oars, and when sea sailing I would consider oars an essential piece of equipment, except, perhaps, in a 'racing machine' where the extra weight and stowage might be too great a problem and where the dinghy could expect to be towed back to base by the race rescue boat if necessary. It is quite surprising how many dinghy sailors cannot row a boat, and this could be serious. The same applies to the use of anchors.

Any boat which sails in tidal conditions should carry an anchor and be prepared to use it. Its use may be limited to anchoring when the wind has dropped and the tide is taking you in the opposite direction to that in which you wish to go, but it might win you the race, and there are other occasions when you will risk being swept out to sea if you are unable to anchor. Anchoring is covered in Chapter Five.

A painter is a piece of rope used for tying up a dinghy, usually from the stem head. For details of knots to use, see Chapters Three and Six.

Fig. 8 shows the special terminology used to describe areas of the boat. It is necessary for you to know these terms as I shall be discussing 'making it go' in Chapter Four.

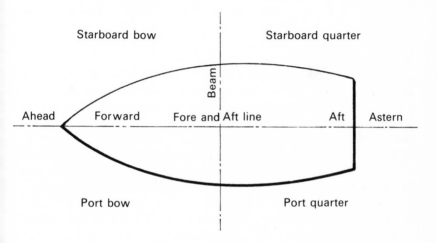

Fig. 8. Areas of boat

THREE

Preparation for sailing

Basic theory

The practical person may find theory at this stage disheartening. Don't be put off. If you can understand one or two fundamentals about a sailing boat before going afloat, you will find that you will be much more in sympathy with your craft, and when you do get afloat the learning process will be much quicker.

Several factors contribute to the easy movement of a boat through the water. Firstly, there is its underwater shape. A typical dinghy will be about three times as long as it is wide and will have a 'sharp' end and a 'blunt' end. Quite obviously the forward end will cut through the water with minimum resistance and the fine 'V' shape forward will make for easy movement through the water. Further aft the boat will be more flat-bottomed. This gives stability, makes for roominess and tends to lift the boat on to the surface of the water, particularly at high speeds; this is called 'planing'.

So, basically, the shape of a boat is conducive to making it go in a forward direction. If the wind is blowing from astern or from somewhere over the quarters, then the boat will be pushed in a forward direction. Unfortunately the wind is often blowing from the side and sometimes comes from more ahead than astern (closehauled sailing). Now, though the boat has been designed to move forwards, it will also move sideways a little when the wind presses from one side or the other. A modern dinghy only has a few inches of hull under the water so there is nothing much to 'grip' the water and provide lateral resistance. We could build boats that are very deep in the water; many large yachts have a deep keel; but in a dinghy this would be cumbersome and reduce its speed. Also there is no need for lateral resistance when the wind is aft; we then require the minimum water resistance. This is known as 'minimum wetted surface area'.

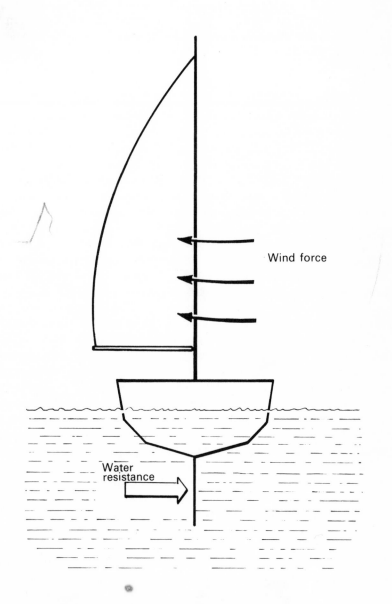

Wind force

Water
resistance

Fig. 9. Lateral resistance

Ideally something which is adjustable is required, hence the centre-board. This is a pivoting piece of shaped wood or metal which can be fully lowered when sideways pressure is greatest (closehauled), and fully retracted when there is no need for it, when running dead before the wind.

Here I have stated the function of a centreboard very simply. Later we will talk more about the intermediate adjustments of a centre-board and its relationship to balance and weather helm.

If any reader is still unconvinced about the need for lateral resist-ance in the form of a centreboard, it can easily be tested in a bath of water. Cut out the rough shape of a dinghy hull from a piece of wood about ten inches long and apply pressure from the side and slightly aft to represent the force acting on a boat by the wind blowing from abeam. Then tack a piece of wood on to the side of the boat (similar in shape to a centreboard) and repeat the experiment. Fig. 9 also illustrates this point.

The second important factor affecting the movement of a sailing dinghy is the shape and setting of its sails. Sails are the engine of the boat, harnessing the wind into a force which will 'draw' the boat forward.

Fig. 10 shows how 'particles' of air travelling along the leeward side of a sail from A to B travel further than those travelling along the windward side from Ai to Bi. This is due to the curve of the sail. Because they travel further the airflow on the leeward side speeds up, thus creating an area of lower pressure on that side of the sail. Because there is a constant attempt to equalize pressure, the force exerted on the sail is from the higher pressure area to the lower pressure area, or, put simply, in a direction shown by the arrows, at right angles to all parts of the sail. The 'average' of all these arrows is somewhere about one-third way back from the leading edge of the sail. It follows that the more the sail can be eased out, the greater will be the forward force acting on the boat and the less will be the side-ways force. When the sail is right out in the running position, the resultant force is entirely in the direction in which the boat needs to travel: forwards, and there is no need to use the centreboard to pre-vent leeway. Conversely when the boat is closehauled and the main-sail sheeted in close to the centreline of the boat, the resultant force is much more sideways from the direction of travel, so the centreboard is fully lowered to give maximum lateral resistance. It is easy to see why the closehauled position is the slowest point of sailing in most dinghies.

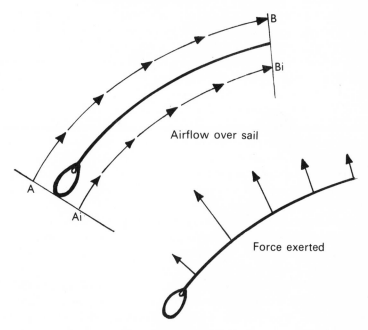

Fig. 10. Effect of airflow on sails

In practice the one important thing to remember about all this is that the extent of the force driving your boat is directly proportional to how far out the sails can be without starting to flap. You must constantly check that your sails are eased as much as possible. It is often better to have a very slight flutter on the luff of a sail than to have it sheeted in too tight.

Safety habits

Don't be over-ambitious. Always leave a fairly wide margin for error. There are many dangers inherent in the sport of sailing and it is to the rescue of unwary adventurers that our lifeboats are called regularly during summer months.

It is essential that all dinghy sailors should be competent swimmers. The R.Y.A. have recommended that participants in sailing be able to swim at least fifty yards in light clothing. This is a minimum and is intended to ensure that anyone who suddenly finds himself ejected into cold water should at least feel at home in it and will not panic but will be sufficiently relaxed to carry out the correct procedures for righting and survival. The survival swimming tests of the Royal Life-saving Society are also very worthwhile and sailors should be encouraged to obtain at least the bronze medal award.

Dinghy sailing, and particularly racing, requires a moderate degree of fitness. I would not wish to put people off but I must warn anyone who has a physical disability or handicap that sailing is not just a matter of lazing about under blue skies and gentle breezes, as many holiday brochure photographs suggest. It can be very strenuous, and wet and cold into the bargain. I have known people without limbs become very competent racing helmsmen, but they tend to be exceptional people with a great deal of courage; and my advice to anyone who is not completely fit is to make sure that you learn with someone who is fully competent and with help near at hand.

Beginners would be well advised to start inland where there is not the additional hazard of tides and currents, where the water is usually more sheltered and where one cannot get very far away from a safe shore.

There are many ways of reducing the risk of accidents. A very important one is to wear some sort of buoyancy garment. There are two types: a buoyancy aid and a lifejacket. The buoyancy aid is exactly what the name suggests: an aid to flotation. Its design presupposes that the wearer will also be able to help himself, that he will be conscious and not in a state of panic. It is really only suitable for experienced people who are not likely to find themselves in the water for very long. The main advantage of the buoyancy aid over a life-jacket is that it is more comfortable to wear and in some models is less bulky. Because of these factors its use has not been limited to experienced sailors and this is to be deprecated. The best buoyancy aids bear the stamp of the Ship and Boat Builders National Federation (S.B.B.N.F.).

Lifejackets, while being slightly more bulky, are essential wear for all novices, children and those who are likely to be away from rescue facilities. They are carefully tested and all bear the stamp of the British Standards Institute. So, when buying, look for the 'Kitemark'. Any garment which does not have this is *not* a lifejacket. The British Standard applicable is Number 3595 (1969). Among other things a lifejacket, when fully inflated, will support an unconscious person in the correct position on his back, with mouth and nose well clear of the water. It will also stand up to the sort of wear and tear normally experienced in boats.

Next on my list of safety points comes the boat itself. Choose the right boat for the job. Local experts can usually advise on this. It becomes particularly important if you are intending sailing in tidal waters.

A subject closely allied to correct choice of boat is the need to use common sense about the weather. You will, with experience, get to know what sort of conditions you and your boat can stand up to, but play it safe at first and don't venture out without someone experienced in the boat, in anything more than Force 3 winds. Force 6 is about the strongest wind that most dinghies will comfortably survive, and then only in experienced hands. If sailing on the sea, Force 4 may be more than enough, for there will be waves to contend with as well as wind. Nowadays there are many aids to foretelling weather. The B.B.C. broadcast shipping forecasts regularly throughout the day; there are local forecasts obtainable by dialling a number given in the front of telephone directories: you can for example dial Portsmouth weather forecast for the Solent and Isle of Wight area. Meteorological offices will supply a forecast on request, and local boatmen and fishermen will often be able to give a rough forecast. Nor should the barometer be neglected. A steady barometer will usually mean little wind, whereas a 'glass' which shows a quick rise or a quick fall will certainly be accompanied by strong winds, for when pressure is changing fast in British latitudes, an unstable weather pattern, probably a low pressure area, is upon us.

In warm summer weather a sea breeze usually blows around our coasts each day from about midday until late afternoon.

When sailing on the sea, beware of fog and mist. Stay ashore if there is any about for not only is there a good chance that you will get lost in fog, but larger craft will not be able to see you and that can be very serious. Contrary to popular belief, you will not be picked up on big ships' radar screens unless you are very lucky.

Just before going afloat, make a habit of doing a quick check on your boat; it only takes about sixty seconds and can save you hours of worry later. A quick look at the boat will tell an experienced eye whether it is seaworthy or not; check for any major damage or weak points. Then, starting at the stem, run your eye over the whole boat from stem to stern. Here are some of the items to check and the order to do it in: forestay, bottlescrews, shrouds, cleat and fairleads on foredeck, painter, mast, halliards, cleats, gooseneck; a look up the mast to see that halliards are not wrapped around the sail or stays or each other; knots in the ends of jib sheets; burgee hoisted, centreboard up and pin in; toe straps adjusted to fit crew and secured; no loose screws on side benches or thwarts; oars and rowlocks and other loose gear tied in; self balers closed, bungs in, rudder and tiller ready, mainsheet and boom ready and tidy, mainsheet horse, pintles and gudgeons all O.K. and finally a quick check of buoyancy compartments to see that all hatches and clips are well secured. I think that it is also essential to carry a bucket and sponge, and a small first aid kit is useful. Some additional gear will be needed when sea cruising.

Many people have been saved from death in water accidents by the 'kiss of life' so it makes sense to learn this simple method of resuscitation.

Clothing

All protective clothing is safety equipment, so it is as well to have the best that you can afford. There is a wide variety available and your fellow club members or fellow sailors will be able to advise you on the type of wear which is most suited to the area in which you sail.

A complete waterproof covering is essential for all who anticipate sailing in Britain. Whether you have a one-piece suit or a separate anorak and trousers is partly a matter of personal preference. The one-piece suit does not allow so many variations of garb; it is either worn or it is not worn! An anorak and trousers are more suited to the British climate, which, being constantly changeable, means that you need to do several changes in a day's sailing if you are not to overheat or freeze. Remember that quite a lot of sailing involves sitting still, getting cold. You are always in the wind, or so one hopes, and this can mean that even on a hot summer's day when others are lying under a scorching sun on the beach, if you are sailing you will probably need a warm sweater and waterproof suit, top and bottom. The secret of enjoyment is to *keep* warm. Once you cool off, it is often difficult to exercise enough to get warm again; there is not room in dinghies to go for a run round!

Even with a waterproof suit one tends to suffer from water down the neck. Keeping the anorak hood up restricts hearing and visibility, so the answer is to wear a small towel, scarf fashion. It also keeps the wearer warm in really cold conditions, when the hood can be raised as well.

If contemplating winter or spring sailing, or serious racing (which will mean that you cannot choose when you sail), a wet suit will be a very good investment. It is made from foam rubber, usually nylon-backed for strength, fits fairly tightly and has high insulative properties which work best when a layer of water is trapped inside the suit. This water quickly heats up to body temperature and gives further insulation. On a fairly energetic day a wet suit can become too hot, but a quick dowsing will solve that problem. Personally, I have found wet suits too hot and sticky for normal summer sailing.

A wet suit can be made for about the cost of normal waterproof clothing, but if purchased ready-made will cost about three times this amount. A suit can be made easily in a weekend.

A few dinghy sailors use dry suits. These are thin, stretchy rubber material which are worn over other warm clothing and they have waterproof seals at neck, wrists, waist and ankles. Condensation is a problem and most small-boat sailors have not found them suitable but they are used quite extensively by the armed forces.

Some headgear is necessary for warmth. A woolly hat is probably the most suitable, although in summer many prefer a cap with a peak to act as a sunshade.

Footwear is largely a matter of common sense. For normal summer sailing plimsols or sailing shoes with a non-slip sole or wet suit bootees (also non-slip) are fine. In colder weather calf-length sea-boots with a pair of warm woollen socks inside are more suitable. It is not necessary to always get wet feet when sailing in winter and I think every effort should be made to find a dry way to board your boat; once feet become wet and cold, then morale drops quickly and winter sailing can become very miserable. The whole body seems to cool off rapidly once feet are wet in cold weather.

Do take plenty of warm clothing when sailing, and if you intend going far from base it is as well to follow the scout motto and 'be prepared'. Take a spare change of clothes in a polythene bag where they will be kept dry. Sailing needs old clothes. Never wear anything smart; it will very quickly be ruined.

Right of way

An international set of regulations controls all craft on the water. Under the rather grand-sounding name of the International Regulations for Prevention of Collision at Sea, this code is mainly for commercial craft under power but there are some rules which directly or indirectly affect sailing boats. I have listed the important rules below and I think that you should at least have read these before venturing afloat on your own for the first time. When you have gained some experience it would be worth reading through the complete set of rules which can be found at the end of this book (see Appendix I). By then you will be able to interpret them more easily.

The important section for dinghy sailors is Part D, the 'Steering and Sailing Rules':

Rule 20

(a) When a power-driven vessel and a sailing vessel are proceeding in such directions as to involve risk of collision, except as provided for in Rules 24 and 26, the power-driven vessel shall keep out of the way of the sailing vessel.

(b) This Rule shall not give to a sailing vessel the right to hamper, in a narrow channel, the safe passage of a power-driven vessel which can navigate only inside such a channel.

Part (b) needs some further explanation. What is a 'narrow channel'? It really depends on the size of the craft. To the Q.E.2 the Solent is a narrow channel! Although she slows to a very slow speed in the Solent, it would take several thousands of yards to stop her, and if you get in her way in your Wayfarer you will most certainly be in great danger. So, again it is a matter of common sense. A sailing dinghy which is very manoeuvreable can often make it easy for powered craft by keeping well clear. This must be done *in good time* so that intentions are obvious before craft get so close that there is danger of collision.

To summarize, then, on this rule: powered craft should give way to sailing boats if they are of similar size, or if they have plenty of room to manoeuvre, but if they are large they may not be able to do so, and common sense must prevail, with early action on the part of a sailing boat who intends giving way. Dangerous spots are in tidal rivers and estuaries and often it is possible for small sailing boats to go into the side while larger boats pass in mid-channel where the water is usually deepest.

Rule 24

(a) Notwithstanding anything contained in these Rules, every vessel overtaking any other shall keep out of the way of the overtaken vessel.

This applies whether you are sail or power.

Rule 26

All vessels not engaged in fishing, except vessels to which the provisions of Rule 4 apply, shall, when under way, keep out of the way of vessels engaged in fishing. This Rule shall not give to any vessel engaged in fishing the right of obstructing a fairway used by vessels other than fishing vessels.

So, we must keep clear of fishing boats. These are required to display either two black cones, one above the other, points together, or two baskets in similar position. In certain circumstances they may display three cones. The reference to Rule 4 concerns vessels which are not under command.

Rule 17

(*a*) When two sailing vessels are approaching one another, so as to involve risk of collision, one of them shall keep out of the way of the other as follows:
  (i) When each has the wind on a different side, the vessel which has the wind on the port side shall keep out of the way of the other.
  (ii) When both have the wind on the same side, the vessel which is to windward shall keep out of the way of the vessel which is to leeward.

(*b*) For the purposes of this Rule the windward side shall be deemed to be the side opposite to that on which the mainsail is carried or, in the case of a square-rigged vessel, the side opposite to that on which the largest fore-and-aft sail is carried.

This is the rule which you will use most. Whatever point of sailing you are on, if you are carrying your mainsail on the port side (starboard tack) then you have right of way over somebody who is on port tack (mainsail on starboard side). The windward leeward rule makes more sense when you have experienced it once or twice, but see Fig. 11.

It is the duty of everyone in charge of a boat, whether it be the captain of a 250,000-ton tanker or you in your fourteen-foot dinghy, to avoid collision, and it is therefore essential to constantly look ahead so that you are not caught out.

These are the only rules that I am going to mention, but there are one or two hints that I can give to beginners to help on the first few trips afloat.

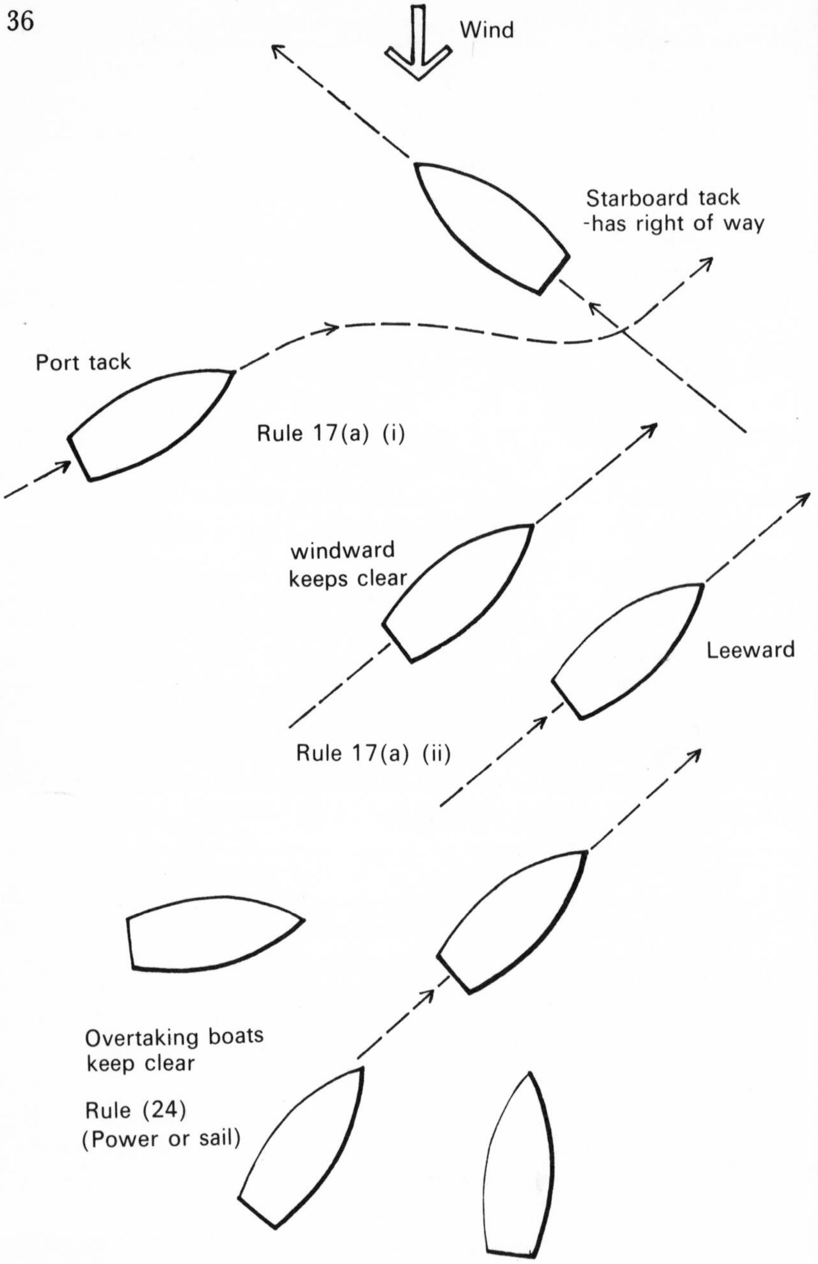

Fig. 11. Right of way rules

Initially you will need plenty of space, so try to keep clear of areas where there is likely to be any commercial traffic, or other sailing boats racing. An inland lake or a quiet river which is not tidal would be ideal. If you do find yourself in a fleet of racing boats it is courteous to give way even though you may have right of way. You will be able to tell when boats are racing as they will be flying a rectangular flag from the masthead instead of the usual triangular burgee.

How to learn

Undoubtedly the best way to start sailing is to find a competent helmsman who needs a crew. Many clubs have special arrangements to put crews in touch with helmsmen; but make it clear that you are a novice – then he cannot complain later! Spend a few weeks crewing before trying the 'driver's' end of the boat. Then, if possible, arrange for a qualified instructor to give you a few lessons. You may decide to go on a course run by one of the many sailing schools dotted around the country. Some of these have been examined and approved by the R.Y.A., and at these schools you are assured of good standards of instruction, adequate boats and so on. Many Local Education Authorities also run courses and these are usually of a high standard. A few elementary courses are run at the National Sailing Centre at Cowes, though there is great demand for the places on these courses and so you would have to book well ahead.

An ideal progression would be:

1. A season's crewing, followed by
2. An elementary course at a sailing school
3. A season's helming (preferably in your own boat)
4. Some crewing for a racing helmsman
5. Racing helming
6. Crewing on a larger cruising yacht
7. Cruising skipper

This plan falls in nicely with age groups and availability of money. Of course you may decide to specialize somewhere along the line, or circumstances may force you to limit your sailing to one type. There are opportunities to attend theoretical and practical courses at all stages and I shall deal with these more fully at the end of the book.

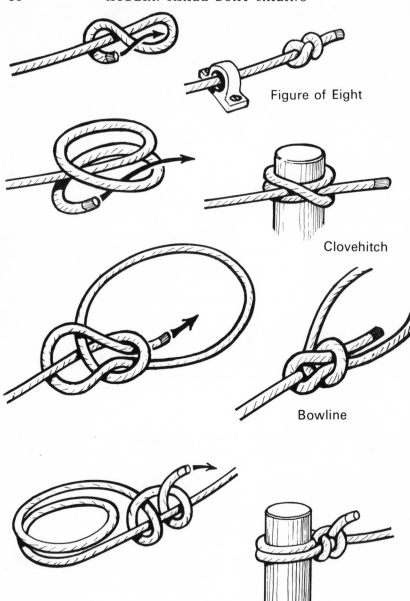

Figure of Eight

Clovehitch

Bowline

Round turn and two half hitches

Fig. 12. Basic knots

Basic ropemanship

Chapter Six deals much more fully with this subject but it is essential to know the four knots/hitches shown in Fig. 12 before going afloat for the first time.

The figure-of-eight knot is used as a locking knot and is tied in the ends of the jib sheets after they have been passed through the fairleads. This stops them coming out accidentally. It can be used in any similar situation.

The clovehitch is used to secure the burgee to its halliard; one near the top of the staff and one near the bottom. It is also used to secure any pole or spar whether the end of the securing rope is free or not. There are two ways of tying it and both should be learnt.

The bowline is most useful for securing loose gear to the boat, e.g. bucket, oars, baler. It is probably used more than any other knot in a dinghy and has the great advantage that it can be easily undone, even when wet.

The round turn and two half hitches is a safe knot used for tying up a boat to a ring or post or for tying a boat down to eyebolts or stakes in a dinghy park.

FOUR

Making it go

The three factors concerned with making a boat move are:

> the wind
> the sails
> the helmsman (driver)
> Let us look at each in turn.

The wind

Strength of wind is all-important for dinghy sailors. If it is too great, sailing will just become a fight for survival. Without any wind a dinghy is a completely dead thing, and, if on the sea, it will be at the mercy of the tides.

Wind strength is described in the Beaufort Scale in forces from 0 to 12 and corresponding speeds in miles per hour. Here is the scale in full:

Beaufort Wind Scale

Beaufort number	Limits of wind speed in knots	Descriptive terms	Sea criterion	Probable height of waves in feet	Probable maximum wave height in feet
0	Less than 1	Calm	Sea like a mirror	—	—
1	1–3	Light air	Ripples with the appearance of scales are formed but without foam crests	$\frac{1}{4}$	—
2	4–6	Light breeze	Small wavelets, still short but more pronounced. Crests have a glassy appearance and do not break	$\frac{1}{2}$	1
3	7–10	Gentle breeze	Large wavelets. Crests begin to break. Foam of glassy appearance. Perhaps scattered white horses	2	3

Beaufort Wind Scale—continued

Beaufort number	Limits of wind speed in knots	Descriptive terms	Sea criterion	Probable height of waves in feet	Probable maximum wave height in feet
4	11–16	Moderate breeze	Small waves, becoming longer: fairly frequent horses	3½	5
5	17–21	Fresh breeze	Moderate waves, taking a more pronounced long form; many white horses are formed (chance of some spray)	6	8½
6	22–27	Strong breeze	Large waves begin to form; the white foam crests are more extensive everywhere (probably some spray)	9½	13
7	28–33	Near gale	Sea heaps up and white foam from breaking waves begins to be blown in streaks along the direction of the wind	13½	19
8	34–40	Gale	Moderately high waves of greater length; edges of crests begin to break into spindrift. The foam is blown in well-marked streaks along the direction of the wind	18	25
9	41–47	Strong gale	High waves. Dense streaks of foam along the direction of the wind. Crests of waves begin to topple, tumble and roll over. Spray may affect visibility	23	32
10	48–55	Storm	Very high waves with long overhanging crests. The resulting foam in great patches is blown in dense white streaks along the direction of the wind. On the whole the surface of the sea takes a white appearance. The tumbling of the sea becomes heavy and shocklike. Visibility affected	29	41
11	56–63	Violent storm	Exceptionally high waves. (Small and medium-sized ships might be for a time lost to view behind the	37	52

Beaufort Wind Scale—continued

Beaufort number	Limits of wind speed in knots	Descriptive terms	Sea criterion	Probable height of waves in feet	Probable maximum wave height in feet
			waves.) The sea is completely covered with long white patches of foam lying along the direction of the wind. Everywhere the edges of the wave crests are blown into froth. Visibility affected		
12	64	Hurricane	The air is filled with foam and spray. Sea completely white with driving spray; visibility very seriously affected	45	—

Assuming inland conditions (i.e. non-tidal), dinghy sailing conditions are from Force 1 to Force 6. Some experienced folk can still keep their craft afloat in Force 7 and even Force 8, but most people would consider that the strains put on hull, sails and rigging are just not worth risking. Even a Force 6 will severely test the skill of a dinghy helmsman. About Force 3 to 4 is ideal dinghy sailing weather and Force 5 will give some hairy planing conditions in most modern dinghy classes. Ideal conditions for a beginner would be Force 2.

Few racing crews seem to 'reef' their sails in strong winds. This means reducing the amount of sail area either by changing to smaller sails or by reducing the size of racing sails. I think this is a pity as a boat which is overcanvassed will be unmanageable and speed is lost. Reefing is, therefore, a seamanlike thing to do and a correctly reefed boat is not only safer but it is faster on most points of sailing. I will discuss reefing fully in Chapter Five.

Apart from normal winds, whose direction will be predicted by the weather forecasters, there are also sea breezes which blow around our coasts during the afternoon. They are usually at approximately right angles (blowing onshore) to the general line of the shore. These occur on a summer's day when the land begins to warm up, so even if there is a lack of wind on a summer morning, don't abandon all hope! A sea breeze may well develop by midday.

For racing, the course will be planned to suit the wind direction

When 'pottering', however, it is as well to consider wind direction before setting out. Usually it is sensible to do the hard sailing early in your trip and have the wind astern to bring you back to base. So if a westerly is blowing, one would set out in a westerly direction and return with an easterly heading.

Wind is the only 'fuel' that I know of which is free. Perhaps this is one of the attractions of sailing, but we do have to pay a penalty for this free facility. It is not possible to sail directly into the wind. Nor is it possible in most boats to sail within approximately a ninety degree arc with the wind direction cutting this arc down its centre (see Fig. 13). We call this the 'No-Go Zone'.

Within the 'No-Go Zone' the wind cannot be induced to blow across the sails in such a way as to exert any driving force. You will know if you are in this sector as the sails will flap even when hauled in tight. If the wind is westerly, to get to a position which is to the west of your starting point you will have to zig-zag along the extremities of the no-go sector. This is known as 'beating to windward' and you will be sailing closehauled.

If the wind is steady and not affected by hills or buildings, it will be relatively easy to beat to windward in this manner but when it is fickle and changeable it is necessary to pay constant attention to small fluctuations in direction in order to arrive at a destination in the shortest time.

The sails

Before going any further we must consider which of the sails shown in Chapter One should be selected for certain wind strengths. For simplicity I will limit the choice to the three which are commonly found on dinghies: main, genoa and jib.

> Up to and including Force 3 – full mainsail and genoa might be carried
> Force 4 – change genoa for jib and reef main lightly
> Force 5 – medium reefed main and jib
> Force 6 – heavily reefed main only, or if sailing down wind drop main and use jib only

This will give a rough guide for a boat like a Wayfarer. Lightly reefed, would be about three rolls, heavily reefed, might be six to eight rolls.

Now, again for simplicity, I will use the bermudan sloop as an

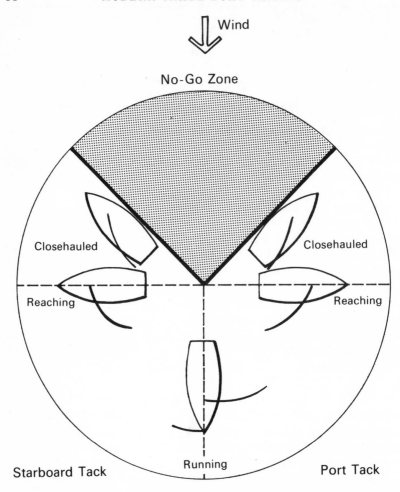

Fig. 13. Basic points of sailing

example and we will consider the respective duties of crew and helmsman. In a boat like the Enterprise the crew sits forward and controls the jib. The helmsman sits behind him controlling the mainsail. Each sail is controlled by a sheet, a rope attached to the clew of the sail in the case of the jib and to the boom in the case of the mainsail.

Providing that the boat is not facing into the 'No-Go Zone', when the sheets are hauled in the sails 'fill' with wind and the boat moves forward. To slow down or stop, the sheets are freed off, the sails then lose the wind and flap and the boat slows. If, in an emergency, the sails have to be slackened quickly, this is called 'letting fly'.

Making a boat move is relatively simple. Getting it to go in exactly the right direction at the greatest possible speed and with safety is rather more difficult. It requires careful and constant adjustments of sheets, tiller, centreboard and body weight. This all comes with experience though much of it is common sense.

In addition to minding the jib or genoa the crew has to balance the boat, move the centreboard up or down and keep a good lookout for other boats or obstacles which are on collision course. These are his general duties. He has a few more specialized jobs which I will mention later.

The driver

I have deliberately called the helmsman a 'driver' to emphasize his function.

In one hand he holds the tiller, or, if leaning out to balance, the tiller extension. It should be held in the hand nearest to the stern of the boat and usually with the hand facing down. In the other hand is held the mainsheet. After some practice it will be quite easy to grip the mainsheet under the thumb or first finger of the tiller hand when hauling on the sheet.

The position of the helmsman and crew will vary but it should always be their aim to prevent the boat heeling over by moving weight from seats to sidedecks, so in strong winds both will find themselves leaning out over the side of the boat with toes tucked under toestraps and thighs on the sidedeck. In light winds the crew may need to sit on the leeward side to keep the boat on an even keel. Helmsmen should always be on the windward side, facing the mainsail. (There are some exceptions to this which I will mention in Part II.)

So far as fore-and-aft positioning of a crew is concerned, while learning it will be quite safe to sit amidships, neither too far aft nor too far forward. Later you will learn to move aft when on the plane and forward when closehauled.

As well as steering the boat and handling the mainsheet, the helmsman must keep an eye on all parts of the boat and be constantly looking ahead so that he can make decisions about course changes and boat handling in good time. He will also be helping his crew to balance the boat by leaning out over the side when the wind demands it.

A good helmsman will sail his craft 'through the seat of his pants'. He should 'feel' the boat and be aware of any fluctuations in course, in wind strength or in movement of his crew. This is achieved through his contact with the side deck, his grip on the tiller and mainsheet and, most important, via the feel of the wind on his face or on any other exposed part of his body. He may feel the boat heel slightly, or surge forward, or a stronger pull on the mainsheet will indicate more wind; the helm may need slightly more strength as weather helm is increased. Also, he will with practice be able to 'read' the water, anticipating puffs and squalls on the surface of the water ahead before the boat is affected by them. The burgee will help him to know the apparent wind direction from its position at the top of the mast.

I have already mentioned the first 'emergency drill' for a helmsman to learn; that is, letting fly. If a boat is heeling dangerously or if it is necessary to stop or slow down, the command 'let fly' is shouted and both helmsman and crew then let the sheets run through their hands rapidly until both sails are flapping violently. They must also take care to move into the boat quickly at the same time, otherwise they will upset the boat's balance and probably find themselves in the water! I urge beginners to practise this technique several times when they first take charge of a dinghy; the ability to let fly quickly will get you out of many jams. The noise of the sails flapping is worrying at first but after a while you will come to associate it with safety.

Points of sailing

Now we come to the essentials. 'Points of sailing' is the name given to the different angles or 'courses' on which a boat sails in relation to the wind direction. Fig. 13 shows the basic points of sailing.

In Chapter Three we considered the factors which make a boat move in the required direction, namely shape, wind direction, angle of sails, rudder, centreboard. I have also stated that the 'No-Go Zone' is approximately ninety degrees. This leaves us 270 degrees of the circle in which the boat can sail. It will sail for half of this sector with the wind on the starboard side and half with it on port side. When it is on starboard tack the mainsail will be on the port side, and when the boat is on port tack then the mainsail will be on the starboard side. As the mainsail crosses the centreline of the boat, we say that we are 'tacking' (sometimes called 'going about') or 'gybing', depending on whether the wind is ahead or astern of the boat respectively.

Two other terms which are related to the side on which the mainsail is carried are 'windward' and 'leeward' (see Fig. 16). The windward side is the one opposite to that on which the mainsail is carried; the leeward is the other side (see also Fig. 11).

For ease in understanding we can, initially, talk about only three basic points of sailing: running, reaching and beating (closehauled).

When running, the boat is being 'pushed' along by the wind. There is no tendency for it to get pushed sideways and, therefore, no need to use the centreboard. In practice a centreboard is sometimes left down just a few inches to give stability. Sails are let out a long way to give maximum forward drive and when the wind is dead astern they are goosewinged: that is to say the jib is held out on the opposite side to the mainsail with the jibstick (or whisker pole) so that it is not sheltered by the mainsail.

A boat running is very unstable. The boom and mainsail are hanging out over the side of the boat, and if there is any choppiness or a fluky wind a boat will tend to roll from side to side. This can become so bad in waves that it will roll right over. It is to prevent this happening that a small amount of centreboard is left down. Careful balance by the crew is essential and on a windy day it will be sensible to keep off this point of sailing.

On a run, if the wind should come from the leeward side, i.e. if the helmsman is not concentrating hard on his steering, the boat is then said to be 'sailing by the lee'. This is dangerous as a gybe may occur without warning. This may be called a 'chinese gybe' as the top part of the mainsail would blow across before the bottom, causing an 'S' shape in the sail. Chinese gybes often end in capsize.

Altogether, running is not the point of sailing to recommend for a novice. It has too many hidden dangers. Not so reaching.

Reaching is, conveniently, the safest and fastest point of sailing. It is the 'happy medium'. The sails are most efficient when in the reaching position. (This will be discussed more fully later.) Reaching covers an arc of about 135 degrees and is sub-divided into close reaching, beam reaching and broad reaching. More of these sophistications in Chapter Ten; for the moment I will discuss beam reaching, with the wind at right angles to the boat.

When reaching, sails will be slackened to approximately the half-way position. There will be some lateral pressure and so the centre-board also will be down to about the half-way mark. It will be important for the crew to keep the boat upright, and in a decent breeze they will probably both need to be seated on the sidedeck.

A boat is usually very stable on a reach and can attain its maximum speed. Sometimes a reaching dinghy will 'lift' on to the surface of the water and go very fast indeed. This is 'planing', and when this happens crew weight should be moved aft to increase the planing effect and sails will have to be sheeted in slightly. Planing in this manner is extremely exhilarating and is the aim of all racing dinghy helmsmen. Later we will look at the use of a spinnaker. As this sail is normally carried on a reach, it is not uncommon to find oneself planing at speeds of up to fifteen knots with the spinnaker bosoming out proudly ahead. These sort of conditions require skill and experience and when achieved give great satisfaction.

The third point of sailing, beating, requires skill of a different kind. As lateral pressure is at its maximum, full centreboard is needed. This in turn causes the boat to heel over more than on any other point of sailing, so crew weight is required to balance and keep it upright.

Sails are hauled in close to the centreline of the boat and this means hard work for the two crew. Add to this the wave problem: you are sailing *into* them all, and you will begin to realize why beating is the slowest and possibly the least popular point of sailing. Unfortunately there always seems to be more beating than anything else because, of course, as I said earlier, in order to get from A to B one has to zig-zag, so travelling twice as far as on any other point of sailing.

Beating requires concentration from the helmsman in order to prevent the boat getting into the 'No-Go Zone' and 'stalling'. Many helmsmen do this by watching the luff of the mainsail. A slight flutter or 'lifting' is the warning signal that you are in the 'No-Go Zone' and prompt tiller action is necessary to keep the craft moving.

When closehauled and the wind changes so that bearing away is necessary, a boat is said to have been 'headed' by the wind. If it is possible to luff or 'point higher', then that is known as a 'freeing' wind. In the northern hemisphere generally the wind will 'veer' (move clockwise) from its normal direction as it gusts and will 'back' (anti-clockwise) from that direction when it lulls, so there is an obvious advantage to be gained from sailing on a starboard tack.

Before going afloat let us just examine one more piece of theory. It is an important item of information that I have deliberately not explained, the relationship of true and apparent winds.

Fig. 14 will help to explain this relationship. A good example of the apparent wind is felt when cycling. Before setting off, a gentle breeze may be felt. This is the true wind. As you mount your bicycle and gather speed, pedalling into the wind, so the wind appears to increase in strength. This is the apparent wind and it is, of course, greater than the true wind because of your movement through the air. Conversely, if you move with the wind the apparent wind will be less than the true wind. This demonstrates the relationship between *speeds* of true and apparent winds, but not direction.

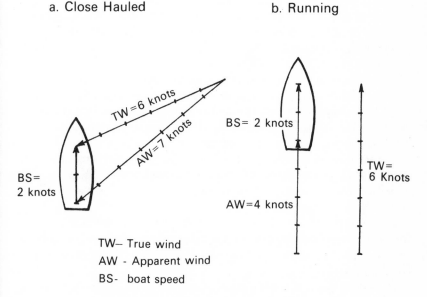

a. Close Hauled

b. Running

TW— True wind
AW - Apparent wind
BS- boat speed

Fig. 14. Apparent wind. a *Close hauled.* b *Running*

We have seen that in a sailing craft it is not possible to sail directly into the wind. The true wind, flowing over the sails of a stationary boat, may be at an angle of, say, fifty degrees to the boat (on the bow). When the boat moves forward the apparent wind will increase, as we just saw in the example of the cyclist. It will also move forward of the true wind and perhaps the burgee will show an angle of forty five degrees. This is because as the boat moves forward it is producing its own wind in addition to the true wind. Fig. 14 shows how this works in relation to boat speed.

It is precisely because of this phenomenon that catamarans, which move very fast in medium and strong breezes, need their sails sheeted in hard even when on a reach. It is also why, when planing in a (mono) dinghy, it becomes necessary to sheet in harder as the boat gathers speed.

Do not worry if you find this confusing. Like most aspects of sailing theory, it may be difficult to understand until you have experienced it in the live situation. In practice all you need to remember is the need to haul in your sheet as you gain speed and slacken off again on slowing down. It is really only critical when planing.

Whether you have already sailed as a crew or not, I am going to assume in Part 2 that you have a working knowledge of sailing terms, in order to get to grips with the essential manoeuvres needed for complete boat control. Here are two more terms that we frequently use (see Fig. 15).

Luffing means to alter course towards the direction of the wind, e.g. from a reach to closehauled, or from a run to a reach. When luffing, sheets are hauled in and the centreboard is lowered more. If the helmsman is sitting in his correct position, facing the mainsail, he will push the tiller away from him to luff.

Bearing away is the exact opposite to luffing, i.e. helm towards you, sheets eased, centreboard raised and the boat moves on to a course which is further away from the wind direction, e.g. from a reach to a run.

When 'tacking', that is when turning the boat through the 'eye' of the wind, a helmsman luffs first until head to wind and then bears away on the new tack until the sails fill and the boat 'gathers way' (begins to move).

If bearing away is continued a gybe will occur, i.e. the stern of the boat is presented to the wind and the mainsail is blown across. If this manoeuvre is not controlled carefully damage can occur or, at worst, a capsize. It is, therefore, more sensible to use tacking as a means of changing from one tack to another during your early sailing days.

For this reason I would suggest that beginners use a figure-of-eight-shaped course to start with, going about (tacking) at each end. To do this you need to find a peaceful stretch of water at least fifty yards wide, with the wind at right angles to this width so that you can reach backwards and forwards across the figure-of-eight.

When coming ashore after your first few trips, it will be a good idea to let fly where there is plenty of space, drop your sails and row to the shore or the moorings. This will save much embarrassment and possibly a few repair bills and insurance claims. If you have to land

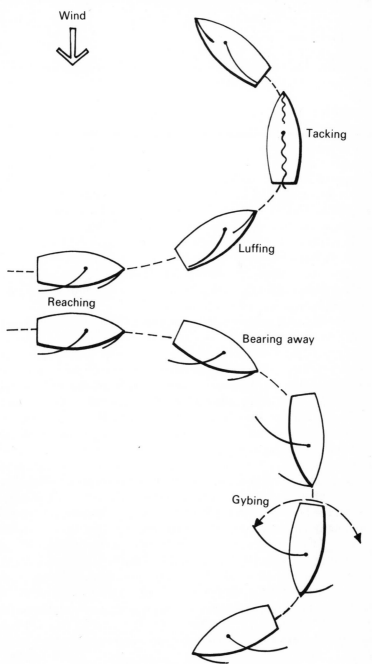

Fig. 15. Luffing and tacking: bearing away and gybing

on a shore, do remember that your centreboard and rudder should be lifted before you touch bottom.

Now we are almost ready to go afloat, so I will finish this chapter with a few practical hints on launching and getting away from the shore.

Launching drill

If a dinghy is kept ashore it will probably be launched by a trolley or road trailer. A launching trolley normally costs about one-third as much as a road trailer but it is only suitable for launching and not for high-speed road travel. Road trailers, as the name suggests, are intended for car-towing and may or may not have sealed bearings on the wheels. Those without sealed bearings do not take kindly to being pushed into the water, particularly sea water. Whichever type of road trailer is used, it is a sensible precaution to rinse in fresh water after a salt-water launching.

Launching trollies are less troublesome and do not usually have bearings, simply an axle with solid hubs rotating on it. An occasional daub of grease on the axles pays dividends.

Most road trailers have adjustable chocks to support the bilges of a boat, and, provided these are adjusted to suit, should give little trouble. Not so all launching trollies, however. I have seen several G.R.P. boats damaged on the bilge strakes because the trolley has not been tailored to suit the boat. In any event boats should be handled very gently when being lifted on or off a trailer or trolley. A dinghy hull is very vulnerable when it does not have the support of water. For this reason one should never get into a dinghy on shore. Boats can often be left partly supported on their launching trollies, providing that the trolley is well forward; the stern and sides can be supported on old car tyres or specially-made shaped chocks.

When about to launch, make sure that the stern is on something soft; lift the bows and push the trolley under to the required position. The dinghy should not be slid on to the trolley. Once on it is necessary to tie the forward part of the trolley handle to the boat, usually with the dinghy's painter. If this is not done, the boat may slide back on its trolley or even come off it completely, probably banging its stern on the ground with a hard 'thwack' as the weight tips aft.

To launch, find a suitable ramp, slipway or gently sloping area of beach without stones or rocks and push the boat on its trolley stern first into the water until it floats off, not forgetting to check that the bungs are in place first! Launching a dinghy of more than 12 ft length is a two-man operation. While one holds the boat's head into the wind, the other returns the launching trolley to its 'parking lot'. It is not necessary to heave and strain when launching. Let the trolley and the water do the work; use brain not brawn and your boat will be much less likely to suffer damage.

Once afloat, a boat should be held or secured from a position at or near to the stem-head. If this is not done and a gust of wind catches it, you will suddenly find yourself sailing off even though sails have not been hoisted, and if you are not in the boat this can present problems!

Some boats have cleats or samson posts on the foredeck, with perhaps a fairlead near the stem-head through which the painter can be led and secured. If this is not the case, a light dinghy can usually be held by the forestay or bottlescrew. Some people will tell you that this will bend the bottlescrew but in more than twenty years of dinghy sailing I have never seen this happen; strains are just not that great. In many racing dinghies there is nowhere else to hold the boat.

Once in the water, secure your boat to a jetty or ring. Most launching sites have something of this nature to make life easy. If no such facility exists then the unfortunate crew will have to get his feet wet, because if he tries to stand on dry land the boat will constantly touch bottom and this should be avoided for several reasons. In cold weather I would not recommend wet feet and personally I take great pains to launch 'dry' on all but the hottest summer days. Wet suit bootees or calf-length sea boots overcome this problem.

If a road trailer is used for launching, it may be necessary to keep the bearings dry for reasons already mentioned. Some road trailers have a tip-up arrangement which facilitates launching and most have rollers on which the keel rests. If it is of the rigid and non-tip variety, push it down to the water's edge until the tyres are just in the water. Place chocks or stones behind both wheels and then, with one person on each side, gently ease the boat towards the water on the trailer rollers. It must be kept central. Beware of the boat going with a sudden rush for the last couple of feet, and make sure that someone is holding the painter!

Where possible it is better to leave the trailer attached to the towing vehicle while launching; it will then be more stable and wheel chocks will not be necessary.

Centreboards should always be secured before launching. Normally a pin is provided for this purpose; it fits through the centreboard and its case.

Rudders should never be fitted until the boat is afloat, and if self-balers are fitted remember to close them before launching.

As many jobs as possible should be done before launching. Sails can be hanked on, halliards and sheets attached, battens slotted into the sail and everything checked and put in its proper place. (See Chapter Three for pre-launch checks.)

Sails should rarely be hoisted before launching. Only when racing is there a case for hoisting first so that sails can be accurately tensioned, but even then it will not be possible in anything other than light wind conditions.

Once afloat the helmsman climbs aboard and hoists sails. Most helmsmen prefer to hoist the main first as the jib flaps about a lot and makes a great deal of noise. However there are advantages in hoisting the jib first which we will discuss later.

When sails are correctly hoisted, check that sheets are free to run. The rudder and tiller should then be fixed in position and the pin removed from the centreboard so that it can be quickly lowered if needed when you set off. The kicking strap too will be fixed to the boom before you set sail, although it will also need adjustments later (see Chapter Ten).

Lastly, before setting off, check that halliards are neatly coiled and hooked over their respective cleats out of the way and that sheets are still free and have locking knots in the end to prevent them slipping through the fairleads (jib sheets) or blocks (mainsheet).

All this time the crew will be holding the boat head to wind. When you are ready, seated with the mainsheet and tiller in your hands, tell him to climb aboard. While he does so you will need to balance the boat. It is quite a good idea to get him to take a turn with the painter around something on shore, bringing the end of the painter aboard with him. Once he is aboard, have a quick look around to check that the immediate vicinity is clear before you set off. As soon as the water is deep enough, get your crew to lower the centreboard to the half-way position; this is a good habit to get into, whatever point of sailing you are going on to and will save much embarrassment. One often sees beginners set off in fine style only to drift ignominiously sideways into the nearest moored craft or jetty because they have forgotten this basic drill. Once away from the launching area you can adjust the board further to suit the point of sailing that you are on.

Plate 1. (Left) *International 5o5 with spinnaker drawing nicely*. Roger Smith

Plate 2. (Right) *International Fireballs racing at Cowes*. Roger Smith

Plate 7. *Good rowing position with feet braced against buoyancy tank.* John Hart

Plate 8. *The position of the hands and oars can clearly be seen.* John Hart

Plate 9. *A Wayfarer sailing backwards. The mainsail is pushed right out to port.* John Hart

Plate 10. *A backwards-sailing boat gathers speed. Careful steering is necessary at this time.* John Hart

Plate 11. *Trapeze in use on a Fireball. Note also the way in which the helmsman is holding the tiller and the bend in the boom giving a flat sail.* Roger Smith

Plate 12. *The Tane class Polynesian catamaran. This class of boat designed by James Wharram and with a junk rig has crossed the Atlantic in 20 days.* James Wharram

Plate 14. (Right) *The Unicorn, an A-class catamaran. A single hander with a great turn of speed.* Roger Smith

Plate 13. (Below) *Snowgoose of Wight, formerly Snowgoose, a well-known racing catamaran, now owned by the author.* Beken of Cowes

Plate 15. (Right) *A 470 dinghy. This popular class is typical of the good modern g.r.p. dinghies that are now being produced. Selected for the Olympics in 1976.* Roger Smith

Plate 16. (Below) *Mirror Dinghies racing at Cowes. This small boat is now the largest British class of dinghy.* Roger Smith

Plate 17. (Above) *Flying Fifteens rounding a mark at Cowes. Designed by the late Uffa Fox this class is somewhat unusual, having a sleek fin-keel.* Roger Smith

Plate 18. *What sailing is all about. The thrill of a good beat to windward on a breezy day.* Roger Smith

Getting under way

I will consider getting under way in tidal conditions in Chapter Eleven. For the moment let us think about getting away from a shore where there are no tidal complications. Whether it be from a beach, a hard or a jetty, the technique will be similar. Letting go from a mooring is a little different.

Wind direction is all-important. If the wind is off-shore or parallel to the shore or any position in between, the routine is straightforward: push the boat off, adjusting sails to suit the point of sailing. It is when the wind is anywhere between parallel to the shore and directly on-shore that difficulties may arise. Before dealing with this, we will differentiate between a 'lee shore' and a 'weather shore'. Do not confuse with the lee and weather sides of a boat. Fig. 16 explains these terms.

A lee shore is the sailor's nightmare. Not only is sailing off a lee

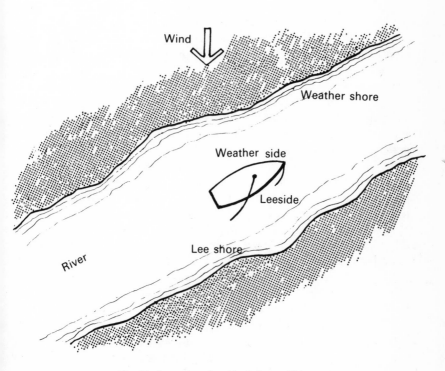

Fig. 16. Lee and weather side of shore and boat

shore more difficult because of the need to closehaul off it, but there are also wave and surf problems on large stretches of water.

With a dinghy it is usually possible for the crew to push the boat out far enough to enable the centreboard to be partly lowered. On a very gently sloping shore it may be necessary to row or paddle out from the shore. An inexperienced person should row out without hoisting sails and tie up to a mooring, post, or if necessary anchor, so that sails can then be hoisted in comfort and without hurry and the boat made ship-shape before setting off.

In a swell or where waves are breaking on the shore it is sometimes necessary to use a permanently fixed line to haul out on until well clear of the danger. This may simply be an anchor with one fathom of chain and a warp, which may be anchored fifty or sixty feet out and the warp secured to some point on land. A red marker buoy should be attached to the rope if it is left permanently in position. This will act as a warning to other craft which could otherwise be in danger of getting tangled up in it. For this reason the use of hauling warps is frowned upon on well-used waterways.

If launching off a stone slip or wooden jetty, care should be exercised; such places can become very slippery especially if in fairly still water.

Letting go from a non-tidal mooring is usually just a matter of backing the jib so that the boat's head 'falls off' to port or starboard, sheeting in the sails, lowering centreboard and dropping the mooring buoy over the quarter so that there is no risk of sailing over it and getting it fouled up with the centreboard or rudder. It is often sufficient just to bring the mooring buoy aft to the quarter, thus making the bows swing off as though tied up from that point. But the backing of a jib is a seamanlike thing to practise and will have many more uses, as we shall see in Chapter Five. See Fig. 17.

A congested area will demand slickness of handling and it is sensible to allow plenty of space during early helming days. The ability to sail closehauled and tack quickly is needed before one tries to launch at Burnham or Hamble on a busy summer weekend. Generally though, when in difficulties and collision seems imminent, two basic techniques should be adopted.

Firstly, let fly. This will slow the boat down and minimize the danger. Secondly, always steer your boat alongside any other craft or obstacle which you are unable to miss; hitting it head-on can result in very expensive insurance claims.

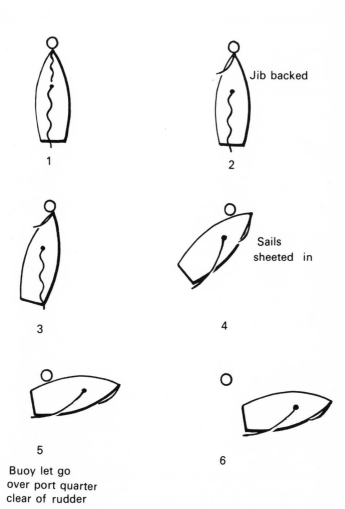

Fig. 17. *Getting away from a mooring*

To close this elementary section, I would refer the reader back to the check lists that I recommended in Chapter Three. A few minutes spent checking before going afloat can save hours of worry later. An experienced helmsman will run through his checks quite automatically, but it is essential to form the habit right from the first time you helm a boat.

FIVE

Seamanship

What is seamanship?

In a sense all that we do in boats can loosely be termed seamanship, but here I am using the word to denote special skills which separate a 'sailor' from a 'seaman', the latter being a person who understands the elements that he is using and will survive in bad conditions because he is able to work from first principles and therefore not only knows when and what to do in a given situation but also knows why he does it.

Seamanship starts ashore with observation and reading and matures when theory has been put into practice afloat. Watching other experienced helmsmen and questioning local people about conditions is a good preparation to going afloat, and the first four chapters of this book should provide sufficient theoretical introduction to the newcomer to sailing to enable him to be a more-than-usually responsive crew on his first time out.

Experience, of course, can only be gained the hard way and it is particularly true of sailing that the more one learns, the more one realizes just how much there is to be learnt.

Where the penalty for mistake can be loss of life, it would be well to caution the novice at this point regarding the word 'seamanship'. Seamanship does not have to be practised on the sea! Indeed a sensible beginner will gain experience on inland waters before progressing to sea conditions which are usually much tougher. Father Neptune will tolerate few mistakes.

The odds and ends which should be found in a seaman's pocket are the hallmarks of seamanship. These should include a shackle key, a shackle, a piece of thin line, a safety pin, a split pin and a knife.

Perhaps to this list a bung might be added as these are all items that a dinghy helmsman will need sooner or later. It is only after a season of sailing the same boat that you will really know exactly what to carry for emergencies.

A real seaman will take great trouble in preparing his boat before going afloat. A frayed sheet or a worn shackle will be replaced immediately and not left until the return. He will carefully check the condition and position of all his gear as suggested in Chapter Three. Let us now look at some specific aspects of sailing which, when well done, separate the seaman from the sailor.

Rowing

This basic, essential skill should be thoroughly mastered before ever sailing is attempted. So if you have just bought a sailing dinghy, get a pair of rowlocks fitted and practise. It is first and foremost a reserve means of propulsion when, for a number of reasons, the wind cannot be used. Do not hesitate to resort to rowing any time when you are uncertain of your ability to control the boat under sail. Drop sails, unship your rudder, leave a little bit of centreboard down and use your oars.

Dinghy oars will be from six to eight feet long and can usually be stowed somewhere in the bottom of the boat. Always fasten them in securely when not in use. A simple clamp made from elastic shock-cord is ideal or, simpler still, two 'tails' of codline to tie around each end of the oar. The oars should be easily accessible.

Rowlocks too should be tied on and conveniently to hand. The modern plastic variety do not seem quite as satisfactory as galvanized but they do save weight and should be adequate for casual use in a sailing dinghy.

Whenever the oars are not actually in use, the oars and rowlocks should be stowed (put away). Rowlocks, particularly, are very injurious to your and other boats if left in position. Sheets can easily foul up on them too. Oars, if left protruding over the side of a dinghy will get broken or slip overboard; they may also damage other craft.

Oars are preferable to paddles for the reasons outlined in Chapter Two. In tidal conditions they are essential in all but out-and-out 'racing machines' during well-organized races.

It is difficult to teach someone how to row by telling them. Find some person who is proficient and learn by watching him. Don't bend the arms too much; let your back do the work. Make sure that your feet are firmly planted on a part of the boat so that the power of each stroke is transmitted to the hull through your body. Take your time and get a good long pull with each stroke. Try to keep both oars equally extended over the side of the boat, and most important, don't forget to glance over your shoulder from time to time to see what is ahead.

Do not overload a small dinghy. Rowing dinghies are usually described as 'pram' or 'stem' dinghies. A pram has a flat front (i.e. blunt) and a stem dinghy comes to a point and has a stem. A six- or seven-foot dinghy will normally only carry two people, whereas a nine- or ten-footer can take three or even four. Seaworthiness depends on how beamy it is and how high the sides are. In calm water inland it may be quite safe to load a dinghy until the water is within six inches of its gunwhale, but in a 'chop' and particularly in a tideway it would be very foolish to do this and eight or ten inches of freeboard would be a minimum.

Because many accidents occur in small rowing dinghies which are being used as yacht tenders, it is sensible to fit buoyancy in such craft and for children and poor swimmers to wear lifejackets. When boarding it is essential to step into the centre and sit down quickly, holding on with both hands while doing so. Many a yachtsman the worse for drink has suffered a soaking or even gone to a watery grave attempting to get into or out of his dinghy!

Sculling

Sculling is a much neglected art. With crowded marinas and harbours it can be a very useful way of propelling your boat when there is not room to get the oars out. A sculling notch in the transom, or if you cannot do this an extra rowlock socket – in either case placed a little to one side of centre if steering gear requires this – will enable you to begin sculling very quickly in an emergency. Fig. 18 shows the technique. The beginner will find it easiest to start sculling with both hands on top of the oar and the blade flat on the water. From this position move the blade gently but firmly to the right, angling it slightly so that it starts to 'dive'. After a few inches, twist the wrist through ninety degrees and pull the blade back across to the other side describing a figure-of-eight shape with the blade in the water. Whenever you go wrong, return to the centre line with blade flat and start again. Ideally ask a seaman to show you how it should be done. If an oar is lost at any time, you will be glad that you mastered the art of sculling. It is very useful over short distances.

When a rowing dinghy is left, it should be pulled well clear of the water; above high-water mark if on the coast. It should be secured with its painter to any suitable ring, post or rail. A round turn and two half hitches is the safest knot for this purpose, although a bowline

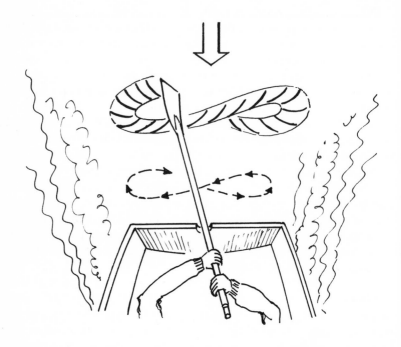

Fig. 18. Sculling technique

is often used. Place oars and rowlocks well inside the boat and make sure that any centreboard is up. If a rudder is carried, remove it and place it on the bottom of the dinghy. In tidal conditions the classic 'mistake' with a small dinghy is to either tie it on too short a painter so that it is left dangling from the quay when the water recedes or, worse still, to leave it alongside a jetty where it can drift underneath and become trapped by a rising tide. After this sort of treatment it is usually only suitable for firewood.

Anchoring in non-tidal waters (*For Tidal Waters, see Chapter Eleven*)

An anchor is not an essential piece of equipment for a sailing dinghy on small inland lakes or reservoirs. There will be some occasions inland, however, when an anchor will come in handy, particularly on rivers with moving water. The inland sailor would be well advised to use his safe, familiar waters to practise the art of anchoring before venturing on to the sea where there can be no doubt about the good sense of including anchors in sailing dinghies. All boats should carry an anchor on the sea.

Be sure to practise in as many different situations as possible; do not leave the acquisition of this seamanlike skill until faced with an emergency.

There are four types of small-boat anchor that come to mind: the Fisherman's, the C.Q.R. (or Plough), the Danforth type and the Umbrella type. Fig. 19 shows these. It also shows the names given to the different parts.

The umbrella anchor is not very satisfactory and while it may hold a small dinghy temporarily it is just as likely not to. Its holding power is not good and it tends to fold up rather easily just at the wrong moment. Its folding characteristics make it easily stowable in a small boat, but really it is not the anchor for a seaman. So I will dismiss it as not worthy of your consideration.

Of the three remaining, the Danforth type is probably the most versatile, and weight for weight the best general-purpose anchor for a small dinghy, so where only one anchor is carried I would opt for this type. It is easily stowed.

The C.Q.R. is the most efficient anchor because of its large area of blade or 'plough share' which becomes buried in the ground. It is particularly good in mud or sand; but on harder ground, e.g. pebbly or rocky ground, it is not quite so reliable.

There are two disadvantages in using a Fisherman's anchor in a dinghy. One is stowage, and the other is that weight for weight its holding power is not so good as the C.Q.R. or the Danforth, and, therefore, a heavier anchor has to be carried. On the other hand if you sail in an area where the ground is hard, it may well be worth carrying a Fisherman's. This has to be dismantled to be stowed; the stock is folded flat along the shank and tied in place. It is the oldest type of anchor and traditionally used by fishermen.

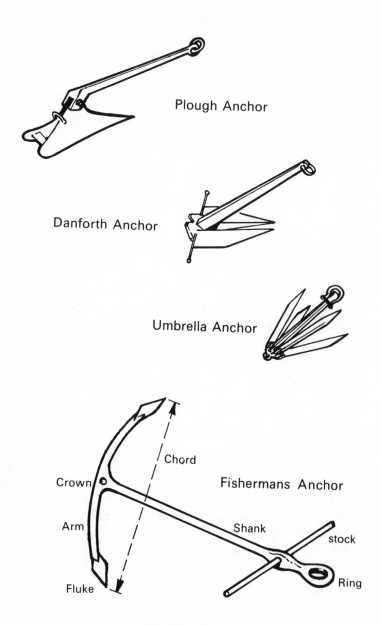

Fig. 19. Anchor types

With all anchors the fluke must dig in. In the case of the Fisherman's this is encouraged by the stock which lies at right angles to the shank. With the C.Q.R. it is by the use of a hinge by which the fluke is attached to the shank, combined with the shape of the fluke.

A short length of chain next to the anchor helps it to lie flat on the ground. With dinghies a fathom of chain and about twelve fathoms of rope is sufficient. It pays to have the chain fairly heavy as its weight means that it will not be lifted up by the warp in a strong blow. I would advise $\frac{1}{4}$-inch chain and $1\frac{1}{4}$-inch nylon rope for a heavy dayboat. Lighter rope could be used with a lighter dinghy.

The weight of an anchor for, say, an Enterprise should be about 5 lb. and for a heavy eighteen-foot day boat, such as a Seafarer, about 20 lb. These figures should enable you to make an approximation of the weight needed for any dinghy up to around eighteen feet.

It is better to err on the side of overweight for anchors, chain and warps, and when you find yourself in that emergency situation, perhaps anchored off a rocky lee-shore in a gale, you will have no qualms about your anchor holding.

Anchoring is frequently badly done. Preparation is essential. If there is any likelihood that you will need to anchor, check your gear as soon as you get afloat or, better still, before launching.

The chain should be fastened to its anchor by a shackle. Galvanized chain is normal and care should be taken to use a galvanized shackle. To prevent the shackle pin from working loose, wire it to the shackle; thread a piece of galvanized wire through the pin eye and twist it around the shackle.

The anchor rope should be tied to the chain with a fisherman's bend (see Fig. 25), and if left permanently attached the rope end can be seized back to the standing part of the rope.

Inboard, the end of the rope must be tied to a solid part of the boat (around the mast is popular in dinghies), and the warp neatly coiled in the bottom of the boat. When not in use the anchor must be tied down well out of the crew's way so that it will not slop about and cause damage as the boat heels and pitches.

Now comes a very important procedure which must be practised before anchoring, mooring, heaving to, reefing and coming alongside can be managed. I refer to 'putting the brakes on' by turning head to wind.

To reach this position, luff the boat slowly until almost head to wind. This means steering it round by pushing the tiller away from you (assuming you are sitting on the weather side). As the boat enters the 'No-Go Zone' the sails will flap and the boat will lose way (slow down). Just before it stops moving completely, bear away just enough to fill the sails again and keep it moving. As you are now closehauled, the centreboard should be fully down. Luff again and lose way. You will find, after a few minutes' practice, that you have complete control over the boat's speed and will be able to approach an object such as a mooring buoy or jetty very slowly indeed. When you wish to stop completely, free off sheets and luff the boat into the head to wind position. As you were previously moving only very slowly, your craft should stop in a very few feet.

Now, back to anchoring. Once the boat has lost way the anchor should be lowered by the crew, very carefully over the bows, passing the anchor warp through a fairlead which should be placed as near as possible to the stem head. On racing-type dinghies this fairlead may not be fitted and it may be necessary to make a strop with a piece of line which can pass around the forestay or stem head fitting and also encircle the anchor warp. It is essential to ensure that the boat swings from a point either at or very near to the stem head.

Once the anchor 'bites', i.e. digs in and holds the boat, the centreboard should be raised and the sails lowered. Many people prefer to lower the jib before starting anchoring so that the foredeck area is clear. This is good seamanship but will depend on how well a boat sails without its jib, and whether you are likely to need it if things don't work out as planned; for example in a crowded anchorage it may be necessary to back the jib (hold it on one side) to blow the boat's head in the opposite direction in order to sail off and have another try at the manoeuvre.

Continue paying out the anchor warp gradually until you have the equivalent of approximately four times the depth of water at that point. This is a rough guide and if you are not sure of the depth, then it is better to let out too much warp rather than too little. This ensures that the warp makes as small an angle as possible with the ground where it attaches to the chain or anchor and this in turn helps to pull the anchor along horizontally, causing it to dig in.

To check that the anchor is not dragging, take a transit on shore. Pick two objects which are in line and see whether they move apart or not. When they do not move apart you can relax and attend to the 'snugging-down' of the boat. If staying for only a short time it will be sufficient to furl sails, or tie them down and either remove the rudder and tiller or lash the tiller amidships to prevent it from flogging about. With a light boat it is best to remove it altogether.

Assuming there is no tidal stream, your boat will swing on its anchor with its head to wind. It may slew around slightly but providing that you have raised the centreboard this will not cause much discomfort.

When choosing an anchorage, it is as well to find a spot which is sheltered by the shore (a weather shore), where the water is not more than fifteen feet deep and where you know the anchor will hold. If it is a busy area, make sure that you are out of any channel or commercial shipping area and do not anchor near to moorings as you will more than likely get your anchor fouled up with someone's ground tackle or buoy.

If anchoring in an area which is known to be littered with old mooring chains, bedsteads or other rubbish, you should 'buoy your anchor' or arrange a tripping line so that should the anchor get hooked it can be quickly released by pulling on the tripping line. Fig. 20 shows how this is done. The tripping line/buoy line should be equal to twice the depth of water as a general guide. This also holds good in a tidal area.

Heaving to

This simple manoeuvre is an extension of the 'slowing down' drill mentioned above and it is necessary to be able to do it in a dinghy as in a larger yacht. It can be used when carrying out repairs, when caught out in moderately strong winds or even in order to wait for your friends to catch you up.

If you only wish to change places in the boat, then a very simple heaving-to position will suffice. Simply get on to a beam reach and let fly so that both sails flap. For longer periods the following drill will be needed.

The technique varies a little from boat to boat and light to strong winds, but the principle is the same. Slow your craft down by using the luffing drill that I mentioned under 'Anchoring' and then bring it to a stop by going head to wind. By fixing a transit on shore you should be able to tell when the boat has lost all way. The aim then is to hold the boat in a bows-to-wind position by balancing the headsail against the mainsail. This is done by backing the jib, not too much at first, and sheeting in the main. The centreboard can normally

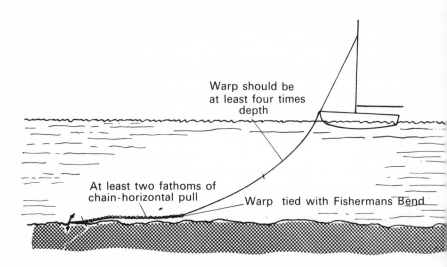

Warp should be
at least four times
depth

At least two fathoms of
chain-horizontal pull

Warp tied with Fishermans Bend

Fig. 20(a). How to anchor

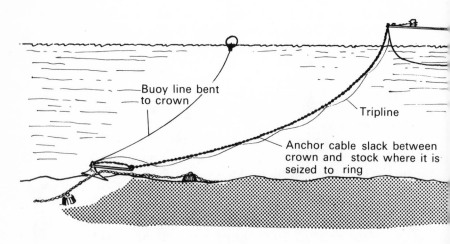

Buoy line bent
to crown

Tripline

Anchor cable slack between
crown and stock where it is
seized to ring

Fig. 20(b). Two methods of tripping a fouled anchor

be left about halfway down but if the wind is strong this could be dangerous and it should be raised rather more.

In light dinghies the mainsail often does not need to be used. Simply put the helm down hard and keep it there and use this to counteract the effect of the backed jib. By trial and error you will find the combination of jib-mainsail-helm which best suits your particular boat.

The boat will eventually settle so that it lies with the wind slightly on the weather bow. In very strong winds the jib will need to be backed only a little and if the head still blows off then lower the centreboard more.

A dinghy such as a G.P. 14 will lie comfortably hove to in wind strengths up to about Force 5. Above this it becomes difficult and rather dangerous, as a stationary boat is very vulnerable to a strong gust which may blow it over, particularly if the centreboard is down.

A displacement yacht with a heavy keel can lie hove to in winds up to about Force 8 or 9. In these conditions the helm would be lashed and storm jib and trysail (in place of the mainsail) would be hoisted. Fig. 21 shows the approximate positions of sails and rudder for a

Fig. 21. Heaving to

dinghy in the hove to position. I must stress again that each craft will vary in its ability to heave to.

In practice the term 'heaving to' is used rather loosely. What I have described is really 'lying to'. Heaving to is when a large boat's speed is reduced in heavy weather by hauling the jib 'aback'. Heaving to in a dinghy is not quite the same as heaving to in a displacement yacht. Do not expect your dinghy to remain in one spot; it will drift quite a bit.

Heaving to is a good position from which to carry out reefing.

Reefing

As the wind strength increases, so should the area of sails carried be decreased. Some dinghy sailors are loathe to reduce sail or reef and often leave it until it is too late. Admittedly, a racing machine often does not have the same need to reef as does a day boat. The racing helmsman will push his boat harder than his cruising counterpart and expects a certain amount of damage to his boat and gear. He will also plane whenever possible and much of the exhilaration of sailing comes in a good blow when a boat like a Flying Dutchman can reach speeds of 15–20 knots on the plane. But reefing is good seamanship and often means the difference between survival and catastrophe. It is no use carrying full sail only to capsize a hundred yards from the finishing line!

The best way to reef a dinghy is to substitute a smaller suit of sails. A Wayfarer, for instance, will handle very nicely in a Force 6 with Firefly sails set. Some classes have two recommended suits of sails, e.g. the Enterprise with its racing and cruising sets. Reducing sail area in this way cuts out many problems. The kicking strap in particular is still functional.

Other methods of reefing are by reef points which are usually found on larger and/or older types of boats, roller reefing and furling. The latter method is used on most modern dinghies. The mainsail is furled around the boom and a smaller headsail is set, perhaps a jib in place of a genoa, or even no headsail at all. In some circumstances, for instance, when reaching or running before the wind in strong conditions, the mainsail is lowered and the jib only is used (see Chapter Nine).

A few boats have a furling gear fitted to the luff of a headsail so that the headsail can be reefed simply by hauling on a rope. The Wyke-ham-Martin gear is a good example of this method. Generally, however, headsails are changed or done away with and it is the mainsail which requires a definite reefing technique.

Firstly, heave to or sail slowly with the jib backed while the mainsail halliard is eased and the sail rolled around the boom. The crew, with practice, can do this job, while the helmsman is left to concentrate on sailing the boat, keeping it on an even keel to make the operation easier. I am not going to suggest here how many 'turns' around the boom one should make; this will vary with types of boat and prevailing conditions. Suffice to say that it would not seem worthwhile to put less than three turns in at a time. The main halliard is then 'sweated up' again and the jib can be attended to if necessary before continuing.

There are a few snags in this method, none of which is of vital importance except when racing.

Most kicking straps attach to a slot in the underside of the boom and cannot be operated when the mainsail is reefed. A simple solution to this problem is to either carry a strop of webbing about two inches wide and two feet long which is rolled into the sail as it is reefed and the outer end attached to the kicking strap, or simply to roll a sailbag into the sail and use the cord to attach the kicking strap. A better method is to use a 'claw' type of attachment for the kicking strap; this encircles the boom, sail and all and can be used whether reefed or not.

Another consideration is the shape of the sail. As the roach is often fairly 'full' on the average dinghy sail, when reefed the after end of the boom will drop lower than normal, leaving very little space for the helmsman to operate. A solution here is to roll in a shaped batten to take up the fullness in the sail when it is furled.

Other problems largely concern the shape and efficiency of a sail, and in many racing classes owners find it necessary to carry a light-weather sail which is full and of a light-weight cloth and a heavy-weather sail which is cut much flatter and is of heavier material. The latter is not so difficult to reef effectively.

If you are lucky enough to have roller reefing gear, remember to lightly oil the working parts occasionally. The operation of this gear is fairly straightforward and can be practised at first in calm conditions, perhaps even on shore. Keep a little tension at all times on the halliard so that the gear handle is pulling against this. It is also a good idea to keep the sail partly filled while reefing so as to keep its wrinkle-free shape as far as possible.

The technique of tying reef points requires some explanation. First tie down the luff cringle to the boom, then the leach cringle which will also be held out to the aft end of the boom in a similar way to the clew outhaul. The reef points should then be tied around the *sail* with a reef knot (see Fig. 25), taking care to get the same amount of tension on each one and gathering up the sail neatly at each point. A cringle, by the way, is the eyelet let into the sail. It will be easier if the boom is supported during this operation.

Mooring in non-tidal waters (*For Tidal Waters, see Chapter Eleven*)

Picking up a mooring involves the same principle as anchoring, i.e. slowing the boat by luffing and turning the boat head to wind to stop. But whereas anchoring does not need to be exact to within a few feet, mooring does, and it therefore requires more precision. In addition it often has to be carried out in close proximity to other craft so more care and skill is required. It would be sensible, therefore, to gain experience in open water with a dummy buoy placed specially for the occasion if necessary.

It is helpful to drop the foresail before picking up a mooring. This clears the foredeck for action and leaves the crew free to attend to the business of collecting the buoy, while the helmsman will have a clear view as he approaches.

Until you are very sure of your ability, have a dummy run before actually picking up the mooring. If you approach on a close reach, i.e. with the wind slightly ahead of the beam, you will have the mooring buoy well in view all the time and it should be picked up by your crew when still on the weather bow.

Whether the pickup is made by hand or with a boathook will depend on the size of boat, but beware! I have seen many crews slide gracefully off the shiny foredeck as the helmsman luffs up to a buoy, forgetting in the delight of his new-found skill, to ease the mainsheet!

After a dummy run you can re-adjust your approach as required. Remember the slowing down routine: luffing and easing sheets. A boat is often travelling much faster than its occupants estimate; it is only when close to buildings, jetties, etc., that a boat's speed can be judged accurately.

Ideally you should lose way and come to a halt with the mooring buoy six inches away from the weather bow. The crew then pulls it aboard and, after passing it through a forward-positioned fairlead, makes it fast to a cleat, samson post or mast while the helmsman should be losing no time in raising the centreboard and lowering the mainsail.

If the mooring is your own and used for a small boat only, it will be enough to secure the boat by a rope, but with all heavy moorings the rope to which the buoy is attached should be pulled in until a chain is reached and the craft moored directly to the chain. If you are using somebody else's (heavy) mooring, pull in the chain, attach your own painter to it, then lower away a little so that the chain is not in contact with your boat. Do not use the buoy rope for this as once this wears out and breaks the mooring ground tackle may be lost for ever. Do also take care to guard against chafe through your fairlead. A piece of plastic hosepipe fitted over the rope should prevent this.

If you are leaving your boat on a mooring, the rudder and tiller should be removed, or lashed amidships in the case of larger craft. Sails, too, should be removed or tied down securely and all loose gear stowed in the bottom of the boat. Do not leave anything dangling over the side except, perhaps, fenders.

Do not under-estimate the amount of skill required to pick up a mooring. If necessary, it is better to drop all sails in open water, get out the oars and row across to your mooring, rather than risk damaging other people's boats in a crowded harbour.

I hope that Fig. 22 will help you to understand the mooring procedure.

Coming alongside

The first rule here is always to approach the lee side of a jetty, hard, slipway, etc., if that is possible. The technique required is similar to that of mooring, except that the point of sailing on which you approach may be forced upon you by the shape of the shore. If possible, a reach or close reach is preferable. Lose way gradually by easing sheets rather than by luffing, but keep enough way on to steer around other craft or other obstructions. If you are carrying fenders place them in position over the side before commencing the run in. If compelled to approach from the weather side, then follow the procedure outlined under 'Lee shores' below.

Approaching from the lee side, try to slide your bows alongside rather than bang the jetty head on, and have your crew ready to fend off forward in case you misjudge the speed of approach. He should also be ready to jump ashore and secure the boat temporarily with the painter. Sails can then be lowered and centreboard and rudder

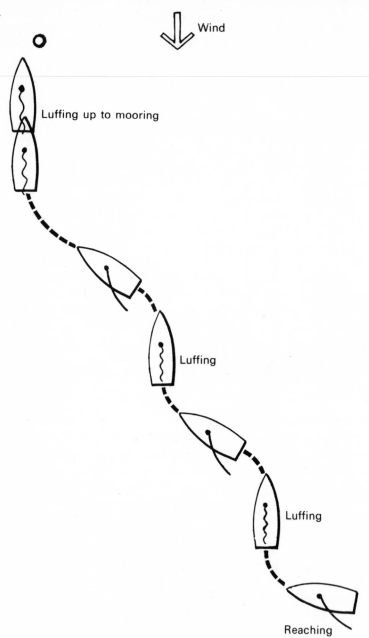

Wind

Luffing up to mooring

Luffing

Luffing

Reaching

Fig. 22. Mooring

attended to. If the landing is only temporary, and someone will be watching the boat, it will not be necessary to remove the rudder, nor to make any more permanent tying up arrangements. If other than temporary, however, the boat should be well secured, as shown in Fig. 23.

In practice it is rarely necessary to leave a light dinghy alongside for any length of time and it is normally unwise to do so. Therefore, the use of springs (see Fig. 23) does not arise. But in the case of a heavy sixteen- to eighteen-foot day boat it may well be practicable to do so.

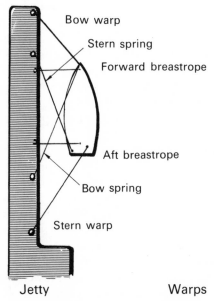

Fig. 23. Warps used in making fast alongside

There are one or two courtesies involved in lying alongside. In the first place most sailing club jetties are intended for landing only and should not be littered with tied-up boats. If it becomes necessary to leave your boat alongside a quay, then the appropriate authority should be sought for permission to do so. This may be a club secretary, a harbour-master or a private owner. In particular, do not leave your boat alongside a commercial quay without first checking that you may do so; you could cause delay and consequent loss of earnings to those who earn their living afloat.

Finally, and perhaps most important, if you do have to lie along-side another boat, do place fenders, and do make sure that you tie on to samson posts or deck bollards/cleats rather than onto some weaker part of their craft. Unless your boat is very small and theirs is large, you should also tie up to the shore so that their mooring warps only take the strains of one craft. And do find out who will be sailing first before going off to the pub for the evening!

Lee shores

These two words will either bring tears to the eyes of even the most seasoned yachtsmen, or induce them to launch into a long history of all their narrow escapes!

I would refer you back to Fig. 16. Let us be sure what a lee shore is: the shore that the wind is blowing on to. The dangers of lee shores are much greater for large boats than they are for dinghies. If blown on to a sandy, muddy or shingly lee shore in a dinghy you will probably be able to jump out and haul your boat out of the water to safety. It is only the rocky lee shore which spells disaster for dinghies and big boats alike.

Nevertheless, there are many good reasons for needing to approach a lee shore with great care, and there will be many occasions when, in a dinghy, you will have no choice in the matter of whether or not to land or launch on a lee shore. So let us look at the problems of landing and getting off a lee shore which does not have the compli-cations of tide and surf. (These hazards will be dealt with under 'Sailing in Tidal Waters', Chapter Eleven.)

Fig. 24 shows a typical approach for landing, and this can be used if the landing place is a beach, jetty, quay or whatever.

Plan ahead; heave to at least fifty yards offshore and directly up wind of your landing point. Drop the mainsail and stow it out of the way, then sail in on jib only, letting it fly when still a few yards away to slow the boat down. Be ready to raise both the centreboard and rudder blade if landing on a beach or slipway and have your crew jump out, though not too soon, to prevent the boat crunching on to concrete or pebbles.

There is an exception to this routine: for an inexperienced person it would be better to drop both sails and row ashore in any but light winds.

When getting off a lee shore it will be necessary to sail away close-hauled and this means that the centreboard must be lowered. Now

here is a problem if launching from a beach. The usual way to overcome it is for the helmsman to get his feet wet. Another way is to row
out, anchor and then hoist sails. If you decide on method one, the
helmsman should hold the boat by the head while the crew hoists
sails, fits rudder and lowers centreboard as much as possible. The
helmsman then pushes off and scrambles in over the quarter. Care
should be taken not to sheet in the jib before the main or the boat will

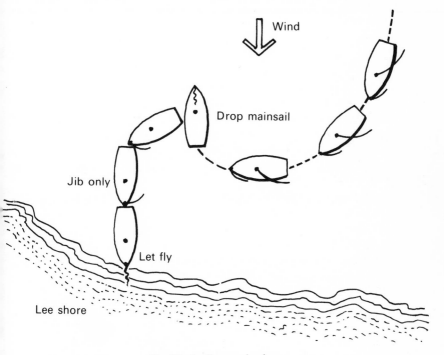

Fig. 24. *Landing on a lee shore*

be quickly blown back on to the shore. Some prefer to hoist the jib
only when safely away from the shore.

In deep water, as from a jetty or quay, it may be possible to sail
straight off, though it can be very difficult to get the mainsail hoisted
as the boom will foul the shore and it is usually much more seamanlike to row away. It saves time in the long run.

In a bay it is often possible to find a part of the bay which is not
a lee shore, so do look around and find the *best* place to launch. With
a straight coastline, of course, you will not have any choice.

Lee shore skills, like many others in sailing, depend upon the helmsman and crew being constantly alert and planning ahead. I cannot stress too strongly the need to be thinking at least two hundred yards ahead all the time you are sailing. By doing this you can anticipate trouble and prevent it. This is the essence of good seamanship.

SIX

Ropework

Types and sizes of rope

Until the 1950s natural fibres were used exclusively on boats, but the years since have seen the development of nylon, terylene and polypropylene. Nowadays very few modern boats still use natural ropes. Apart from one or two special situations I will assume that we are going to use man-made fibre ropes as these have great advantages in strength and handling qualities over the older types.

A confusing number of trade names are given to synthetic ropes, but the two most common materials are terylene and nylon. Nylon is strongest and has a great deal of stretch (up to 40 per cent of its length before it breaks). Because of this elasticity it is unsuitable for halliards or headsail sheets, although the stretchiness is an advantage when used as an anchor warp or for mooring.

Terylene has much less stretch than nylon and a pre-stretched terylene is manufactured specifically for halliards.

Both terylene and nylon can be bought in a threestrand 'laid' form and also as a plaited rope, i.e. an inner core covered by a continuous outer sheath. The plaited variety is easier on the skin and is, therefore, often used for sheets.

The properties of synthetic ropes are as follows: they do not absorb moisture to any great extent; they are very strong, will not rot and can be handled as easily when wet as when dry. They also have a much longer life than natural fibres, so repaying their initial higher cost.

In Britain rope is categorized by the measurement of its circumference. The following table shows the sizes commonly used in boats up to about eighteen feet, and their respective breaking strains:

Circumference (inches)	Sisal	Manilla	Poly-propylene	Terylene (H.T.)	Nylon
$\frac{1}{4}$	46 lb.	75 lb.		310 lb.	
$\frac{3}{8}$				510 lb.	
$\frac{1}{2}$	240 lb.	280 lb.		650 lb.	700 lb.
$\frac{5}{8}$				875 lb.	
$\frac{3}{4}$	520 lb.	635 lb.		1,250 lb.	1,650 lb.
$\frac{7}{8}$	728 lb.	896 lb.		1,700 lb.	
1	0·48 tons	0·59 tons	0.94 tons	1·00 tons	1·31 tons
$1\frac{1}{8}$				1·25 tons	
$1\frac{1}{4}$	0·63 tons	0·78 tons	1·40 tons	1·56 tons	2·05 tons
$1\frac{1}{2}$	0·94 tons	1·18 tons	2·00 tons	2·19 tons	2·94 tons

More knots

In addition to the basic knots shown in Chapter 3, you should learn the reef, sheetbend, double sheetbend and fisherman's bend if you want to be a complete seaman. These knots will cover most of the situations which you are likely to meet in a small boat. Fig. 25 shows how they are tied.

Each knot has a specific use, e.g. the reef knot for tying reef points, the fisherman's bend for attaching an anchor to its warp. In addition to this specific use there will be many other situations where it can be used. So try to form the habit of using the correct knot for each job; this is good seamanship and will help you to avoid accidents.

Here are some uses for each knot shown:

The reef is now only used for reef points and for tying battens into batten pockets. It is not as safe a knot with synthetic rope as it was with natural fibres. For this reason it is a sensible precaution to tie an extra half knot after you have tied the reef, making the sequence: right over left and under, left over right and under, right over left and under. Pull the ends tight after each 'under'.

A sheetbend is a very useful knot and can be used in almost all situations where two ropes are joined together. When one rope is thinner than the other, a double sheetbend is used. Take care to get the ends of the two ropes coming out on the same side, otherwise you will have a left-handed sheetbend which is not so secure, particularly in synthetic rope.

The fisherman's bend is the anchor knot but it can also be used in any situation where a round turn and two half hitches is used. It is safer than the latter as the greater the pull on it the tighter it locks.

Reef

Sheet bend

Double sheet bend

Fishermans bend

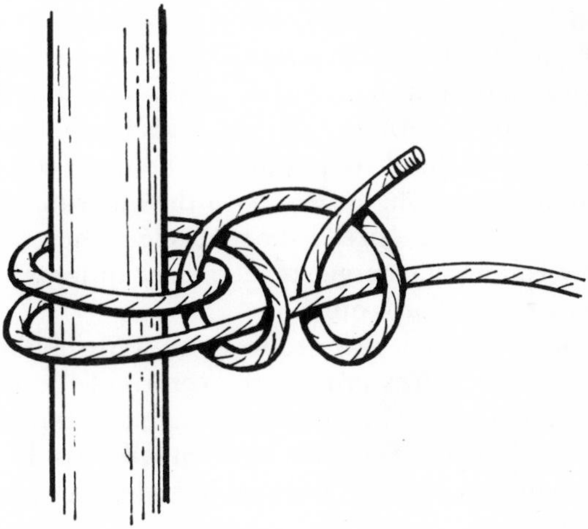

Fig. 25. More knots

Rope handling

Treat all the ropes in your boat with respect. Every one should have a correct place and be coiled and cleated carefully so that in an emergency you will know exactly where to find each halliard, sheet or warp.

Modern dinghy cleats come in many different models. Most of them are self-jambing so that it is rarely necessary to put a locking turn on a halliard. With a two-horned type always make a complete turn before doing figure-of-eight turns. With the jambing type just one turn is sufficient and the remainder of the halliard can then be coiled and hung loosely over the cleat by passing a loop around the coiled part.

Synthetic ropes do not shrink when wet as hemp does, so it is perfectly all right to make a locking turn if the cleat is fairly large and of the non-jambing variety. Another method is to use a slippery hitch (simply a loop passed under the previous turn). This has the advantage that it can be quickly released.

When making fast to a post, a bargees' hitch is very seamanlike. It is also quick and safe and easy to let go in a hurry. Take two turns around the post and then pass a bight (loop) of rope under the standing part of the rope and over the post, then another bight in the opposite direction and over the post, and finish off with a round turn.

If making fast to a ring, a clovehitch with a loop in one end is a good temporary method; but if the boat is to be left, then a round turn and two half hitches should be used, or even a fisherman's bend.

Most laid ropes are 'right-hand lay' and should be coiled clockwise. A laid rope is normally three strands and the strands are twisted together into a spiral. When coiling, hold the coil in one hand and give each new coil a slight twist with the other hand. All the coils should be about the same size. Take some care when coiling. It will certainly repay you in an emergency, e.g. in a capsize when you might have to release the halliards quickly.

Coiled warps which are to be stowed should be finished off with two or three turns around the centre of the coil and then the end passed figure-of-eight fashion through one end of the coil.

A skill often neglected in modern sailing is the use of a heaving line. This can be a lifesaver and should be learnt early. One end of the line will be a 'monkey's fist' to give some weight to the end which is heaved. You will need to get someone to show you this complicated

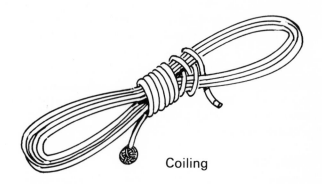

Coiling

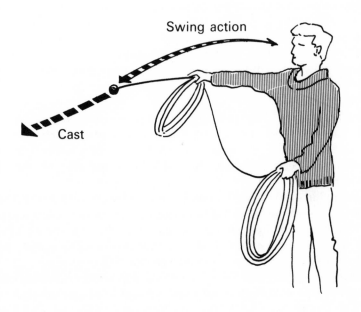

Swing action

Cast

Fig. 26. Heaving line

knot or spend a winter evening sorting it out from a good ropework book. If you do not know the monkey's fist, tie two or three bunched up figure-of-eight knots in the end of the rope; it is almost as good.

When heaving, split the carefully coiled line into two parts with the monkey's fist in your best throwing hand. Throw this end in the way that a discus thrower does and then open the other hand so that the second part of the coil can 'snake out' as the weight comes on it. It is essential, of course, to make sure that the inner end of the coil is tied on before heaving, otherwise the result is the same as lowering an anchor and chain which is not secured. Both can be rather expensive mistakes! See Fig. 26.

Whippings

Diagram 27 shows the four types of whippings required in the syllabus of the R.Y.A. Intermediate Certificate. As there are many good books on this subject I shall leave the reader with these excellent illustrations and recommend him to learn, if possible, from an experienced seaman.

With the advent of synthetic ropes it must be recognized that there is not the same need for whippings as there used to be. A whipping is made to prevent the end of a rope from unlaying or fraying. This can be achieved just as effectively on a synthetic rope by burning the ends and rolling while melted. With practice a good, quick and neat seal can be made which will be even more permanent than a whipping.

Splicing rope

A splice is either used for joining two ropes together (long or short splice), for sealing the end of a rope as in a whipping (back splice), or for making an eye in a rope end (eye splice). In practice I have found it only necessary to use the eye splice regularly and this is shown in Fig. 27.

Much nylon and terylene rope is now plaited, and while the manufacturers take great delight in insisting, by the use of attractive display boards, that this rope can be spliced, in fact it is rather difficult to do so, and it is only in laid rope that splices will normally be made so this factor further reduces the need for skill in splicing.

I would emphasize, that it is very necessary to master the art of eye splicing, because a modern dinghy will have at least four eye splices on it. The halliards attach to the sails by an eye splice and shackle. The mainsheet may be eye spliced to its lower block, and the kicking

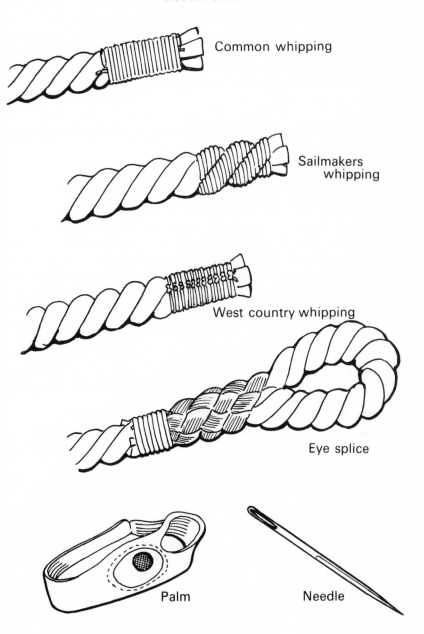

Common whipping

Sailmakers
whipping

West country whipping

Eye splice

Palm   Needle

Fig. 27. Whippings and eye splice

strap will almost certainly have an eye splice on it. If you have lanyards instead of bottlescrews, these will be eye spliced to the shrouds, and loose gear, such as buckets and balers, can be secured to the boat by an eye splice, at least at one end.

A splice is much stronger than a knot and is more permanent. Splicing should be practised regularly particularly 'splicing the mainbrace'. This is the very seamanlike habit of issuing an extra rum ration to all the crew! It really has nothing to do with rope.

Splicing wire

This skill, if done by hand, is difficult and not without its hazards. Nowadays it is normally only done by professional riggers and sailmakers. Otherwise, it can be done by machines. This is called 'talurit' splicing, and I expect that if you examine the wire splicing on your dinghy shrouds and forestays you will find a small, compressed collar near the eye and thimble splice. Almost all small boat wire splicing is now done in this way. It is very quick, not expensive and certainly much neater than can be managed by hand. Most sailmakers, riggers and many yacht chandlers have talurit machines and can carry out a repair to your shroud or halliard in a matter of minutes.

Talurit splices have one disadvantage. They often leave a small but sharp fringe of wire ends protruding from the end of the collar. This should be covered with an inch or two of rigger's tape to prevent sails, sheets, etc. from catching on it.

Many larger yachts have swageless terminals on standing rigging. This is a sort of screw-on-barrel end which grips the wire end of a shroud tightly as the barrel is screwed up. These are very good, though rather expensive and not used much on dinghies as yet.

Throughout this book I stress the need to acquire seamanship skills as I feel that these are often lacking in modern dinghy sailing. I do feel, however, that it is not necessary to stick to the old methods of whipping and splicing when there are now modern and perfectly good ways of achieving the same, or even better, results. If you own a Thames Barge or an 'old gaffer' it may be quite a different matter, but then this book is not written with such owners in mind. It is written for the modern dinghy sailor.

SEVEN

Boat maintenance

During the season
Hull

Careful attention to a few details during the season will save you spending a great deal of time on winter repairs.

It is important to realize that a boat out of water is not in its natural element and it needs special chocking and ventilation.

Support a dinghy evenly on its keel with a chock fore and aft. A car tyre makes an excellent dinghy chock, or scooter tyres, being much easier to handle. If the boat has self-balers, leave them open and arrange the chocks so that water will run out of them. Otherwise chock the boat sloping towards the bung holes and leave the bungs out. Many craft have a stern buoyancy tank, in which case it is necessary to leave two sets of bungs out to drain it.

Besides fore- and aft-chocking, consider lateral support. The boat should not heel to one side, and supports placed under the bilge strakes (usually one each side is sufficient) will prevent this.

Very often a dinghy can be partly supported on its launching trolley but the drainage considerations must not be forgotten. It will be necessary to pull the trolley out a little and place a chock under the stern.

Fibreglass boats do not take kindly to contact with concrete, and much damage can be done by allowing parts of a G.R.P. hull to either scrape along or bang down onto a concrete slip or quay. In the absence of anything softer, even a piece of wood will prevent damage if placed between the boat and the concrete.

Many people consider a boat cover a worthwhile investment. For dinghies, the boom-up cover is the most suitable type. This uses the boom in its normal position to form the ridge of a 'tent' which easily sheds rainwater. As well as protecting the boat from rain, it will protect varnishwork from sun, which, particularly in salt air, will do a great deal more damage than rain. See Fig. 28.

Next comes ventilation. This is much more important in wooden boats than in G.R.P. Make sure that air can get to all parts of the hull. This means removing any buoyancy tank hatches or inspection covers and perhaps bungs as well. It also means ensuring that there is a flow of air under a cover.

In practice the problems of ventilation are not so acute in dinghies as they are in larger yachts which are locked up sometimes for weeks at a time.

The windage area of a mast adds up to several square feet. For this reason it is always necessary to tie a boat down when it is left ashore. Some club dinghy parks have ringbolts provided for this purpose, but if this is not the case you will need to drive a couple of stakes into the ground, set at an angle rather like a tent peg. The rope ends can be tied down with a round turn and two half hitches and a clovehitch used for around the mast. It is not sufficient just to run a turn around the mast as this will still allow the boat to blow over.

When leaving a boat it may be tempting to 'cheese' sheets and painter down on the deck. This looks very shipshape and smart but, in fact, is not a seamanlike practice. It leaves the rope stiff and difficult to handle and makes a terrible mess of a varnished deck after only a few weeks. It may even permanently mark a fibreglass deck if the atmosphere is dirty. So it is better not to leave ropes on the deck at all; leave them coiled loosely in the boat. All rope should be coiled loosely so that it can dry out naturally.

If a boat is parked in an area where the air is polluted, or if you sail on salt water, it is advisable to hose down with fresh water after each sail. Salt will dry on the hull, ropes and sails, and leaves an abrasive surface similar to sandpaper.

Dirt, too, is a problem. It will become engrained in paint or varnish, or even on a fibreglass deck, so that it may be necessary to wash the boat *before* going afloat. It depends where you sail, how rich you are and how much you care for your boat as to how much time you will need to spend on this sort of maintenance.

If any boat is kept afloat for long periods, it will be necessary to treat the bottom of the hull with a coat of antifouling. This is a special paint which resists marine growths, worms in particular.

Try to be alert for weaknesses, and spot them early. Frequently check that rudder fittings, cleats and fairleads are secure, and if you find a loose one fix it there and then. A longer screw or a nut and bolt to replace a screw should do the job.

It is also essential to check the standing rigging, sails, battens and shackles regularly. Normally once the habit is formed you will do this automatically every time you use the boat. The old proverb 'a stitch in time . . .' is very true where boats are concerned. I shouldn't be surprised to find that it was a sailor who first coined this phrase.

Fig. 28. Chocking and tying down

Rigging

If rigging is correctly adjusted when the mast is stepped it will probably not require any further adjustment for a season. In a new boat, however, there will be quite a lot of stretch in new rigging.

When stepping the mast initially, a certain amount of trial and error will be necessary.

The experts in most racing classes have found the best setting for standing rigging and it is usually common knowledge, so if you buy a class boat check with other owners for advice.

If no information is available, set the mast up so that it is vertical and central, i.e. not leaning to either side. You can use the main halliard as a plumb line for this operation. Set up the forestay in this position, then tighten the shrouds the same number of turns each and this will give the mast a slight rake aft which should be about right. Before starting this operation, make sure that the boat is exactly horizontal as it will be when afloat and without anybody aboard.

In the case of a boat which has a mast stepped on deck, e.g. the Enterprise, ensure that the standing rigging is fairly tight, otherwise the whole lot may jump off the deck in a chop. I can recall this happening on the starting line in a club championship race!

A word about bottlescrews. These will have locknuts to prevent them unscrewing. Do not put any faith in these. Thread a piece of stiffish wire through the hole in the centre of the screw and bend it around the top and bottom to be sure that the screw cannot come undone. Having done this, cover with rigging tape or Scotch tape to prevent sails or sheets chafing on the wire. Lanyards are much easier to use and to replace, and they cost far less than bottlescrews. If you use lanyards, tie a few good half hitches to secure the ends well after setting up your rigging.

Most people take sails off their boat but leave the running rigging in the boat, complete with stopper knots. Rope is expensive and it is much better to undo the knots, wash in fresh water and hang up to dry in the garage at home.

Don't forget to check shackles, clevis pins and safety pins regularly. The pins of soft metal shackles wear out surprisingly quickly.

Sails

Ideally terylene sails should never be folded but hung up loosely in an airy building out of sunlight. Unfortunately not many people have a twenty-foot-high sail loft in their homes, but with a little ingenuity something can be worked out.

If the sails must be folded, keep the folds to a minimum and take care not to kink the wire in the luff of the headsails. Many headsails have a clear, see-through, polythene panel near their foot which will eventually crack if folded. It is possible to make the folds across the sail and keep this panel in one fold.

Battens must always be removed from sails and stored flat.

When sails are used in a salt atmosphere, or if they become sprayed with sea water, they should be washed in fresh water. Sea water will leave an abrasive deposit on the sails, and the terylene stitching, which stands 'proud' of the cloth, will eventually fray.

Out of season

Storage

With the arrival of G.R.P. the problems of winter storage have become less acute. A glass boat will probably survive even if left out in the open throughout a winter. The only danger is that of ice, which can crack a hull apart. So care should be taken to keep water out by providing a cover or turning the boat upside down. Careful and even chocking will minimize the risk of the hull warping, although a well-cured G.R.P. hull should not suffer in this way unless very badly treated. In any event the boat should be kept off the ground, if only to keep it clean. Before laying up for the winter, it should be washed in warm water with a little detergent added, then dried before being stored, and any buoyancy hatches and locker doors left open so that air can circulate. A cover will help to keep a boat clean as well as protecting the wooden parts, so even with G.R.P. it is advisable to use one if indoor storage is not possible. A good polishing with a hard wax will also pay dividends.

A wooden boat needs more careful winter storage. Plywood boats should be stored under cover in a dry atmosphere and chocked evenly at bows, stern and amidships. Carvel and clinker hulls should be under cover whenever possible but should preferably be left in the open air so that they will not dry out excessively, when warping and splitting of planks may occur. In all cases the boat should be at least six inches off the ground, and care should be taken to prevent rain-water entering. Light dinghies up to about fourteen feet can be inverted, but with heavier and larger craft it is usually best to store them the right way up with supports along the keel at about every three feet.

A clinker hull will need a few days to 'take up' when it is put back in the water. It will be very leaky at first, but as the planks absorb moisture they will swell, sealing any gaps.

A boat should never be left on its side. This will cause distortion and serious damage can result. A small dinghy, such as a Mirror, can, however, be stood up vertically against a wall on its transom.

Masts should be removed from the boat and hung up with supports every few feet so that the whole mast is horizontal without any curve. It may, alternatively, be placed on a rack with supports similarly placed along its length. In practice it is difficult to provide completely even support, and for this reason the mast should be

turned over on to its opposite side at approximately monthly intervals. Metal masts should, if possible, be stored indoors in a dry
atmosphere, but a wooden mast is better out of doors, though under
cover. If allowed to dry out too much, a wooden mast will develop
'shakes', i.e. slits along its length. Most old wooden masts have some
shakes, caused largely by the sun. Small shakes are not serious and
can be filled with a filling compound. A shake should not be confused
with a compression fracture which would show across the mast. This
could be very dangerous and, under load, the mast may snap without
warning. A similar fracture can occur in metal masts but may not be
so easily seen.

All standing rigging should be removed from the mast and washed
in fresh water. When dry it can be wiped over with an oily cloth and
vaseline smeared on. Coil loosely, label and hang up indoors for the
winter. The grease will need wiping off before re-rigging, otherwise
sails will be marked.

All rigging should be inspected before storing away and replacements made or repairs done. Stainless steel wire will last several years
if looked after carefully, whereas galvanized wire will only last about
two seasons. Running rigging should be discarded when it becomes
either worn or too stiff to handle. With synthetic fibres this may be
after three or four season's use. Often halliards and sheets wear only
at certain points. It is not necessary to discard the whole rope. Either
reverse it or cut off a worn end. Halliards can usually be reversed so
that the worn part becomes the 'tail', which does not take any
strain.

Terylene sails should be washed and dried, then hung loosely in an
airy room out of direct sunlight. Alternatively they may be folded
carefully and loosely and stored in the sail bag. Again, it is advisable
to inspect them carefully before storing, and to carry out any necessary repairs. The areas which receive most wear are batten pockets,
headboard, clew outhaul and the luff.

Cotton sails can be stored in a similar way and must be very dry to
avoid mildew and rotting. They will be better if not exposed to the
air, but neither should the bag be completely sealed.

The rudder, tiller and other small items of gear should be cleaned
and stored sensibly indoors in such a manner that they will not warp
or twist. All shackles and clevis pins should be examined for wear,
and a drop of light oil applied to them.

Painting and Varnishing

Modern developments in paint and varnish technology have proved a boon to the small-boat owner. It may well be unnecessary to re-paint or re-varnish more than every second year if polyurethanes are used. However, if one accepts that half the fun in boat owning is the 'messing about', there is some excuse for the enthusiastic owner who spends more time painting his craft than actually sailing her.

The thorough preparation of surfaces is all-important. Sanding down, filling any small cracks or holes with 'stopper', washing off any dirt or grease, are all prerequisites for a good finished surface.

When applying paint, choose warm weather and a dust-free wind-less day, and use a good quality brush.

Varnishing is very similar to painting, but it is very important not to varnish in cold or damp weather as the finished surface will then carry a 'bloom'.

Whether using paint or varnish, all prepared wood must be thoroughly dry. In some cases this will mean cleaning off old paint or varnish with a scraper and leaving for several days before applying a new coat. It is, therefore, a job that should not be hurried.

Normally if wood is bared, a coat of primer will be needed, then two or three undercoats before the final top coat.

If painting over an old (painted) surface, make sure that you use a similar paint. For instance, never mix polyurethane with ordinary paint. The same applies with varnish.

Simple repairs

G.R.P.

Here is the greatest advantage of glass-fibre boats. Repairs are simple, quick and cheap.

Most iron mongers sell fibreglass repair kits but, if possible, obtain matching gel coat (the outer shiny surface) from the manufacturers of your boat, otherwise colour matching is very difficult. One problem here is that the gel coat only has a shelf life of about six months.

Small dents and scratches are filled by simply mixing a little gel coat resin and filling with a wooden spatula. Overfill to allow for shrinkage and sanding down afterwards. Once dry, the surface should be trimmed with the appropriate surfoam plane, sandpaper and finally wirewool. The latter gives a very polished finish. A final polishing with a metal polish will give a good gloss finish to the surface.

Where the strength of the material has been affected, build up layers of resin and glass-fibre mat on the inside of the hull, waiting until each is dry before applying the next layer. After two or three layers, apply gel coat to the outside and smooth off as before.

Quite large holes can be repaired with practice; up to three or four inches across, or even more where the shape and strength of the hull is not badly affected, e.g. on side decks. If the topsides are damaged, however, it may be preferable to have the repair carried out professionally.

Take care to remove any paint, grease, dirt or moisture before starting on a repair.

Glass-fibre tape and resin can also be used to repair tillers, spinnaker booms and jib-sticks. Simply clean off any paint or varnish and apply the tape well soaked in resin. Two layers are normally sufficient.

Any part of a G.R.P. hull which is likely to be subjected to strain or rubbing should be strengthened with wooden battens, bonded to the inside of the hull, e.g. the bilge strakes of a Wayfarer, or anchor points for fittings. Dry and unpainted wood strips or blocks are glassed into position with resin and glass mat.

Where any additional gear is fitted, like cleats or fairleads, wooden backing plates can be used under a G.R.P. deck or on the inside of a hull. The extra gear is screwed or bolted through the fibreglass layer and into the wood. This prevents any cracking on the area and gives a solid form for the screws to 'bite' into, in addition to strengthening the hull at that point.

It is also possible to repair quite large holes by bolting a wooden plate on the inside of the hull first. This should be waxed, and should cover the hole completely. Layers of chopped strand mat and resin can then be built on this and finally a gel coat before sanding down. Afterwards remove the plate and lay several layers of fibreglass on the inside of the hull to strengthen. These should well overlap the repaired area. Bolt holes can be filled with a resin paste made from resin and Polyfilla.

Here are a few simple rules for using fibreglass:

1. Temperature should be between 15 and 25 degrees centigrade.
2. A dry atmosphere is desirable.
3. Avoid doing work in direct sunlight.
4. Make sure that the surface on which the repair is to be

carried out is absolutely dry. This is particularly important if a wooden boat is being repaired with fibreglass, and heating should be used over a few days if necessary to dry out the area to be repaired.

5. Only mix enough catalyst and resin for immediate use.

6. Use acetone for cleaning brushes and tools.

7. If an accelerator is used, it must never come into direct contact with the catalyst, otherwise an explosion will occur. Mix them into the resin separately.

8. Make a 'no smoking' rule when fibreglassing. Resins, catalysts and accelerators are all highly inflammable.

Plywood

Plywood for marine use should be stamped B.S.S. 1088. This ensures that it is weatherproof. It is rather more expensive than ordinary plywood.

Damage to plywood rarely results in a neat hole; it normally splits in several directions. Before repairing, it is necessary to cut away all the damaged area. This is best done by drawing and then cutting out a diamond shape to include any of the damaged part. The new piece is 'scarfed' in. Edges of the hole should be sloped with a chisel or surform tool and a new piece of wood cut to exactly the same size, with its edges sloping the opposite way to that of the hole.

The new piece is then glued into position with a good resin glue with either a pressure plate or screws to hold it in position until it is set hard. If screws are used, they can be withdrawn later. For extra strength it may be desirable to glue a second, larger backing plate of plywood to the inside of the hull. This will depend on the size and position of the hole. It should not be necessary on any hole smaller than about four inches across unless it was close to a chine, transom or stem.

Where there is much damage, it may be necessary to replace a whole section of plywood. This is not beyond the capabilities of an amateur but it would be advisable, if doing this for the first time, to seek the advice of a professional boatbuilder, or perhaps a more experienced friend. Remove all traces of the old section very carefully so that neighbouring sections are not damaged. Paint and varnish on the neighbouring sections must also be removed so that new glue will bond. The new sheet should be identical in shape to the old one, although it should be five to ten millimetres larger so that it can be planed and sanded down to make a good fit after glue has set. It should be fixed by glueing and screwing.

Any repair joins can be filled with a filler cement and, when dry, sanded down carefully, new wood being primed and then painted as described earlier.

Beware of buying old plywood boats. After some years, plywood is liable to delaminate, particularly if moisture has been allowed to get at the hull. Also, unless the end grain has been well protected throughout its life, it may be that the inner laminations will have become soft and pulpy. So careful inspection of areas around hog, keel, transom, stem and chines is essential.

One way of protecting plywood hulls is to coat with glass-fibre. While this is perfectly acceptable for a cruising boat, it would add too much weight to a racer.

Clinker, Carvel and Moulded Wood

In my view the repair of these craft is not something that an amateur can easily accomplish. It requires a knowledge of and skill in boat-building and should sensibly be left to the professional. Because of the difficulties and expense in having these types of hulls repaired, ply-wood and G.R.P. have developed very rapidly in recent years. The boat owner who wants to sail his craft and spend the minimum of time on maintenance will wisely opt for a G.R.P. boat.

EIGHT

Survival

Practice of survival techniques

Just as the development of new materials has given rise to new thinking in boatbuilding technology, so does the type of modern dinghy produced require a different type of approach to survival philosophy.

For instance, a modern planing dinghy is *expected* to capsize from time to time, so self-balers and transom flaps have become standard equipment and the average racing dinghy helmsman will have developed an effective and quick righting drill which probably will not even necessitate him getting wet above the knees!

The beginner, however, should not fall into the trap of assuming that righting drill, man overboard skills and other survival methods, do not need practising.

Lives could undoubtedly have been saved on many occasions had some knowledge and experience of the required skills been obtained before foolhardy beginners put afloat. Serious sailing accidents happen mainly on the sea but inland areas, too, have trapped the unwary.

Survival in cold water

By 'cold' water I mean the water experienced around the shores of Britain and on inland lakes and rivers for the majority of days in a typical British summer. Winter temperatures are much lower, and survival then will be a matter of minutes rather than hours.

'Immersion exposure', that is the lowering of the body-core temperature by exposure of the skin to cold and wet simultaneously, is a very real danger at any time of the year in Britain and should never be underestimated.

Although exceptional cases of survival have been known, the average life expectancy of someone immersed in the sea off our coasts without specialized protective garments (e.g. a wet suit) is between twenty minutes and four hours. Personal factors such as whether a person panics, how fat they are, their age, all vary the survival time. Women tend to survive better than men.

It is now known that a person who keeps still in the water will not cool down nearly as quickly as someone moving about. The action of water moving over the surface of the skin has a very great cooling effect. Any clothing, particularly waterproofs, will provide insulation, trapping a layer of *still* water between it and the body.

While death may not occur for several hours, the period during which a normal person can usefully assist himself to survive will only amount to about thirty minutes at the maximum and may possibly be as little as ten.

There are two essential rules for a person who finds himself in the water:

1. Stay with the boat always.
2. If you cannot right the boat, tie yourself to it and relax, keeping as still as possible.

The 'stay with the boat' philosophy has been proved time and time again. If the shore is only a matter of *feet* away, then it may be permissible to break the rule but, remember, distances over water always appear less than they really are, and in survival tests even strong swimmers have been unable to complete fifty yards in water temperatures of less than forty degrees F. So the water temperature is all-important.

Another reason for staying with the boat is that it can be easily seen by rescuers, whereas a single head bobbing about in even quite small waves is very difficult to see. Furthermore, if the worst happens and you become unconscious, you may still be rescued if tied to the boat and wearing a fully inflated lifejacket.

Wet suits improve survival chances dramatically and if you take part in winter sailing it is essential to wear one. Besides being windproof they insulate by trapping water inside the suit. This layer of water quickly warms to body temperature. An overall or boiler suit should be worn over the top of a wet suit to protect it. Fortunately wet suits can now be made by the D.I.Y. man for about the same price as a set of waterproofs.

It is possible that in the near future even better insulating material than neoprene will be developed and it may be cheaper and lighter.

The R.A.F. and R.N. are constantly researching this subject. At present survival suits for aircrew are produced but they are very expensive and quite out of the reach of dinghy sailors. However, I am sure that technology will come up with a thin and cheap material with very high insulative properties before very long.

Prevention, of course, is preferable but if an accident cannot be prevented, then certain aids for attracting rescue can be employed.

If sailing alone on the sea, some form of distress flare must be carried. These flares can be bought at any chandlery store and consist either of a red hand-held flare for use close to the shore, or red rocket flares which can be seen several miles away. Sets of mini-flares can also be purchased but as they only rise to about 250 ft. they are not very useful; they also require a firearms certificate.

Lifejackets have whistles attached. The whistle can be used to blow S.O.S. (... ——— ...) or code flags N and C can be hoisted.

If no distress equipment is carried and you can stand on your upturned boat, then raising and lowering the arms at the side of the body is also a distress signal. Remember to face the direction from which you might be visible.

All of these methods are *international* signals for use in distress. Others, including those for use in larger craft, can be found in the International Regulations for Prevention of Collision at Sea, Part F, Rule 31. (See page 181).

It is also an advantage to know single letter signals of the International Code. These are 'Urgent and Important Signals' and can be used to notify other craft of danger, or may inform you of some hidden danger. For example, the letter 'U' means 'You are moving into danger'. One hour per week throughout the winter is sufficient to make you familiar with all the letters of the Morse Code.

Capsize righting drill

It is impossible to lay down a method which will be one hundred per cent successful with every type of boat. I will firstly detail a method which I have used extensively over the past few years and which I have found works well with the majority of modern dinghies up to about sixteen feet in length. Afterwards I will recommend one or two amendments to suit particular classes or types of craft. Like many other aspects of dinghy sailing, this method is relatively new and was developed primarily for boats of light displacement and a large amount of built-in buoyancy.

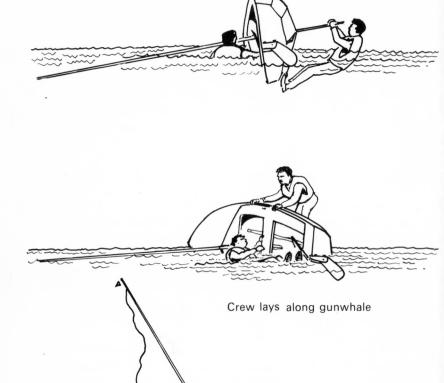

Crew lays along gunwhale

Crew "Scooped" in

Fig. 29. Righting after capsize

I hope that you will have tied in all loose gear before going afloat. If so – prepare to capsize. Here is the drill:

1. Maintain contact with the boat at all times.
2. When in the water after a capsize, check verbally and in a loud voice, that all the crew are in a safe position. You may not be able to see each other and this is most important.
3. The helmsman then goes to the centreboard while the crew moves to the transom (to avoid being trapped under the boat should it invert). As soon as the helmsman steadies the boat by grasping the centreboard (putting some weight on it, even though he may not be able to climb on to it), one crew member moves to the mast side and passes the jib sheet over the upper gunwhale to assist the helmsman in righting. During this time any additional crew members move to the bows and hold on there.
4. The helmsman should, if possible, then climb on to the centreboard and, keeping his feet near the hull, lean back holding the jib sheet until the boat begins to come up. The crew on the mast side should retain contact with the boat but *not place any weight on it*. As the lower side of the boat begins to come out of the water, this crew man lies in such a position (close to the boat) as to be easily 'scooped' in as the boat rights. Do not try to right the boat until all crew members are in position.
5. Often it is possible for the helmsman to climb aboard off the centreboard at the same time as the crew is scooped up. If this is not possible, however, the crew slackens off all sheets and then helps the helmsman to climb aboard. Additional crew members can then also be helped aboard.
6. Regain control of the boat immediately; you may be sailing into the side of an expensive yacht or getting tangled up with a racing fleet!
7. Bale out or open self-balers and sail away.
8. Check all gear, particularly halliards and sheets, to make sure they are not streaming over the side.

After three or four practices in fine, warm weather with help near at hand, you will find that it is very easy. Now here are my suggestions for those boats (or people) with whom there will be special problems:

1.   If you are not successful at righting the boat *first* time, fully inflate your lifejacket before trying again. If you leave it until later you may not be in a fit state to do so.

2.   Very often either the helmsman or crew, or both, will be able to climb out on to the centreboard as the boat goes over. In this case it is just a matter of careful balance and no one needs to get wet. Lean backwards on the centreboard, and as the boat comes up climb quickly over the gunwhale and into the boat. This is the way that most racing helmsmen do it.

One warning: If the mast has already touched the water it is too late to climb over on to the board. In trying to do so you will make the boat 'turn turtle' and perhaps get yourself trapped under the upturned hull. You should, instead, drop into the water, so taking your weight off the 'wrong' side of the boat.

3.   If a boat does become inverted, the first aim is to bring it back on to its side so that the righting procedure outlined above may be used. To achieve this, lean on the centreboard with toes on the gunwhale, or use a jib sheet to gain extra leverage. Do not bounce but apply constant weight. Some boats come up very slowly; it may take several minutes.

4.   The 'roll-in' method is designed to get at least one person on board. If the boat is righted and all the crew are in the water, it will be necessary for one person to go to the stem and hold on, acting as a sea anchor, while the other climbs aboard, probably over the stern, using a loop of the mainsheet to step in if necessary.

5.   If the helmsman is small and the crew large, it may be necessary to change duties by mutual agreement so that the heavier person always does the righting and the lighter one is scooped. Even if you cannot climb on to the centreboard, whoever rights the boat it is essential to lift the trunk clear of the water so that as much of the weight as possible is on the centreboard.

6.   With a heavy boat, particularly one with a gaff-rig, it may be necessary to lower sails before righting. In this case the crew releases both halliards and lowers the mainsail (the jib will normally come down on its own), and reports verbally to the helmsman on completion; while the helmsman balances the boat by placing his weight on the centreplate to avoid inversion. Proceed then as above.

7. Boats with only a small quantity of buoyancy will only take one person aboard initially. If more than one climbs aboard, then water comes in through the tiller port in the transom or through the centreboard case. In this situation one person in the boat should bail (furiously!) while the other holds the boat head to wind at the bows. It may even be necessary to plug the centreboard case with clothing or a rag if the boat is of an older type with inadequate buoyancy. One should take the greatest care not to capsize this sort of craft.

A boat which is full of water is very unstable and great care must be taken not to tip it up again. If at all possible, make sure that you get at least one person aboard as the boat comes upright. He or she can then balance it while the other crew climb in. If nobody gets aboard, the boat may sail away and a potentially dangerous situation results.

It is all-important to expend only the minimum amount of energy during righting drill, as fatigue follows very quickly, particularly in very cold water. For this reason the drill should be thoroughly practised during the early days of learning to sail.

Speed in baling and getting the boat under control is, likewise, of prime importance. Capsizes often occur in crowded harbours where an out-of-control boat can be a very dangerous thing.

If self-balers are fitted, the water will drain out quickest on a reach. It will not drain at all if the speed of the boat is less than about three knots.

Small catamarans are becoming increasingly popular and do sometimes capsize. The method of righting is peculiar to this type of craft. Assuming that it has inverted completely, the technique is to sink the forward end of one hull by standing on it and making the boat 'loop the loop'. It will then normally land the right way up. Members of the Amateur Yacht Research Society (A.Y.R.S.) have experimented with righting quite large cats by flooding one hull and then pumping it out when righted. There is undoubtedly room for much more research on this interesting subject.

Generally it is not possible for an average boat's crew of about twenty stones combined weight to right anything much larger than a Wayfarer, although experienced racing crews frequently capsize and right boats as large as a Flying Dutchman. Water surface conditions are a decisive factor, together with wind strength. It may be very difficult to right even a fourteen footer in short steep seas, whereas there would be little difficulty in getting a National Eighteen up on a calm lake.

There is always the possibility that, for various reasons, it will not be possible to right a dinghy. If this happens the correct survival procedure may make the difference between life and death. You should:

1.   Check that all lifejackets are fully inflated.
2.   Tie all crew members loosely to the boat either with the lifeline on lifejackets or with sheets.
3.   Instruct crew to relax and keep still.
4.   Fire distress flares or make other distress signals at regular intervals.

Man overboard

In what situations is a man likely to fall overboard from a dinghy? The answer to this question is probably 'in any situation'. A helmsman or crew can easily miss hooking his toes under the toe straps as he leaps for the side in a sudden gust. Or a crew member may be knocked unconscious by the boom as it comes across.

There is one situation which can be rather tricky: that of the single-hander. There is quite a lot to be said for all single-handed sailors wearing safety lines to attach themselves to the boat, even in dinghies.

The dangers of falling overboard in tidal waters, where there will be waves and tidal streams, are of course much greater than inland. A person in the water, even in two-foot waves, will soon disappear from the view of his companion in a dinghy. So quick action is necessary. At all costs one crew member must keep an eye on the man in the water and should keep pointing at him so that the helmsman can steer towards him.

There are basically two methods of doing an 'about turn'. The fastest is to gybe and round up in a circle; the other to bear away, tack, bear away and round up.

The second method is slightly slower but much safer if there is only one person left to handle the boat; it avoids gybing which, in windy conditions, can be risky. See Fig. 30.

Whichever method is used, take care to round up with the man on the weather bow. If he is on the lee side in any sort of choppy condi-

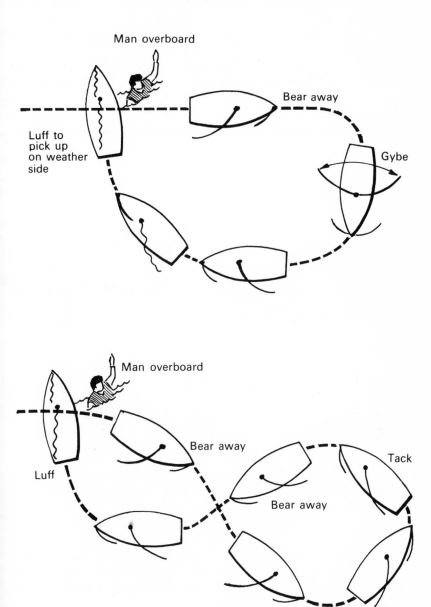

Fig. 30. Two methods of return for man overboard

tions, he could be seriously injured as the boat bangs down on top of him. Once contact is made, heave to while he is helped aboard.

A person with saturated clothing is very heavy to lift, and the lever principle can be used here. Heel the boat and lift the 'victim' on to the gunwhale so that his trunk is well over the side deck. Then move across to the other side of the boat, so raising the deck with the casualty on it. He will probably be able to slither into the boat at this point. If he is unconscious, tie a line around his armpits and heave him in.

Fig. 31. Retrieving a person overboard

An alternative method (see Fig. 31) is to let him climb in over the transom. You can lower a loop of the mainsheet or make a 'ladder' of loops with the painter, for him to step in, but do not be surprised if he finds this too difficult.

If your man overboard is very heavy or unfit, or both, you may have to face the fact that you will not be able to get him back aboard;

so if you are alone in the boat in this situation, don't waste time and his energy trying. If you are reasonably near to the shore, fasten a line around his chest and tow him ashore (face upwards, please). If you are not near a shore and if there is no other help at hand, then you have only one alternative: capsize the boat and get him aboard by the scoop method. It may sound drastic but it is the only logical thing to do.

Jury rigs

Choose a fine day with a gentle Force 2 breeze blowing. Row yourself out into the middle of a safe 'pond', having first removed your mast, centreboard, rudder and tiller, and see if you can arrange a jury rig which will enable you to sail first on a run (easy), then on a reach (harder) and finally closehauled (who says it's impossible?). This will test your initiative, prepare you for a real survival situation and probably teach you more about your craft than you have learnt to date.

Look around the boat. What can be used to replace these essential pieces of gear?

With some ingenuity a mast of sorts can be made from an oar. Not all the sail can be set, but enough to sail on a reach at least.

Another oar would serve for steering. After all, this is the way that many natives of the Pacific Islands steer their craft even today. It should be tied to the transom for easy handling.

If you carry floorboards, it may be possible to push them through the centreboard case. If this is not wide enough, then lash them to the side of the boat like a lee-board and this will (perhaps) enable you to sail closehauled. In practice you would be very unlucky if all these items of boat gear were damaged in one foul swoop. There is usually some mast left after a breakage and with an oar lashed to the top of it quite a lot of the original sail area can be set.

Oars *or* floorboards, *or* even, in dire emergency, a thwart will suffice for a daggerboard, and that should still leave one oar for steering.

While on the subject of jury rigs, let us look at one or two other calamities that are likely to befall you.

A frequent one is the broken shroud. If spotted quickly, it should be possible to go about on to the opposite tack, so taking the weight off the broken side while temporary repairs are carried out and before the mast comes crashing down. If a lanyard is left permanently attached to the bottlescrew and chainplate, very slightly slacker than the bottlescrew, then the weight of the mast will be immediately transferred to this should a breakage or failure occur in the bottlescrew or shackle.

A broken boom is no great tragedy. It is usually possible either to use the mainsail loose-footed, or drop it and run for a lee shore under headsails only.

The wise cruising sailor will carry one or two spares and will have examined all his gear before setting out so it should never happen! It

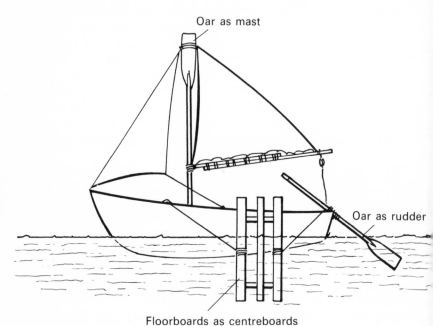

Oar as mast

Oar as rudder

Floorboards as centreboards

Fig. 32. Jury rig

will probably be the racing helmsman who, anxious to win, will push his craft that little bit too hard. In practice this *is* when the damage occurs and this factor is borne out by insurance companies who often ask higher premiums for insuring masts and sails while racing.

The only real essential is propulsion. When we remember that several people have actually rowed across the Atlantic and recently a couple completed the first Pacific row, there should never be any real cause for concern if all boats carry a good pair of oars and rowlocks.

Handling under tow

The reader may be excused for thinking that handling a small boat under tow is not really a matter for inclusion in a chapter on 'Survival'. But he would be quite wrong. If you had been towed at close on fifteen knots by a fast patrol boat in a fourteen-foot dinghy (he thought he was going slow), you would appreciate that this heading is aptly placed.

The maximum safe towing speed for dinghies is about eight knots. Five knots is much more comfortable, while three is ideal. Make sure, before accepting a tow, that your 'Sir Galahad' knows this.

The towing warp must be attached to something solid and firmly fixed. The ideal is a good strong samson post on the foredeck. Alternatively the mast or a thwart will do. Always lead the warp through a fairlead well forward. If this is not available, be very careful to steer a straight course.

When under tow, sails should be dropped, centreboard fully raised and the crew weight placed well aft. In the absence of a rudder, a planing dinghy will tow easily if the crew sits in the stern. Never go forward to the foredeck while being towed. Always steer a straight course behind the towing boat. This is particularly important if towed in two lines abreast, as if boats are steered outwards, away from each other, this puts a greater strain on the boat and on the towing warp, and will appreciably slow down the towing craft. If this is a typical club rescue boat of fairly low power, towing half a dozen craft, it can be very frustrating for the skipper.

When turning, follow the same curve as the tow boat, and remember, if in a tideway, that you may have to 'over steer' to miss moorings, etc., which the leading boat easily cleared.

In choppy or rough sea conditions it is common practice to weight the tow line midway between the two craft. This acts as a shock absorber and prevents sudden jerks on waves.

NINE

Controlled sailing

General boat control

Boat control will develop with experience but it is possible to hasten the acquisition of skills by the practice of particular techniques. Some of these special techniques will be described in this chapter. You should be thinking about principles constantly while practising these techniques, for it is only when the principle is fully understood that a helmsman will become proficient enough to act quickly in any given situation.

One of the more important principles in sail-boat handling is that of the 'pivot'. All boats pivot around a central point, the Centre of Lateral Resistance, and can be handled much more effectively, therefore, through adjustment of main and head sails than by the rudder. 'Balance' is all-important. In order to understand how the boat balances around a central point, we must refer to Fig. 33.

'C. of E.' stands for Centre of Effort and is the 'averaging out' of all effort exerted on the sails. 'C.L.R.' is the Centre of Lateral Resistance.

When the C. of E. and the C.L.R. are on the same line, i.e. the C. of E. is directly above the C.L.R., then the boat is perfectly balanced, having neither lee helm nor weather helm (Fig. 33). Theoretically, this is ideal but in practice just a small amount of weather helm is preferable for (a) safety, and (b) good tiller control.

If the C. of E. is aft of the C.L.R., then the boat will have weather helm, i.e. if the tiller is not held, the boat will luff by itself. If the C. of E. is forward of the C.L.R., it will have lee helm and would bear away if left to its own devices. This is dangerous as, if for example, the helmsman fell overboard before the crew could take hold of the tiller, the boat would have gybed.

What affects the position of the C. of E. and C.L.R.?

Let us take the C. of E. first.

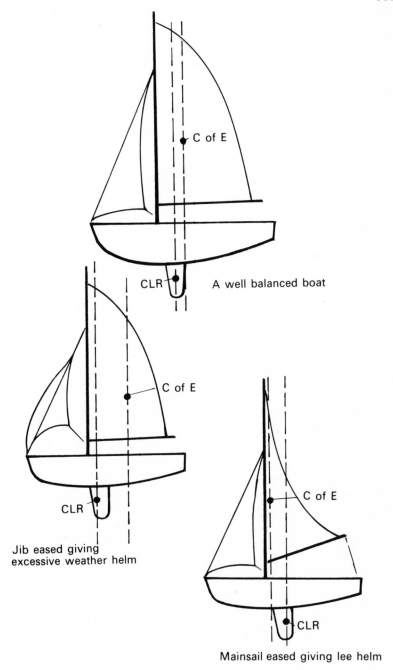

C of E

CLR

A well balanced boat

C of E

CLR

Jib eased giving
excessive weather helm

C of E

CLR

Mainsail eased giving lee helm

Fig. 33. Weather and lee helm

The position of the sails decides where the C. of E. will be. If the sails are moved forward as they are when sheets are eased, then the C. of E. moves forward and vice versa, so that a closehauled craft will have a C. of E. much further aft than one on a run.

And the C.L.R.?

In a dinghy the position of the C.L.R. is chiefly dictated by the underwater shape of the boat, and when heeled over it may be quite different to its shape when on 'an even keel'; the position of the centreboard too, is important (when pivoted up or aft it will effectively move the C.L.R. aft). The position of the crew will also affect the underwater shape of the hull.

Following from the above, it will be realized that to correct excessive weather helm we may:

(a) ease the mainsail/sheet in the jib;
(b) raise the centreboard more;
(c) move the mast forward (a more permanent correction);
(d) move crew aft;
(e) keep the boat upright, or heel it to windward a little.

To counteract too much lee helm:

(a) ease the jib/sheet in the main;
(b) lower the centreboard more;
(c) move the mast aft;
(d) move crew forward;
(e) heel the boat a little to leeward (as in roll-tacking; see Chapter Ten).

Having looked at the principle in theory, let us examine the practical implications.

If you buy a 'One Design' dinghy, such details as the position of the mast and size of centreboard will be unalterable. You can only hope that the designer has done a good job. So you are left with the following ways of controlling the boat:

1. adjustment of main and headsail sheets;
2. raising and lowering the centreboard;
3. fore-and-aft movement of helmsman and crew;
4. sideways movement of ditto to keep boat upright or heeled.

There are, admittedly, one or two minor and more sophisticated adjustments on racing craft but basically it is a combination of these four things which enable you to accurately control your boat. I shall now deal with some of the specific techniques which will help you to obtain good boat control. Constant practice in uncrowded water will pay handsome dividends.

Sailing without a rudder

Choose a calm day for your first attempt and have the oars and rowlocks handy just in case! If possible keep out of tidal water at first.

Get into the middle of a good big space, heave to using sails only, then remove the rudder and tiller.

Make all adjustments gently and a little at a time, but quickly. Sail away on a beam reach first with sails in the correct position and try to keep in a straight line by using your weight to heel the boat to leeward if you need to luff, and to windward to bear away. Afterwards repeat the course on the opposite tack. You will discover that quick but stealthy movement is necessary.

Having tried the heeling method, now experiment with sheet adjustment, sheeting in on the mainsail and easing the jib to luff, and vice versa to bear away. Unconsciously you will be trying all the time to get the C. of E. exactly over the C.L.R.

After considerable practice, test yourself from A. to B. Make the boat follow a straight line to a fixed point. Beam-reaching is easiest. After some practice try broad-reaching and, finally, beating. Sailing closehauled without a rudder is quite difficult. You will need to keep the craft on an absolutely even keel. The slightest amount of weather helm caused by heeling to leeward will make it luff very quickly. When you start beating, try sailing with both sails flapping slightly on their luffs and gradually tighten up.

After some practice of this skill you will probably decide that heeling the boat one way or the other will be the best way to make minor (and quick) modifications to course, but sheets will need to be used for more permanent changes.

When you eventually replace the rudder, try to continue to sail the boat in this way so that the tiller always feels 'light'. Any movement of the rudder to steer the boat causes reduction in speed, however slight.

Should you ever find yourself unable to use the rudder through damage, an oar or paddle can be lashed to the transom and will be quite easy to steer with, providing it goes down into the water at least as deep as the rudder blade does.

If you later decide to race, you will find that this practice has given you a useful introduction to 'roll-tacking' as well as helping you to sail the boat at its fastest.

Sailing backwards

In crowded harbours, narrow rivers or when racing, this technique once mastered can often get you out of trouble. It will also prepare you for the occasion when you 'miss stays', get 'into irons' and find yourself sailing backwards unintentionally.

The shape of a dinghy and the points of attachments of the sails are not so well suited to making it go backwards. Nevertheless, it can be done quite easily.

The essential requirement is to bring your craft exactly to the head-to-wind position. In order to achieve this you must know where the wind is coming from, and here the burgee can be very useful.

Choose a fairly light wind for your first try. Keep the transom out of the water by moving forward. Once the boat is head-to-wind and stationary, instruct the crew to push the boom out as far as possible and hold it there. Raise the centreboard to quarter down and, keeping tiller amidships, wait for the boat to move before 'backing' the jib in a similar way to the mainsail. The jib can be backed with a sheet.

Tiller movement is critical, as you will quickly discover. Only slight movements are necessary and the tiller will work in the opposite way to that which it does when the boat is moving forwards. Providing you keep the wind dead ahead, this 'reverse running' should not be difficult; but if you accidentally slew onto a 'reverse reach', you will soon be in trouble. After some practice, it should be possible to sail in the ninety degree angle of the 'No-Go Zone'.

If several boats take part, it can be good fun to make up an obstacle race which can include sailing backwards, sailing without a rudder and other tests of seamanship such as heaving to and anchoring. You will learn a lot about your boat and get a great deal of enjoyment out of the exercise. I should warn, however, that sailing backwards or sailing without a rudder (no oar) is very difficult in waves or wind strengths of more than Force 3.

Formation sailing

Here is another skill which will rapidly improve your boat-handling ability. If you can get a minimum of three boats and a maximum of

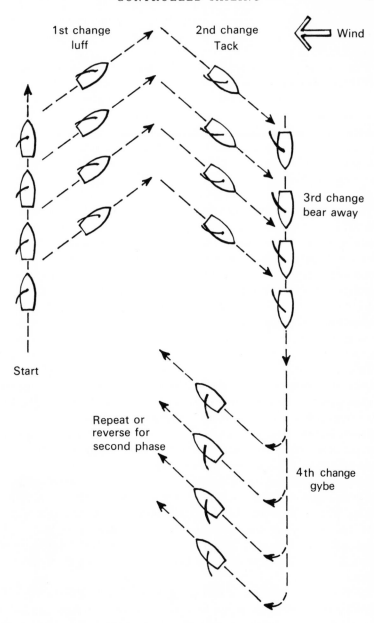

1st change
luff

2nd change
Tack

Wind

3rd change
bear away

Start

Repeat or
reverse for
second phase

4th change
gybe

Fig. 34. A simple formation sailing pattern

six, formation sailing will do wonders for your boat control. It will help to ensure that you are alert, well-orientated and skilful in the various manoeuvres that you have learnt.

Fig. 34 shows the simplest type of pattern for formation sailing. A leader boat is appointed and he will have the basic plan in his mind (or on paper pinned to the thwart). He should also carry a whistle which is blown *loudly* every time he changes his course.

When the whistle blows, all boats do exactly what the leader is doing. Sometimes they will be following him in line-ahead formation, sometimes sailing parallel to him in line abreast and sometimes he will be at the back of the line.

Very quick reactions are necessary and all participants will learn to handle their boats automatically. In particular it will be necessary to control the *speed* of each craft so that they can be kept the same distance apart. On a reach or a beat, boats can be slowed by easing sheets and on a run to sheet in will reduce speed.

All will need to sail a very 'tidy' course, following exactly the route taken by the boat ahead and almost anticipating any change of direction. If the whistle is blown a couple of seconds *before* a change in direction, this is more likely to happen.

As crews become more proficient, it will be possible to progress to true formation patterns as shown in Fig. 35. This is best controlled from a power boat and on a given signal the next part of the sequence takes place. Signals can be flags, shapes or hoots on a hooter or bell. If the latter, it should not be used where commercial traffic may misinterpret the signals as Rule of the Road Signals.

Or again, a specific boat may give the lead. It can be marked distinctively with red sails, etc. Whichever method of control is adopted, everyone will need to learn the sequences and have a diagram of them pinned to a thwart.

At Cowes Week some years ago, a team from the National Sailing Centre put on a display of formation sailing under the direction of Timothy Short, culminating in a mass capsize. This was highly spectacular and caused much amusement ashore. Sailing is not normally a spectator sport; perhaps this idea might be used on regatta days?

However, my purpose in including it here has nothing to do with its value as a spectacle. It is a way in which boat control can be improved and is a very good method of training for those with a little helming experience.

Sequence 1

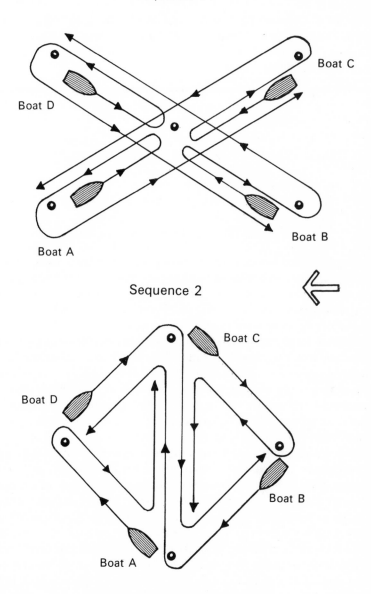

Sequence 2

Fig. 35. Advanced formation sailing patterns

Heavy weather sailing

Sailing dinghies in bad conditions of wind and sea is not something which anyone should *plan* to do, but sooner or later you will be caught out and it is only sensible to prepare for that occasion.

By heavy weather I am referring to wind strengths of Force 6 and above. Here are a few do's and don'ts:

1. Do always set out prepared for the *worst* conditions.
2. Don't ever leave protective waterproof clothing behind because the weather is fine.
3. Do always check your boat's gear before leaving shore.
4. Do always get a weather forecast if sailing on tidal waters.
5. Do always wear lifejackets and tie them securely.
6. Don't delay reefing if the weather deteriorates.
7. Do turn back if conditions are worse than expected.
8. Do obtain local advice before launching in a strange area.
9. Don't ever leave the boat in the event of a capsize.

I have included heavy-weather sailing in this chapter because it is in bad conditions that people tend to forget about boat control and get out of control. Quite a small dinghy can stand up to very strong conditions of wind and sea if it is in good condition and the rigging, sails and fittings have been regularly maintained.

The most important single factor in heavy-weather sailing is the decision to reef. Get those reefs in early and do remember the need for a temporary kicking strap (see Chapter Five). There is more than one way to reef. In very strong winds the best way is usually to drop the mainsail and sail for the nearest shelter on a broad reach under jib only. Or, if you are forced to beat to get to shelter, use the reefed mainsail only.

When cruising in dinghies there are several ways in which you can prepare for the ultimate survival situation. Fit a 'righting rope' under each gunwhale. This comes out through a hole in the side of the boat just under the gunwhale amidships and can be held in place under the gunwhale on each quarter by fixing partly cut away pieces of rubber or plastic tubing. When a capsize occurs, the rope on the upper side can be quickly released and used to right the boat (as in Chapter Eight).

Another safety device is a simple harness for both crew members. Use a length of 1½-inch rope ten feet long with a double bowline on

one end which should have a large and a small loop. The large loop
fits around the chest under the armpits, and the small one around the
neck (loosely!). The other end should be secured to mast or thwart.

While a man overboard in a Force 3 on inland water is merely an
annoyance, a similar occurrence in a Force 6 where there may be
four-feet waves is very serious. It can be extremely difficult to get a
man back into a dinghy in these conditions.

A sea anchor is another useful addition for those who cruise in
small boats. Its function is to keep the head of the boat pointing into
the waves and able to ride out bad conditions. It must be said, how-

Fig. 36. Use of sea anchor on a dayboat

ever, that this would be very limited in an open boat; sea anchors are
really more useful for bigger craft when used from the stern. A
dinghy would normally be better off running for shelter. Fig. 36
shows how a sea anchor is used.

Frank Dye, a famous dinghy cruising sailor, had a drum of terylene line attached to his mast tabernacle on his Wayfarer 'Wanderer'
for his sea anchor. On his trip to Norway in 1964 he used it effectively
in Force 8 and 9 winds.

When sailing in heavy winds it is advisable to raise the centreboard
somewhat even when beating. If a wave and a sudden gust hit the
boat at the same time, a boat with full centreboard will almost certainly go over; it cannot 'skid' at all as a boat with little or no board
will.

Boats larger than dinghies will use the techniques of heaving to and 'lying ahull' in gales. This they can do in safety as they are completely enclosed and also bigger and heavier than dinghies, usually with self-righting keels built into their design. Providing there is plenty of sea room, i.e. that a lee shore is not close enough to be a hazard, they will have few worries.

Dinghies cannot use these techniques for more than short periods. They would either overturn or fill up with water, being too small and too open. Their lightness is also a disadvantage.

One other technique which all sailing boats, large and small, can use is that of dragging warps. In extreme conditions when running for safety under 'bare poles', i.e. no sails set, a boat can be slowed considerably by dragging a rope or ropes behind her. The rope should be fixed with an end attached to each quarter, so making a 'U' shape in the water. This produces an effective 'drag' on the water and the speed of a dinghy which can be potentially dangerous in big seas may be reduced by as much as half.

TEN

Advanced techniques

I hope that anyone who has learnt to helm a boat will find this chapter useful. The additional equipment discussed and the techniques involved in using it will, however, be of particular use to those readers who intend racing.

Would-be racing helmsmen should become fairly competent at general helmsmanship before progressing to the racing 'scene' where quick and automatic reactions and split-second timing are prerequisites for success. It is also desirable to get some racing experience as a crew before moving into the 'hot seat'.

Sail control

Numerous theories about sails and aerodynamics have been advanced. Some experts disagree and new research is being constantly undertaken and new information promulgated for our edification. It is, in short, very easy to become confused. Because of this I shall try wherever possible to confine myself to the practicalities of sail and boat control and leave theorizing to the experts.

Sails are the boat's engine. Paul Elvstrom, one of the world's most successful racing helmsmen, never paid much attention to the hull of his boat, even racing in Olympic competition with poorly-painted hulls. His sails, however, were sacred and he would spend hours just trying to get rid of one small crease.

The flow of air over the two sides of a sail must be smooth and unbroken by any irregularity of surface.

Modern racing-dinghy sails can be adjusted in many ways. Take a mainsail. The three sides: the luff, leach and foot, all have their particular means of adjustment. The luff has a halliard at the head and a sliding gooseneck at the tack to tighten it. It may also have a Cunningham Hole with which to gain extra tautness in strong winds. The leach will normally have a leach line which can be set before the race to best suit prevailing wind conditions. Different types of battens are used to gain extra stiffness in the roach.

The foot of a mainsail has the most adjustment of all. All dinghies utilize a clew-outhaul but many modern racing craft have adjustable clew outhauls fitted to the boom. On some this incorporates a drum which can be adjusted by the helmsman while sailing.

Kicking straps, too, have developed in recent years and many modern boats have very powerful kicking straps which are capable of bending both boom and mast quite considerably.

Additionally, centre mainsheets and sophisticated traveller arrangements on the horse have made it easy to obtain the required sail shape for varying wind conditions.

What are the sail shapes required, and how can these be achieved with modern gear? In order to answer this, we need to remember the theory mentioned in Chapter Three.

The useful driving force is exerted at approximately right angles to all parts of a sail. Fig. 10 shows that a sail is most effective near to its luff, not only because it is tall there but also because the luff has a better angle to the wind (known as the angle of incidence) than does the leach and, therefore, gives more forward drive. But we all know what happens when we luff too much: the sail 'stalls'. The luff shakes because the wind is not filling it, and the boat loses speed. In strong winds we can go closer to the wind providing we can flatten out the sail and prevent that special part next to the luff from stalling.

The point at which a sail stalls is very important. Strong winds, particularly when sailing closehauled, need flat sails, and light winds require rounded, full-bellied sails. If wind can be induced to flow over a well-curved sail, more force will be produced because of the greater pressure differential on each side of the sail (Chapter Three). So in light winds we use well-curved sails. In strong winds, the stalling of a well-curved sail will occur much earlier because air is moving too fast to get 'around' the big curve, so flatter sails are necessary.

Heavy-weather sails are made in a heavier cloth than light weather sails, to stand up to the stronger forces exerted on them. Most people cannot afford two sets of sails and so a compromise suit for most racing dinghies is of medium weight and not too flat nor too full. It is with these sails that all our sophisticated adjustment gear is of most use.

To flatten a medium-cut mainsail we need to bend the mast back, pull the centre of the boom down and tighten the sail at two of its three corners (see Fig. 37). This is done by sheeting down on the kicking strap, tightening the clew outhaul and tightening down on a Cunningham Eye. The bending forwards of the middle of the mast and boom particularly assists in flattening.

There is one other aspect of sail adjustment that needs mentioning. If a sail is pulled in towards the centre-line of the boat at its clew, the force exerted at the leach (at right angles to the sail, remember) is

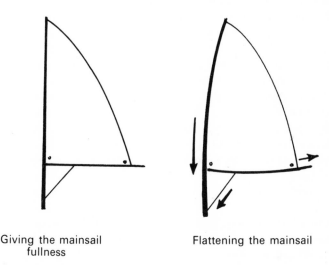

Giving the mainsail
fullness

Flattening the mainsail

Fig. 37. The kicking strap and sail shape

actually going to be driving the boat backwards as it will be past the right angle to the centre-line of the boat. This is where mainsheet travellers come in. By slackening off a traveller, the mainsail can be kept tight but the above problem is overcome and the sail is flattened. In strong winds the traveller will normally be right out at the edge of the transom and in lighter winds it will be pulled in closer to the centre-line of the boat, so assisting in making a fuller sail.

Where a centre mainsheet is used, the sail can be set for a particular point of sailing and then the traveller is 'played' in the puffs, i.e. eased a little as each strong gust hits the boat. This is one of the main advantages of centre mainsheets.

A centre mainsheet is placed on a track amidships so that the helmsman has the tiller behind him in one hand and the mainsheet in front of him in the other. It often attaches to the boom by a 'C' shaped claw or by anchor plates to which the pulley blocks are fastened. Once a helmsman has become used to the centre mainsheet it is usually preferred in racing dinghies. Great pressure can be exerted on the boom at the right place, causing less distortion.

Disadvantages of a centre mainsheet are that it fills up the centre part of the boat, that the sheet cannot easily be held in the other hand when sheeting in, and that either the sheet or the tiller have to be let go when tacking. In fact the tiller is normally sacrificed, as a tack can be controlled easily by good mainsheet handling.

Now to the headsail sheets. All sheets, main, jib, genoa and spinnaker, now have jambing cleats built on to or into their fairleads or blocks. This is essential when racing, as there are many jobs to be done in a racing boat apart from sheet handling. The most common type of adjustment on headsail sheets is a combined sliding fairlead-cum-jambing cleat.

It is important that a jib or genoa is sheeted at the correct angle to the mitre-seam of the sail (the seam bisecting the clew). This setting varies but will be somewhere in the region of seven degrees lower than a continuation of the mitre-seam through the clew with the average genoa. When reaching and the sail is eased out, it is also necessary, therefore, to slide the adjustable fairlead forward whereas when closehauled the setting will be further aft. In light winds also the jambers will be set further forward to give a fuller sail, and further aft in a strong breeze.

In addition to this sheeting angle, the width of the 'slot' between the headsail and the mainsail is important. If it is too wide, the airflow will not be speeded up enough and there will be a lack of power and consequent lack of boat speed. If too narrow, the mainsail will stall earlier and again speed will be less than the possible maximum.

Headsails are very efficient compared to the mainsail. In the first place they are usually set on a wire stay which causes a good deal less turbulence to the airflow than does a mast with shrouds at each side of it. Secondly, they affect the flow of air around the lee side of the mainsail (the slot effect) and when set correctly give about one-third more drive to the mainsail than it would otherwise achieve. Fig. 38 will help to explain this.

In the case of a cutter rig (more than one headsail) this latter effect is further emphasized by additional slots. Look at the curve of any well-set headsail and you will recognize the perfect curve of a bird's wing – which surely must be one of nature's most efficient creations.

So do not underestimate the usefulness of headsails. In addition to speed they also give the helmsman more control of his craft, e.g. when heaving to, or if stuck 'in irons'.

A drastic mistake which beginners often make is to leave the weather jib sheet partly taut after tacking. This pulls the sail across towards the mainsail and spoils the slot. It is very important to always free the weather sheet completely after going about, and also to keep an eye open for it fouling up on cleats, mast and so on.

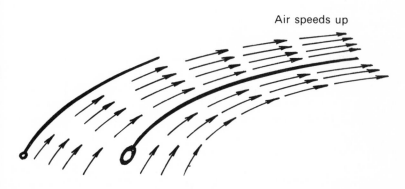

Air speeds up

Fig. 38. The slot effect

The degree of sophistication in sail shape has even led to the introduction of zip-footed mainsails. These have not been widely used, but this development does accentuate how much importance some people place on the need for sail shape to suit conditions. The flat shape of a zipped-up zip-footed mainsail can be converted to a full-bellied sail by unzipping and vice versa.

The control of jibs and genoas has also been aided by tensioning devices such as the mast lever which is pre-set to suit race conditions. The sail halliard is simply hooked on and the lever locked, so that the luff of the sail can be tensioned scientifically and not just by guesswork.

In Fig. 38 it will be seen that the part of the genoa which is overlapping the mainsail is approximately parallel to the mainsail in this closehauled position. This is the normal position although some sail plans benefit from having the genoa a little tighter. If too tight, the mainsail will begin to 'lift' (flutter on the luff) and speed will suffer. The aim should be to obtain the narrowest gap possible without causing the mainsail to lift, and remembering to ease both sails out as far as possible on any point of sailing. Jib (or genoa) and main must move together; it is useless having a well-eased main if the jib is tight, so causing the main to lift.

In racing craft a self-furling jib or genoa will be a great help. This is simply a spring roller attached to the forestay, which, when a line is released, automatically furls the sail around the forestay. For boats with a spinnaker, this gear is almost essential; it can save much time.

Spinnakers

These are race-winning sails but are not necessary on a boat which is to be used primarily by the non-racing helmsman. Many of the out-and-out racing machines have a spinnaker but quite a few of the one-design classes do not, e.g. the Enterprise.

Fig. 39 shows the various parts of a spinnaker and its gear. As the spinnaker boom changes sides, on gybing, so the names of the sheet, guy, leach, luff, clew and tack are changed. This sometimes causes confusion to beginners.

A spinnaker is made up of a large number of panels and represents the ultimate in the sailmakers' art. There are numerous different 'cuts' and types. Once a sailmaker has found a successful shape, he tends to stick with it; so with spinnakers, more than with any other type of sail, it is easy to recognize a particular sailmaker's style.

Being made from very light terylene or nylon material, spinnakers fill in extremely light airs.

Nowadays they are used on a run, a broad reach and a reach and, even occasionally, on a close reach.

Spinnakers require much practice in handling. Hoisting is usually a combined effort for helmsman and crew. It will vary from one boat to another, but here is an outline of the drill:

1.   Crew attaches halliards, sheet and guy to the sail and the boom to the tack, remembering to keep everything outside standing rigging.
2.   Helmsman holds boat steady (preferably on a run) and balances to avoid heeling.
3.   Crew hoists the sail while the helmsman holds the sheet and

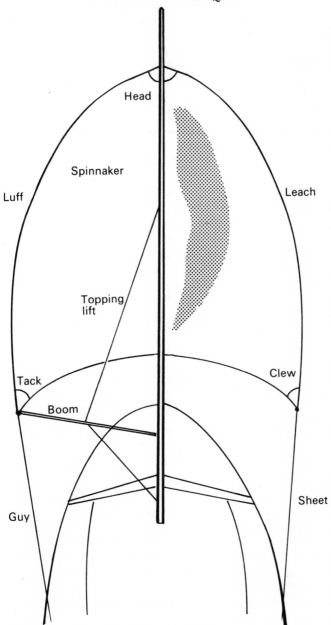

Fig. 39. Parts of a spinnaker

guy to prevent sail getting out of control. Some helmsmen prefer to hoist while the crew check the sail as it goes up. The helmsman will normally stand up during this part of the operation, steering with the tiller between his knees.

4.   Crew clips topping lift to boom and boom to mast. On dinghies the topping lift and the downhaul are one and the same thing.

5.   Helmsman sheets in on guy, making it fast on weather side, then on the sheet to trim the sail.

6.   Crew takes over the spinnaker sheet and balances the boat.

It is often necessary for the helmsman to let the mainsheet go during this operation. At all costs he must prevent the boat from heeling as it is quite unstable with the spinnaker set and would quickly capsize.

Many racing dinghies have a spinnaker 'chute' (a funnel arrangement) fitted in the foredeck to allow quick hoisting and lowering, and a retrieving line leading from the centre of the spinnaker allows it to be pulled into this very quickly.

Once set, the spinnaker must be 'played' by the crew to gain maximum speed. This should be done via the sheet and not the guy. Occasional resettings of the guy may be necessary, but generally it should be sheeted back until the boom is as near to a right angle to the centre-line of the boat as possible and cleated. Any spilling of the wind must be done via the sheet: playing of the guy can result in capsize.

When first using a spinnaker, choose a day with a light breeze and keep on a run. Later, when you have become proficient at hoisting, lowering and gybing with a spinnaker set, will be the time to attempt reaching.

To gybe, first get the boat on a dead run, keep it on an even keel, then gybe the mainsail. While the helmsman holds the spinnaker sheet and guy, the crew unclips the boom from the mast, fastens it to the new tack, unclips from the old tack (now the clew) and clips into the mast. While he does this, the helmsman lets the spinnaker go across the boat to the new weather side. The crew then takes over the sheet and guy and resets them both.

Care must be taken to keep the boat dead before the wind throughout the operation. Gybing fast and on different points of sailing will come later as confidence is built up.

To lower the spinnaker, first unclip the boom from the mast, then from the tack. The helmsman then eases the sheet and the tack of the sail is pulled in to the mast, the foot 'bunched' and the sail lowered. Normally the helmsman will handle the halliard while the crew stows the sail away.

When handling a spinnaker, it is necessary to remember that the two basic principles of headsail handling still apply, i.e. the sail is controlled by its sheet and the tack is kept in a fixed position to enable an even flow of air over the sail to be maintained.

The stowage of spinnaker booms can present problems which have to be solved by each class. The Cherub class has a pole too long to stow in the boat so it is slung under the main boom when not in use. Generally though it will be possible to stow it in the cockpit.

Trapezes

Why is trapeze equipment necessary?

As racing dinghies have had more and more sail piled on and become narrower to make them go faster, the trapeze has become necessary in order to counteract the extra heeling incurred through these speed-inducing factors. The further out crew weight can be moved, the ligher the weight required to keep the boat upright. It is a logical progression from sitting out.

A trapeze is a very simple piece of boat equipment. It consists of two parts: that worn by the crew (the belt) and the wires attached to the boat.

The belt is rather like a corset which supports the whole trunk and is adjustable on the shoulder and waist straps. It culminates in a large metal or nylon clip in front of the body. This in turn clips on to the metal fitting on the wires which are suspended from each side of the mast from the same point as the shrouds. Additionally there are handles incorporated in the wires to facilitate swinging out and in.

A boat with a trapeze can rightly be regarded as wholly a racing boat. The Internation Flying Dutchman, 505 and 470, are good examples of trapeze boats. They are both exciting and difficult to sail, requiring agility as well as expertise and a fine sense of balance as well as strength.

Most crews who trapeze wear wet suits as they rarely get through a race without receiving a dowsing. Good communication between helmsman and crew is necessary if the craft is to be kept upright.

Capsizes often occur to windward because a crew did not get back into the boat quickly enough.

It is difficult to teach the use of a trapeze; this is one aspect of sailing where practical experience is all-important. 'Get afloat and have a go' is the best possible advice for any would-be trapeze artist. Here are one or two tips, however, which may help.

As soon as a trapeze is in action, the crew's weight must be kept on it. Slide out over the side of the boat in a relaxed position so that you hang rather like a sack of flour from the wire. Face forwards, slightly, and straighten the forward leg first. It is this leg which remains braced most of the time. If your helmsman accidentally luffs and you do not have the forward leg braced, not only will you suffer a ducking; you will possibly gyrate around the forestay as though it were a maypole!

Feet should be kept apart to balance, particularly in strong winds. By bending your knees in the lulls, your body weight can be brought closer to the boat without the need to come right in.

It is essential to have a suitable clip on the harness which can be quickly unhooked, as you will need to unhook, duck under the boom, hook on again and swing out, all in about six seconds when beating to windward in a strong breeze.

Handling a spinnaker and a jib on a reach in a medium breeze from a trapeze is probably the most difficult skill in sailing, and much practice is required before you can expect to be really proficient; but the thrill of riding a trapeze boat on a fast plane will prove well worth the effort involved in learning these new techniques.

Toe straps

The function of toe straps is simply to keep both helmsman and crew in contact with the boat when leaning out over the side to balance. They must be comfortable and fit the people in the boat. This means that normally they must be easily adjustable.

Even when sitting on the sidedeck, feet should be under the toe straps; a temporary lull in the wind can otherwise result in a man overboard. They should be securely fixed and the two halves should be independent of each other so that when the helmsman sits in his crew does not shoot out another six inches! Most new boats will have toe straps fitted and these may need to be re-fitted to suit your own requirements.

Self-bailers and transom flaps

Any light planing dinghy will benefit from having self-bailers fitted. They are generally a metal fitting placed in the bottom of the hull about one-third way along from the stern. They rely on the Ventura principle for operation: when open and the boat is moving at more than about three knots, the water moving past the hull creates a sucking force or vacuum which draws water out through the bailer.

Many self-bailers have non-return flaps fitted, but these tend to leak when the boat is stationary so it is safer to close them when not in use.

Another type of self-bailer is the transom flap. This is either a hinged flap on the lower part of the transom or a hole filled by an ordinary plastic funnel. When opened, particularly after a capsize

Fig. 40. Transom flaps. Horizontally hinged and vertically hinged

and if the boat can be sailed fairly fast, a large quantity of water can be self-bailed as the apertures are much larger than in a hull self-bailer. They therefore bail much quicker than a self-bailer but must be correctly positioned, i.e. low and central on the transom, and in most classes they only bail when there is a lot of water in the boat, as after a capsize. The self-bailers will cope with the dregs which transom flaps cannot shift.

As a gallon of water weighs ten pounds, the need to keep boats constantly bailed will be appreciated, particularly when racing.

Fig. 40 shows two types of transom flaps in current use. The vertically-hinged type are very vulnerable when on land, and it would be preferable to select the horizontally-hinged variety whenever there is a choice.

Centreboards, rudders and tillers

There is a bewildering choice of types available for modern racing dinghies, and while the shape and size of centreboards is often controlled by class rules, much freedom is allowed on rudders and tillers.

The centreboard should be regarded as a necessary hindrance which produces drag. By paring it off to a thin trailing edge and rubbing down carefully until quite smooth, extra speed will be gained. Care, too, should be taken to fill any holes or cracks in it as these cause added turbulance and extra drag.

The same applies to the rudder blade. In addition it must be easily controllable so that it can be lifted and lowered at will. The rudder stock should never be allowed to enter the water through bad boat trim as this will cause considerable extra drag. Strength, too, is important and it should be well-fixed to the transom with pintles and gudgeons, preferably through-bolted.

Centreboards must function easily. Whether metal or wood, controlled by a tackle or just a piece of rubber hose as a friction pad, they should be correctly adjusted so that they can be raised and lowered with ease and can be relied upon to stay in any position.

If in doubt about whether to raise a rudder blade, leave it down. The boat is much better controlled with it down and it is really only in light winds when running that it is worth lifting a rudder to reduce drag.

Rudders which have a shockcord as a downhaul need checking from time to time. Shockcord stretches, allowing the blade to rise when going fast. A temporary expedient is to tie a knot in the cord until a new piece can be fitted.

It sometimes happens that a rudder will float off its pintles in a capsize. This can be prevented by fixing a little plastic safety catch or a thin piece of rubber tubing on the bottom pintle.

Generally the designer will have produced the best shape for his rudder blade, but in classes where some freedom is allowed it will be as well to try and find out what shape the winning boats are using, as the one fitted may not be the best for racing. The aim should be to use the smallest blade which is effective.

Tillers need to be strong and have a good swivelling universal joint on the extension. The laminated-wood type are good, though some light metal tillers are now being produced which cut weight and may be as good.

Do check class rules before making any alterations or you could end up with an out-of-class boat.

Some tiller extensions are badly designed and catch the mainsheet when going about or gybing. I personally like the pear-shape or a well-rounded knob. The small 'T' bar type is not good.

Performance and speed

This is a big subject about which some very good books have been written. Here I intend to detail just a few of the basic facts which the racing helmsman in his first or second season may find useful as a check list.

Weight, both in the boat and on the helm, is a serious handicap. When racing, it is necessary to first prune the boat of all non-essentials and make do with fittings lighter than the cruising day-boat sailor would consider safe. Most racing dinghy classes have a minimum weight and it should be the aim to get down as near to that as possible.

A boat which is light on the helm has little drag and will go fast. Try to reduce weather helm to an absolute minimum, first of all by getting a well-balanced boat by trial and error, and secondly by keeping it upright when racing. A slight angle of heel will give weather helm in most dinghies, particularly chine boats, and as soon as this is counteracted on the helm the brake is applied.

Next think about the sails. Unfortunately old sails are not usually very fast. A new set will be needed probably every second year if you race regularly. Treat sails carefully, folding them along panels, not kinking wires in headsails or bending plastic windows, checking that battens are a good fit; and don't stretch the sails too tightly at the corners. It is only in strong winds that sails need to be pulled out at the tack and clew. Many people make the serious mistake of pulling sails out to the black bands even in light winds and the creases at three corners give them away immediately.

Let us now look at each point of sailing and consider how to get the best out of the boat.

When running, the boat should be absolutely upright and all movement must be cat-like. Do not move too far aft, a common mistake. Keep an eye on the water flowing off the transom; if the transom is in the water there will be unnecessary drag. Ideally, the base of the transom should be just touching the water, but not digging in at all.

Except in strong breezes the crew will be seated on the opposite side to the helmsman. When running dead before the wind the jib would be goosewinged, or if a spinnaker was carried the jib should be dropped. The helmsman will need to concentrate very hard to avoid sailing by the lee which can result in a 'chinese' gybe. It is here that the burgee will be most helpful, particularly when sailing in waves, as slight fluctuations in course are unavoidable and a quick glance at the burgee every few seconds will ensure a safe course.

On this point of sailing the centreboard will not be needed to prevent leeway so normally it can be fully raised. However, in strong winds and/or waves of more than a few inches it will be advisable to keep it approximately quarter down as this helps to stabilize the boat which might otherwise rock from side to side.

In light winds on a run it will be advantageous to heel the boat and the crew will need to sit to leeward to hold the boom out. Even the slightest movement will slow a boat down in very light conditions and it is the patient helmsman and crew who usually win, not the ones who keep changing course.

In very strong winds a boat may plane on the run. This is dangerous, as spilling the wind is very difficult if the boat heels too much. Contrary to instinct, the answer to this is to sheet in the mainsail, but taking care not to gybe. By sheeting in, the sail area presented to the wind is reduced. It can only be a temporary expedient and there will be a lot of pressure on the tiller, and much strength and skill is required to keep the boat on a straight course. It is preferable to tack downwind using broad reaches. This will probably be faster. When conditions get so strong, it is often the boats that manage to stay upright which win the race!

Now let us look at reaching. This is the delight of dinghy sailors. It is safe, fast and exhilarating. If a spinnaker is carried it is pure delight, although this adds to the risk of capsizing in strong winds.

Generally the centreboard will be around a quarter to three-quarters way down, depending whether a boat is broad reaching, beam reaching or close reaching respectively. With a spinnaker up, the centreboard would need to be further down in light winds on a beam or close reach as the lateral pressure will be greater. Careful balance is then even more important.

The fore-and-aft position of the crew when reaching and not planing will be similar to running, but the transom and wake must be watched for excessive 'trenching'.

As reaching is a fast point of sailing, constant attention must be paid to the luff of the sails. Lifting must not be allowed, and note that as speed increases the apparent wind moves ahead and sails will have to be sheeted in. If the wind is sufficient to plane, this can best be achieved by coming onto a close reach, keeping the boat on an even keel. As she lifts on to the plane slide the crew weight aft and bear away a little. Do not make the mistake of moving back before she planes; sitting on the transom of a non-planing boat is a sure way to slow it down.

Once on the plane, less centreboard will be needed as the faster a boat goes the less she slides sideways. While planing, constant attention to balance, sail trimming and course steered will be necessary.

Closely tied in with planing is the ability to sail fast on waves. By throwing your weight forward just over the crest of a wave, the boat can be induced to 'surf'. If already planing it may not be advisable to go into an area of waves (if there is a choice) as there will be parts of each wave where the boat will come off the plane, e.g. when going 'uphill'. When the waves are a long way apart, it would probably pay to use them, as planing speed would be increased on about two-thirds of each wave. For more information on this fascinating subject see *Sailing: Wind and Current* by Ian Proctor.

When coming off a plane the sheets must be eased; the apparent wind moves aft.

And so – on to closehauled sailing. This can be very hard work. Indeed if it is not, then probably the boat is not going at its maximum speed. Even in medium winds the helmsman and crew will need to be concentrating very hard on balance. Constant movement in and out is necessary to keep a boat on an even keel and much energy must be expended when leaning out.

The centreboard should be right down, sheets hard in and the sails constantly watched for any signs of lifting. Generally the crew should be further forward than on either of the other two points of sailing.

When to luff and when to ease sheets a little is the constant dilemma. It is connected with the whole business of racing tactics and one's position in relation to other boats. This is outside the scope of this book, but as a general guide it is worth noting that in the northern hemisphere the wind veers (moves clockwise) in the gusts. Therefore the advantage that starboard tack gives is not just right of way, which is a racing rule as well as a 'rule of the road'. If well up to a mark on starboard tack it would pay to ease sheets a little and gain speed, but this would rarely pay on port tack as one would be 'headed', i.e. turned away from the point one was making for.

Again I would stress the need not to sheet in too hard in light winds, particularly when closehauled. The sails can be eased a little, the traveller hauled in towards the centreline to give maximum belly to the sails. This is called sailing the boat 'full and bye', i.e. with no lifting of the sails.

So much then for the points of sailing. Because many seconds can be saved in a race when tacking and gybing, let us just consider one or two points which may help to achieve efficiency during these manoeuvres. Both should be practised in light, then medium, then strong breezes before starting to race.

Tacking requires good balance and good sheet handling. When a boat is tacked efficiently there is hardly a flutter of the sails. A helmsman should have few problems when tacking from one closehauled course to another; he simply keeps the mainsheet tight throughout the operation. Fluttering of the jib, too, can be reduced to a minimum if the crew holds the sheet right up to the point where it is just beginning to 'back', then lets go quickly and hauls in on the other side immediately it fills on the new tack. Both helmsman and crew must move across the boat so that it is kept in perfect balance.

Racing helmsmen 'roll-tack' in medium and light airs. This means that they delay moving until the boom swings across, so heeling the boat and making both sails 'fall' on to the new side; this is particularly helpful in very light conditions as it speeds the tack up.

When tacking from a point further off the wind, first make sure that the centreboard is down and then sheet in on both main and jib, letting the tiller go and hauling the mainsheet in with both hands. The speed of the manoeuvre can be controlled by the speed at which the mainsail is hauled in. The combined effect of sheeting in the main and heeling the boat causes the boat to tack very quickly. If tacking from a run, care must be taken not to sheet in too quickly or a capsize could result. Similarly, strong conditions can have the same effect. After a little practice you will begin to 'feel' the boat and know how fast to sheet in.

Gybing is, if anything, more difficult to do well and it should not be attempted in strong conditions; say above wind strengths of Force 3, until you are very used to a boat.

Make sure that the centreboard is up or nearly up. If it is down the boat can 'trip over' it and capsize, but if it is up the boat will skid sideways in a strong blow.

Ideally keep on a straight course while gybing. Haul in on the mainsheet until the boom is over the quarter. Then get the crew to pull the mainsail across. As it crosses the centre line, ease the sheet so that it can run out. This takes the weight of the sail. Cross over to the other side of the boat as the boom crosses over, correcting the helm slightly (tiller towards you) as you do so.

At first it will probably be necessary to bear away a little to make the boat gybe, but with practice it should be possible to carry out the manoevure without losing any speed or altering course. Careful balance is necessary, and in medium and strong winds you will have to throw your weight across the boat as the boom slams across, to counteract the heeling tendency. Keep the boat on an even keel at all times when gybing, and capsizes will be rare. I hope, however, that they will not be so rare that you never perfect a righting drill!

ELEVEN

Sailing in tidal waters

Boats for sea sailing

Quite obviously there are many sizes of sailing boats suitable for tidal use. Generally one sees as many fully-decked boats afloat on the sea as one sees day-boat types. Many excellent books have been written about cruising in seagoing yachts and in this chapter I shall confine myself largely to dinghies and day boats.

Small light dinghies like the Enterprise or Mirror are more suited to sheltered inland water. Nevertheless, providing one is cautious, these modern boats can be used safely in certain circumstances on the open sea and in estuaries.

Usually weather conditions will determine whether or not one sails. There is the racing dinghy situation too, and in most cases dinghies taking part in club races will be escorted by powered safety boats and will therefore often sail in somewhat stronger conditions than if they were sailing alone.

In addition to racing dinghies, there are many heavier more sea-worthy craft under eighteen feet which are specifically designed for sea/estuary sailing, e.g. the Salcombe Yawl, Yachting World Four-teen-foot Day boat and the Seafarer. For camping–cruising and coastal 'pottering' these craft are ideal.

Safety rules

A Force 4 wind on an inland lake is quite comfortably dealt with in a small dinghy, but on the sea there are many other factors which can make sailing in a Force 4 quite a dangerous business. For instance, if sailing off a coast which is a lee shore, even getting afloat may be difficult. If there is a strong ebb tide running against the wind, seas (waves) will be short and steep and if not carefully handled may capsize a fourteen-footer. At best the going will be very wet.

Generally where there is a good expanse of sea to windward the seas will have room to build up and they will be large compared to those on a smaller piece of water.

If cruising, including day-cruising, it is wise to notify the coastguards. A form (C.G. 66) can be obtained from Coastguard Stations, and information such as colour, size, sail number, E.T.D. (estimated time of departure) and E.T.A. is asked for. If you do not have time to obtain the form, a telephone call to the coastguard station nearest to your point of departure will suffice.

As a boat progresses along a coast it will be 'passed along' from one coastguard station to another. In clear weather it will be constantly under surveillance from the shore.

Should plans be changed because of weather or for any other reason, it is essential to telephone the coastguard again immediately on landing. This could save a very expensive sea and air search.

Except when racing, always carry distress flares as mentioned in Chapter Eight, and it is a good idea to avoid sailing close to lee shores in bad weather. This would include calm conditions when you might be unable to sail away from a dangerous shore.

Calm conditions on the sea can be almost as dangerous as rough conditions. It is very easy not to notice the strength of a tidal stream which may be carrying you away from the shore and out to sea. The tide ebbs for approximately six hours (with some local variations in channels and estuaries) and a dinghy may be many miles off shore before the flood starts. Even with oars it may not be possible to row against a spring ebb tide which can be as much as six knots in the Bristol Channel and even four knots in the Western Solent.

Additional clothing is necessary when sea sailing. The old scout motto of 'Be Prepared' is very good advice. Full waterproofs, top and bottom, as well as some spare warm woollens in a polythene bag should always be carried. Spare, dry footwear, too, is a real morale booster after you have been sitting still for three or four hours waiting for a wind. Emergency food, including a hot drink, is also a sensible idea.

Now we come to a whole new problem for sea sailors which you will hardly have met inland: commercial shipping and the signals used by them.

In almost any harbour there will be local byelaws such as speed limits and out-of-bounds areas. Naval harbours such as Portsmouth have a special set of signals, details of which can be obtained from the appropriate Queen's Harbourmaster Offices. Apart from these special regulations, the passage of all craft (that is, you in your twelve-foot dinghy as well as larger merchant ships) will be subject to the I.R.P.C.S. (International Regulations for the Prevention of Collisions at Sea).

You will need to know a few of the more important International code flags and Morse code signals and their meanings. The urgent and important ones are the single letter signals (see colour diagram). For example, Morse letter 'E' means: 'I am altering my course to starboard' – turning right to the landlubbers!

While talking about safety, a word about fog. Fog is the plague of all seagoers. Large and small ships alike have been sunk after collision in fog. The small-boat sailor is particularly vulnerable as he can be mown down by larger craft without even being seen.

However, small boats have one great advantage safety-wise: they can go where larger craft cannot – in shallow water.

I have three rules for sailing in fog:

1.   D O N ' T, but if caught out,
2.   Anchor in shallow water; or
3.   If practicable, get ashore as quickly as possible.

By carrying a radar reflector high up in the rigging there is a chance that your small boat will be visible on big-ship radar, but do not rely on this. On the other hand, large navigation buoys will be visible on radar screens and, while it is illegal to tie up to these, in an emergency it would be safer to risk a fine than drift about in a shipping channel.

Tides

Fig. 41 gives quite a lot of the information that you will need to know about tidal terms. Let us look at what makes tides and how it affects us sailors.

The moon circles the earth, and the earth, with its moon, circles the sun. Tides are caused largely by the 'pull' of the moon's gravity on the earth and, to a lesser extent, by the sun's pull. When the earth, moon and sun are in line, we get the greatest pull and therefore the highest and lowest tides. These are called 'spring' tides and occur twice per lunar month approximately.

When the moon is at right angles to a line connecting the sun and earth, the pull is weakest and 'neap' tides occur. At this time the moon is also farthest away from the earth, so lessening still more the pull which it exerts on earth.

The moon's pull on the earth is about $2\frac{1}{2}$ times greater than the sun's pull, and it revolves around the earth every 29 days. The earth revolves around the sun every 365 days. The sun, moon and earth are in line every $14\frac{1}{2}$ days, at new and full moon.

As the earth also revolves every twenty-four hours, we get two high waters and two low waters approximately during that period. Several variations and fluctuations are caused by specific local conditions, but we can consider those separately.

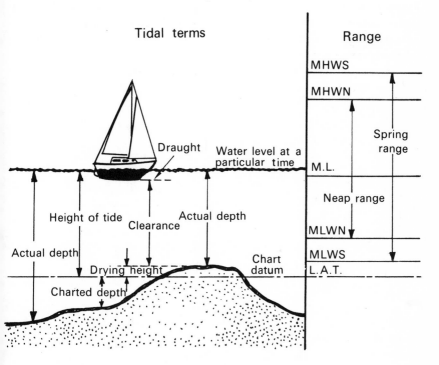

Fig. 41. Tides

This type of tide which we experience in Britain is called 'semi-diurnal'.

The 'range' of a tide is the difference between high water and low water. 'Height' of a tide is the height that a high water reaches above a theoretical low water, called 'chart datum'. The chart datum is the lowest predicted astronomical tide (L.A.T.). Only one or two exceptional tides each year will be below chart datum. This is useful because all depths on a chart are given *below* chart datum, and they are, there-fore, the shallowest water that is normally likely to be encountered.

As the tides flow and ebb (the level rises and then falls), large amounts of water are moving in the direction of the flood or the ebb. This creates tidal streams and for practical purposes these will behave rather like a current in a river. If sailing with a tidal stream, you will reach your destination much more quickly than if sailing against it.

The strength of a tidal stream will vary depending on how near to high or low water it is, and also how near to spring or neap tides they are. I have already said that the range is greatest at spring tides and least at neaps, and it follows, that the strongest tidal streams will also be at spring tides.

Here is a 'rule of thumb' guide to estimate the strength of a tide for each hour of the flood or the ebb. It is known as the 'Twelfths Rule'.

In the first hour of a flood or ebb,
the range will be 1/12 of the total
In the second hour of a flood or ebb,
the range will be 2/12 of the total
In the third hour of a flood or ebb,
the range will be 3/12 of the total
In the fourth hour of a flood or ebb,
the range will be 3/12 of the total
In the fifth hour of a flood or ebb,
the range will be 2/12 of the total
In the sixth hour of a flood or ebb,
the range will be 1/12 of the total.

From this can be seen that the greatest rise or fall (or speed of tidal stream) will be during the middle two hours (third and fourth) of a tide and the least (and weakest) the first and sixth hours nearest to high and low water. Here is a typical example:

Range of tide for day: 24 ft
Depth of water from chart: 6 ft
You wish to know how deep it will be at 1300 hours and the time of low water is 0900:
Range divided by 12 = 2 ft
1300 is four hours of flood, i.e. 9/12 of total range:
9 + 2 ft = 18 ft
18 ft + actual depth of 6 ft = 24 ft
Depth of water at 1300 hours = 24 ft

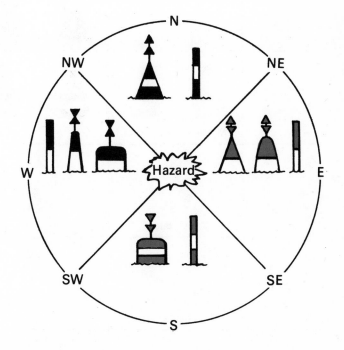

Fig. 42. Cardinal system of Buoyage

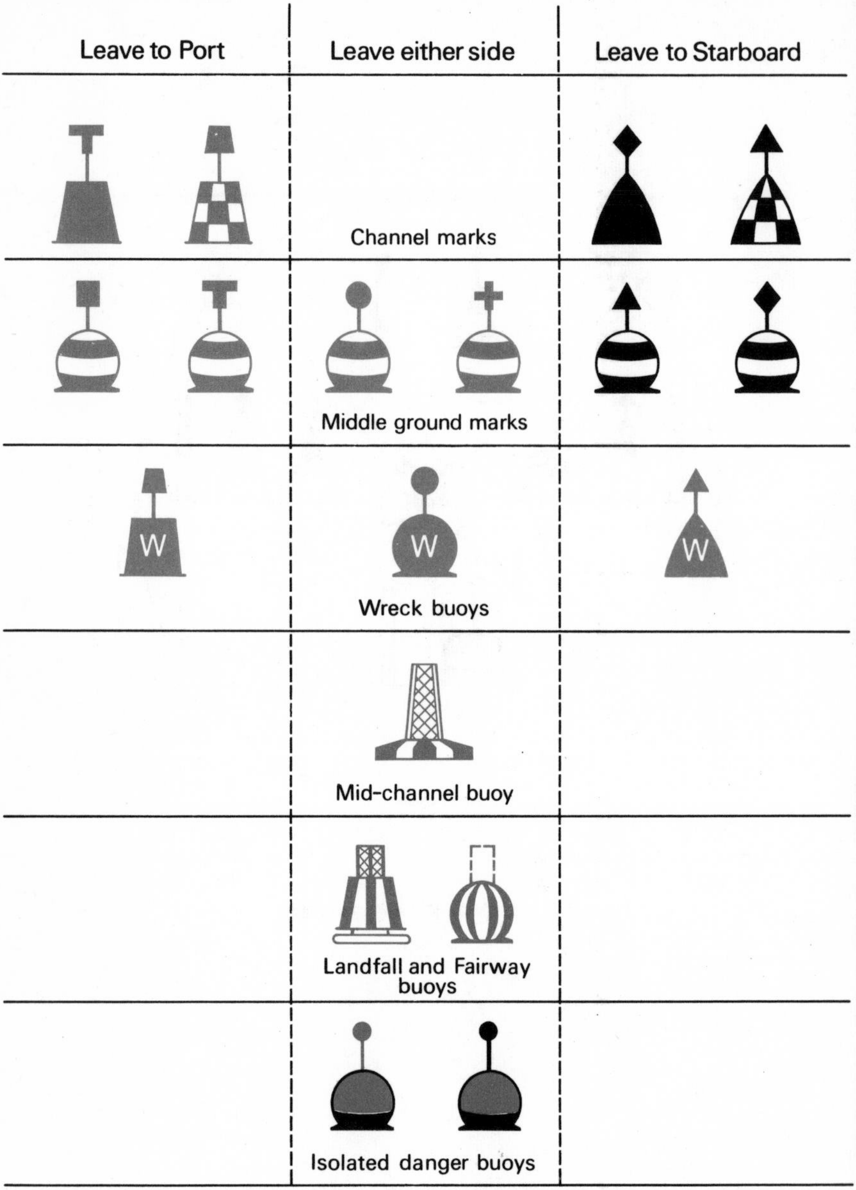

Leave to Port	Leave either side	Leave to Starboard
	Channel marks	
	Middle ground marks	
	Wreck buoys	
	Mid-channel buoy	
	Landfall and Fairway buoys	
	Isolated danger buoys	

Fig. 43. Lateral Buoyage System

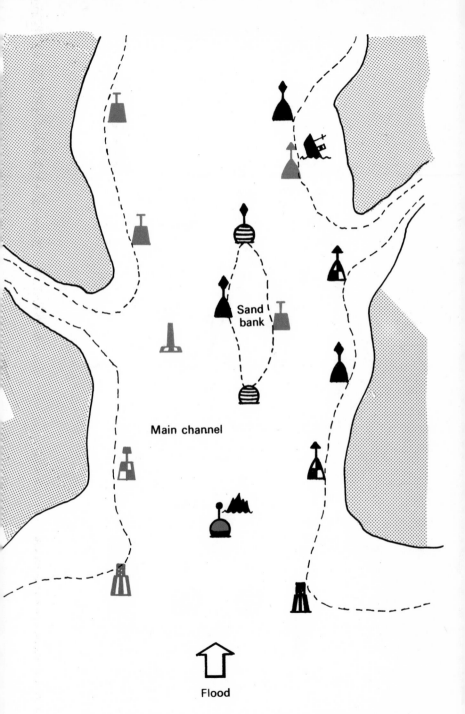

Sand
bank

Main channel

Flood

Fig. 44. Example of Lateral System

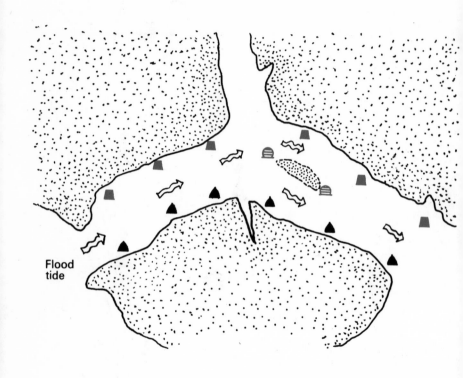

Fig. 45. Buoyage in the Solent

This is only a general guide but it is surprisingly useful in areas not complicated by estuaries, etc. In addition to enabling us to work out depth, it gives a general guide to strengths of tidal streams.

One should always plan to sail with a tidal stream if possible, but if not, then sail during the fifth and sixth hours when it is weakest and when it is getting near to turning. Often people do not realize the importance of this. We will look at two examples:

Example 1. A fourteen-foot dinghy will average about three knots in a Force 2 breeze (varying with the point of sailing).
Imagine this boat sailing
(*a*) with a 2 knot stream against it, and
(*b*) with a 2 knot stream in its favour.
In (*a*) its speed is 1 knot; in (*b*) it is 5 knots, so to cover a distance of 10 miles will take either 10 hours or 2 hours. This example is quite typical in every way.

Example 2. Now imagine the same boat, same speed, but with a tidal stream of 4 knots (fairly typical in the Western Solent at spring ebb tides).
In the case of the boat travelling with the stream, it will move over the ground at 7 knots, taking approximately 1½ hours to complete the journey; but if it is going against the stream, although the boat would be moving *through the water* at 3 knots it would actually be going *backwards, over the ground*, at 1 knot!

In estuaries and channels tidal streams are strongest in the middle where the water is deepest, so when sailing against a stream some advantage can be gained by sailing near the shore. Where there are bends, the outside of a bend will always have the strongest stream (as in the case of a river current). On the inside of bends there may even be places where there is a reverse eddy and the water will be moving in the opposite direction to the main stream. This can also be used to advantage. An excellent example of this can be found at Cowes. During the strongest part of the ebb in the river Medina there is a flow upstream on the western side of Cowes Harbour from approximately the Island Sailing Club to the chain ferry which crosses the river at the narrowest point.

Tides will present the inland sailor with many problems when he comes to convert to sea sailing. They have far-reaching effects which in some cases are quite subtle and will not be obvious to the newcomer. The combined effect of wind and tide, for example, often catches out the unwary. Let us look at this twin factor.

Waves are caused by the wind. When wind blows on the surface of the water it builds up wave height increasingly with greater distance. Most inland water is not more than a few hundred yards across, and even on large lakes like Windermere, or reservoirs such as Grafham Water, there is rarely a clear mile for waves to build up. Occasionally strong winds do blow along the length of a large piece of inland water and then we get waves which may be two or three feet high. This is rather rare, and generally inland water tends to be relatively calm when compared with the sea. When winds blow across large areas of sea there is no protection for the surface of the water, and it is then that big waves (usually called seas) build up. In the open sea they will be as high as mentioned in the Beaufort Wind Scale in Chapter Four.

Furthermore, when the tidal stream is moving in the opposite direction to the wind, the seas become steep and quite dangerous to small boats if the wind strength is more than Force 3 and the stream more than about two knots. A knot, by the way, is one nautical mile per hour, and a nautical mile is approximately 2,000 yards, a little longer than a land mile.

If the wind and tidal stream are moving in the same direction, the height of waves will be much less than expected and small boat sailors may not realize how strong the wind is.

There is one further situation which is potentially dangerous to the dinghy or day-boat sailor: when there is no wind and a strong ebb tide. The R.N.L.I. are often called out to rescue people who have sailed into a strong tidal stream and been swept out to sea – not always in sailing dinghies either; a surprisingly large number are on inflatable air beds!

The predicted heights of high and low waters which can be obtained from tide tables can vary. Low atmospheric pressure and a strong wind in the same direction as the main flood tide will cause an abnormally high tide and may also keep it up for longer than normal. This will also have the effect of producing a faster ebb.

Conversely, high pressure and wind against tide will produce lower high waters than predicted and may also give lower low waters. This is important if sailing in an area where you are only expecting the minimum depth in which your boat can float.

You must obtain accurate information about depth, buoyage, type of bottom for anchoring and so on before sailing in a new area, so it is necessary to know a little about charts, where all this type of information can be found.

Charts

A chart is simply a map of the coast and sea bed. On it is found a hundred and one pieces of useful information which are essential to safe navigation even of a dinghy.

As with maps of land areas, charts come in different 'brands' and scales. The projections also vary.

The Admiralty have a most comprehensive international set of charts covering most sea areas of the world. These charts contain a vast amount of information, not all of which is essential for people sailing very small craft. They also produce the 'Y' series for yachtsmen which cover many harbours and areas used for sailing around the United Kingdom and English Channel coasts.

A firm catering more for yachtsmen is Stanfords. Their charts are coloured, are easier to see 'at a glance', and additionally have compass courses to steer from one harbour to another.

Imrays also produce charts for yachtsmen which are similarly coloured, though not quite as clear as Stanfords. It is really a matter of looking around and trying different types to see which suit you best. In many cases, for areas away from the popular sailing grounds, the Admiralty chart will be the only one available.

If making coastal passages where much information about harbours and anchorages is required, a large-scale chart will be necessary. For longer sea trips, e.g. cross channel, small scale will be appropriate.

Projections, too, will vary even among Admiralty charts. You will need to know whether your chart is 'Mercator' or 'Gnomonic' projection. In the case of the 'Mercator', the curved surface of the earth, having been projected onto a flat surface, has a distorted scale. To make up for the east-west distortion, the lines of latitude will be more widely spaced towards the north and south poles than they are at the equator. The important practical implication here is that when measuring distance on the latitude scale at the side of the chart care should be taken to use the scale exactly adjacent to the area of the chart in use, otherwise the measurements will be inaccurate.

A nautical mile is equal to one minute of latitude at the equator and, therefore, you should never measure distance on the longitude scale, i.e. across the top or bottom of the chart, as minutes of longitude do not represent a nautical mile.

In order to read maps it is necessary to know the meanings of all the symbols and abbreviations used. The same is true of charts and in the case of Admiralty charts these are listed on Chart 5011. There are a multitude of these and some 'swotting' is necessary.

Until recently depths were given in fathoms and feet, the larger figure representing fathoms. A depth of 6_4 meant a depth of 6 fathoms and 4 ft or 40 ft (6 ft = 1 fathom); 0_5 = 5 ft, and so on. Charted depths are now being given in metres but it will be some years before the conversion is complete. Remember that all depths are shown below chart datum so will usually be minimum depth.

An hour or two spent investigating an Admiralty chart with the help of Chart 5011 will quickly enable you to become familiar with this fascinating subject.

Much information about tidal streams is given on Admiralty charts and also on some others. Small 'diamonds' with a capital letter in them show places where the speed and direction of the tide has been measured for every hour of the flood and ebb at both spring and neap tides. A table relating to these will be found in a corner of the chart and by interpolating for periods between springs and neaps fairly accurate estimates of tidal streams can be made.

It is also possible to purchase tidal streams atlases which give similar information which is readily visible simply by turning to the appropriate page.

On each chart will be found a true compass rose. Older charts will have a second inner compass rose notated to magnetic north in the year that the chart was printed. More recently only the true compass rose (north being the north pole) has been shown. In all cases, the magnetic variation, i.e. the difference between true and magnetic north, will be given so that compass courses can be taken from the chart. It should be remembered that magnetic variation is gradually decreasing in U.K. waters at the rate of approximately six minutes annually.

Buoyage

The two types of buoyage found in European waters are the Cardinal system and the Lateral system. Although the Cardinal system is widely used in many European countries, it is not used in U.K. waters, and I shall deal here only with the Lateral system which is used around our coasts. Details of both types will be found in Figs. 42, 43 and 44 (between pages 142 and 143).

Wherever coastal water is navigable by merchant craft, it will usually be buoyed by Trinity House. This organization is responsible for buoyage throughout the U.K. In some small harbours and estuaries, buoyage is the responsibility of local harbour authorities, and in these cases navigation marks may not be of the same type as those used in the Lateral system. In really small harbours (many suitable only for yachts), only posts or 'withies' will be used.

To understand the Lateral system of buoyage one must first know the direction of flow of the main flood tide around our coasts. This is from west to east along the English Channel to the Thames Estuary, from south to north up the Irish Sea and the west coast of Ireland, around the north of Scotland in a clockwise direction, and from north to south down the North Sea.

There will be places where the main streams meet, causing somewhat peculiar tidal situations, e.g. off the Thames Estuary and at the northern end of the Irish Sea. The Solent has a flow from west to east but the stream also flows into Portsmouth Harbour around the south–east of the Isle of Wight, giving somewhat unexpected streams in the Eastern Solent and also giving Southampton a double high water.

Simply stated, the Lateral system buoys channels with starboard hand buoys on the right when approaching with the main flood tide and port hand buoys on the left. Starboard hand buoys are conical in shape, black or black and white chequered, and if they are numbered they have odd numbers. Port hand buoys are red or red and white chequered, can-shaped, and have even numbers. Figs. 43 and 44 show these in full.

Sometimes there will be shallow ground in the centre of a channel. The sides of this will be marked with port and starboard hand buoys and the ends of it with spherical middle-ground buoys. These may be red and white (horizontal stripes) or black and white depending on which side the main channel is.

For practical purposes in small boats these large navigation marks are ignored as they are usually well offshore and mark channels which big ships can navigate. They will be in five or six fathoms of water and there will be no danger of the dinghy helmsman scraping his centreboard on the bottom in that depth!

Rather, the buoyed channels are areas to *keep clear of*, because while in them we may present a hazard to larger commercial craft. When entering a harbour which we do not know, however, it is sensible to sail up the edges of the channels (keep right) to avoid rocks, sewage outfalls or shoal areas.

The three types of buoy mentioned above are the ones most frequently seen. These mark channels. One or two additional buoys which show particular parts of channels are as follows:

Mid-channel buoys showing deep water in mid-channel and only used in big channels, e.g. the Solent; these are pillar-shaped buoys with a flat base and have vertical black/white or red/white stripes depending on which side they are to be left.

Landfall buoys are similar to mid-channel buoys but much taller, and mark the entrance to a channel from seaward. They are often well off-shore. They have the same colours as mid-channel buoys.

There are three other buoys in the Lateral System which the small boat sailor will need to know; they mark specific hazards. They are: wreck buoys, isolated danger buoys and outfall or spoil ground buoys.

Wreck buoys are always green with the word 'WRECK' written across them in white. Shape will depend on which side they are to be left.

Isolated danger marks are spherical, coloured red, white and black horizontally and normally mark rocks. They should be given a clear berth at all times.

Outfall and spoil ground buoys are important to dinghy and dayboat sailors as they often mark the outward limit of large-diameter heavy iron sewage pipes. Sometimes these are also concreted, but in either case they can cause much damage to a small boat and as they are right by the shore, in shallow water, they are one of the worst hazards for us dinghy sailors. Buoys are yellow-topped and may be any shape.

In addition to shape, colour and numbering some buoys carry topmarks and are lit. Topmarks are shown in Fig. 44 but as the lights on navigation marks is a somewhat complicated subject I shall recommend the reader to study a chart before making a night trip. Night sailing should only be undertaken by very experienced sailors.

In small harbours the buoyage of channels will usually be of a similar pattern to the lateral system of buoyage. That is to say that port hand marks will always be red and can- or barrel-shaped and starboard hand marks black, or occasionally green (particularly when posts are used). Reference to charts will indicate at a glance what type of buoy to look for.

In Fig. 45 (between pages 142 and 143) I show an example of buoyage in a well-known area, the Solent. Note that, as the main flood stream flows west to east throughout seven-eighths of the Solent (both western and eastern), the channel buoys may not be as you would expect if approaching from the eastern side. Here is a case where reference to the chart is essential. Note, too, that the main channel passes to the south of Ryde Middle, the shallow middle-ground area in the Eastern Solent. The middle-ground buoys indicate this, being predominantly red in colour.

Buoyage may at first sight appear very complicated, but once the principles of port, starboard and middle-ground shapes and colours are understood the rest will quickly become apparent.

Compasses

All boats which sail on tidal waters should carry a compass. The cheapest serviceable type for small boats can be bought for about £4, but you can pay as much as £30. Within this range there is a large choice.

Several firms make a dual-purpose type of compass which can be either fixed or used as a hand-bearing compass. In a small boat which does not have much ferrous metal in it, this sort of compass is ideal. It is fixed to a bracket which is lined up with the centre-line of the boat for use as a fixed steering compass, and unclipped, then fixed onto a 'handle' when it becomes necessary to take hand-bearings of objects from the boat, to fix its position.

For a little more money, a good fixed grid compass with a swivelling bezel can be obtained; and where the boat is to be used predominantly for day-cruising this type would be advisable as a steering compass. It will be 'gimballed', i.e. it will stay horizontal even when the boat heels or pitches. The more expensive versions incorporate a 'beta light'; this does not require batteries and is similar to the luminous paint found on watches.

As with most navigation equipment, you will get what you pay for. The expensive compasses will be better damped and more accurate. They will also be easier to use.

If your boat has an iron centreplate or carries an outboard motor, you will need to be very careful about positioning a steering compass and also about where you stand when taking bearings with a hand-bearing compass. It may be necessary to obtain expert advice from a professional compass adjuster and even 'swing the ship' to see how much the metal on board affects the compass needle on different courses. This effect is called 'compass deviation', and if you learn about navigation you will need to learn how to allow for deviation when plotting a course to steer. You will also learn to allow for variation (the difference between true and magnetic north). In this book, I will limit myself to mentioning the two ways in which a compass can be used for day-cruising in an area such as the Thames Estuary or the Solent.

The first concerns the steering compass (fixed), and the second the hand-bearing compass.

To get from point A to point B, first look at the chart and obtain the *true* compass course by passing a parallel rule through the two points and then moving the rule to the compass rose. Now, to use this course you must first make allowance for variation (*add* the variation in Britain), then allow for deviation (if any), and finally allow for the strength and direction of the tidal stream. The latter may not be very easy but you will not need to be very accurate providing you can see the shore on both sides and it will be a useful exercise to see how good your arithmetic is.

If visibility is poor and you cannot see the two shores, or the weather forecast suggests fog or strong winds, then you would be foolish to sail. No small boat, sailing for pleasure, should set sail in poor visibility.

Having made all the adjustments to your true course as I have outlined, then you have your 'course to steer'. If you have a grid compass, set the course on it and steer your boat round until it is on course. Constant glances at the compass will be necessary to keep her on course. If possible your steering compass should be placed in front of you where it will be easy to see while also keeping an eye on the sails.

To use the hand-bearing compass, hold it up at eye level at arm's length. Line up the object which you are taking a bearing on with the 'sights' on the compass, moving your whole body and keeping a stiff arm, and then read off the bearing in degrees. To 'plot' (draw) this on the chart you will need to deduct variation (in British waters) and then, by using the true compass rose and drawing the bearing line through the object with parallel rules, you will have a 'position line'.

One position line is not much use as you could be anywhere along it, but by obtaining a second and preferably a third you will be able to obtain 'cross-bearings' or a small triangle on the chart which will show your position.

This is the main use of a hand-bearing compass. Always choose objects which are easily visible and clearly marked on the chart. They should not be too close to each other. In the case where two objects only are used, they should be about 90 degrees apart, and with three there should be about 60 degrees between each. Bearings must never be opposite each other (180 degrees apart).

Taking a bearing in a small boat is no easy job and it needs much practice to become proficient. Try to get amidships and let your body move with the boat. At best it is doubtful whether accuracy can be obtained to nearer than 2 degrees, and usually it will be around 5 degrees of error.

Rules of the road

Full details of the right-of-way rules will be found in Appendix I, pages 169–182. In Chapter Three I outlined the most important rules for small boats and I will reiterate what I said there. Do give yourself plenty of space at first. Avoid crowded harbours, and whenever possible keep out of shipping channels until you are familiar with all aspects of right of way. Do take avoiding action early if you intend giving way, and do find out whether there are any local harbour regulations in force. Often all these things can be checked at the local sailing club or harbour-master's office, or with the local Cruising Association boatman.

Before going afloat it would be wise to become familiar with sound signals given by commercial craft. Part E of the I.R.P.C.S. details these, but here are the ones that you are most likely to come across.

> One short blast (Morse letter 'E'): 'I am turning to starboard.'
> Two short blasts (Morse letter 'I'): 'I am turning to port.'
> Three short blasts (Morse letter 'S'): 'My engines are going astern.'
> Five short blasts: This is a warning that the vessel making this signal has right of way and you are expected to keep clear.

Quite frequently one long blast will be given, and so far as we are concerned in our small boats it can be interpreted as meaning the same as five short blasts.

Morse letter 'D' (— . .) is also used and means: 'Keep clear of me; I am manoeuvring with difficulty.'

It is possible that if an outboard motor is carried, you will find yourself with sails down motoring back to harbour. Even if your sails are still up, if you are motoring you are classified as 'a vessel under power' and Rules 18 and 19 apply. Simply summarized, they state that if you are aiming for head-on collison with another powered craft both boats should alter course to starboard to pass each other port to port. If two power-driven boats are crossing each other's courses, the boat which has the other on its starboard side should give way.

I mentioned Rule 24 – the overtaking rule – in Chapter Three, but I must now draw your attention to Part (b) of that rule which defines what is an overtaking boat (see Appendix I, page 179).

Nautical almanacs

These books contain a great deal of useful information about tides, buoyage, harbours, and navigation which is invaluable to the cruising sailor whether he be the owner of a fifty-ton schooner or a Wayfarer dinghy. Probably the best known and most useful for small boat sailors is *Reed's Nautical Almanac*; *Brown's Almanac* is another, more suitable for the cruising yachtsman who is doing more than harbour-hopping as it contains more information about navigation.

These publications of over a thousand pages are somewhat difficult to follow at first, and it would be wise to buy one for your wife (or husband) for Christmas so that you can spend the winter evenings from January to March finding your way around it!

More about lee shores

In Chapters Four and Five I briefly mentioned inland lee shores and the safe way for inexperienced sailors to get off them. Now a word about tidal lee shores which will often have the additional hazard of surf.

Launching through surf requires quick thinking and quick action. More often than not someone will have to get very wet. In a light dinghy, however, after some practice it will be possible to keep dry above the legs. The technique is to launch the boat with both sails hoisted, bows first; push it out just far enough to get the rudder blade down fully; jump aboard and sail away on a close reach with a little bit of centreboard down. On each wave the boat is luffed to a close-hauled position and a little more centreboard pushed down until the board is right down and a closehauled course can be sailed, away from the shore (see Fig. 46).

With a chine boat and a helmsman who is very familiar with his craft it may be possible to sail the boat closehauled in quite shallow

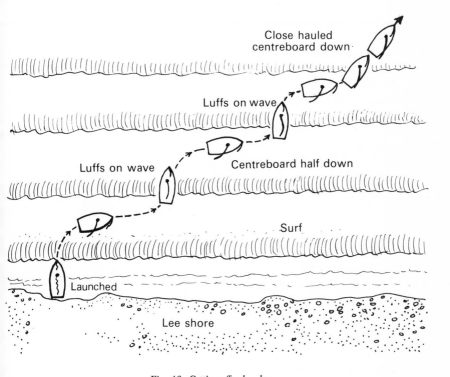

Close hauled
centreboard down·

Luffs on wave

Luffs on wave　　　　Centreboard half down

Surf

Launched

Lee shore

Fig. 46. Getting off a lee shore

water providing that it is kept heeled at almost 45 degrees. The chine gives a certain amount of 'grip' and more centreboard can be lowered as the boat is heeled. This is easier in strong conditions than in light as the crew then do not have to heel the boat; the wind does it for them.

In biggish surf it may be necessary to have a launching party, i.e. a few people in wet suits or swimming costumes who can stand waist-deep in the sea and push boats off while the crew keep dry. This method can also be used for landing in waves of more than a few inches high.

When landing, if a lee shore is a sandy beach, it is possible to sail straight up on to the beach providing the bottom of the boat is well protected with keel and bilge-strakes and the rudder and centreboard are raised at the appropriate moment. This would not be advisable with a highly polished racing dinghy; its chances of winning thereafter would be minimal!

Anchors should be used for landing in surf whenever there is no help available. On a tidal beach they can be retrieved later when the water has receded. Round up into the wind in deep water, drop anchor, lower sails, remove rudder and raise centreboard; then pay out the anchor warp, so easing the boat gradually into the shore. It will be possible to get very close in a small dinghy although it will be advisable to step out before the boat touches ground in order to protect it.

There is one other technique which is used for getting off a lee shore. It is called 'kedging' and is only really applicable to larger craft with a fixed (deep) keel.

On going aground, a small anchor, known as the kedge, is taken out to windward by the yacht's tender (a small rowing boat), or by another boat. The kedge is dropped and the yacht then hauls itself out on the kedge, sometimes using a winch or capstan to achieve this. On a falling tide this would hardly be possible as the boat would be stuck hard before kedging could commence, but on a rising tide or slack water it is usually possible.

Rough water hazards

In certain places and at certain times in the range of a tide there develop patches of rough water or 'overfalls'. These will be shown on the chart and generally should be avoided by small boats under eighteen feet. They are produced by the shape of the coastline, by bars and ledges on the seabed or by the meeting of two tidal streams, sometimes by a combination of these factors. Generally the water will be turbulent and the seas steep or very steep. Two examples are at the western end of the Solent by Hurst Narrows and off Portland Bill, the latter being the most famous 'race' for British yachtsmen. Although sea conditions quite close may be placid, these areas can be very turbulent and should be given a wide berth. It is essential to study a chart before sailing so that their whereabouts is known.

More about anchoring and mooring (*See Chapter Five for basic procedures*).

In addition to the general procedure for anchoring mentioned previously, there are several special considerations when anchoring or mooring in tidal waters.

If the tide is 'slack', that is to say if it is high or low water and there is no movement (tidal stream), the method would be the same as on inland water.

When the tide is flooding or ebbing, however, there are three possible situations:

wind and tide together;
wind against tide;
wind across tide.

In the first case the procedure is straightforward. Only the relative strength of the tide must be considered, e.g. if picking up a mooring in a three-knot tide it will be necessary to sail right up to the mooring before letting fly, otherwise the boat will not reach the buoy but start to drift backwards almost as soon as the sails are released. But in all other respects, proceed as outlined in Chapter Five.

When the wind is against the tide, it is first of all necessary to decide which way the boat will lie when you have anchored or moored. Will it lie with its head facing the wind (wind rode) or will it lie facing the tidal stream flow (tide rode)?

One way to determine which way it will lie is to notice what is happening to other moored or anchored boats nearby which are of similar type to yours. If they are wind rode, then the tidal stream is fairly weak and you should come head to wind and pick up your buoy (or drop anchor) as described in Chapter Five. It will be best to approach across the tide on a reach, and some practice will be necessary. Get your centreboard up and drop sails as soon as you are moored or anchored.

If the boats nearby are tide rode, then you will need to adopt a very different method of approach. Get up wind of your mooring or anchorage, heave to and quickly drop the mainsail, then sail downwind under jib only, to pick up the mooring. This is similar to the method adopted for landing on a lee shore.

When the wind is across the tide, one of the above methods can be adopted depending on whether the wind is slightly against the tide or slightly with it, i.e. diagonal to the tidal stream. If it is exactly at right angles to it, then it would be best to drop the mainsail and sail downwind and across the tide to the mooring.

Anchorages are shown on charts and these should always be consulted when visiting a new area. Popular harbours will have much debris and old ground tackle on the sea-bed, so always buoy your anchor (see Chapter Five).

Picking up a mooring as a visitor, is quite acceptable providing you go ashore and obtain permission if you wish to remain on it. Many harbours have visitors' moorings which are described in local 'pilots'. These are guide books to the harbour facilities and can be bought at yacht chandlers and some bookshops.

Never anchor in a channel. You may well be mown down and sunk! At night a white light should be displayed in the forward part of your boat when anchored. This should be clearly visible all round the horizon. By day you are also required to hoist one black ball in the fore part of the boat, but in practice very few people in small boats do so (see Rule 11 of I.R.P.C.S.).

To conclude this chapter on tidal sailing I would like to stress the need to plan ahead. In particular make sure that you secure a weather forecast before planning a day out on the sea. Freak storms sometimes creep up on us unawares. but most bad weather will be forecast on the B.B.C. shipping forecasts. If the times of these are unsuitable, telephone your nearest weather information centre (see telephone directories). When anything above Force 4 is forecast, think very carefully about sailing; and remember that winds of this strength, if in opposition to a spring tidal stream, can produce some very nasty conditions.

Go well prepared, both in experience and equipment. This means good, warm waterproof clothing, and a boat suitable for the job. And do always leave a note of your intentions with someone on shore.

TWELVE

Where next?

In this final chapter I shall summarize the recent developments in sailing craft, including one or two extreme types like the multihulls, and also point the way forward for those readers who wish to know more about how to specialize in dinghy racing or cruising.

Developments

In some ways the 'racing machines' of today affect the family cruisers of tomorrow, much as Grand Prix racing cars affect the family saloon car. This only happens in sailing to a limited extent – more in the design of go-fast equipment than in the shape of the boat.

The amount of cash available for advertising also affects the sales of a particular type of boat. An example of this was the Mirror dinghy which, fortunately for the sailing public, was a good design.

A few designs during the 1960s caught on even though they were quite unsuitable. These were mainly the small family cruiser type with bilge keels. 'Bilge-keelers' (a shallow keel on each side) in the 17 ft to 22 ft range were probably the fastest-growing type of craft in the last ten years. Their popularity was due to several important factors: price, trailability, size and the fact that they could be sailed on shallow estuaries and grounded easily when the tide went out. Some of these boats are quite unsuited to deep-sea sailing, having a poor windward performance and being generally too small for off-shore cruising. Fortunately they are mainly used in sheltered estuaries and along the coasts.

Mono-dinghies have not developed much in the past ten years. Numbers have increased tremendously but fundamentally new designs have been few. One exception is the Fireball, designed on scow lines, and this boat has quite a following.

In Britain the continental influence has been felt in the last two or three years. This has given boats like the '420' and '470' a well-deserved place on the British racing scene. The only really new developments, however, have been in multihulls, mainly catamarans. The international 'A' and 'B' classes have received a great boost from world-wide multihull publicity and recent years have seen many experimental types of trimarans, proas, and recently, hydrofoils. Let us look at one or two examples of these 'extreme' types.

Catamarans

Probably the oldest type of sailing craft known, they, together with proas, originated in the Pacific. The Polynesian races were expert at handling catamarans and at least one British designer, James Wharram, has used ancient Polynesian principles to design a range of 'cats' with South Sea names like 'Hina', 'Tangaroa' and 'Tehini'.

These craft are constructed as 'V'-shaped hulls, held together by beams only, with no rigid 'wing' between them; just a slatted deck. The beams are attached in a non-rigid manner by using large rubber washers. The principles are that:

(*a*) they can be easily and cheaply constructed by amateurs from flat sheets of plywood;

(*b*) the hulls will give a little under stress and so reduce strain;

(*c*) water can splash up in between the hulls, avoiding the pounding effect which one gets in more conventional cats.

Other designers of cats, such as Prouts with boats like the Shearwater class (the most popular cat class), have stuck to rigid construction and have relied on a very strong method of building called 'cold moulding'.

Another large cat builder, Sailcraft Ltd., has adopted this method but in some of the smaller classes like the 'C' classes, built for the 'Little America's Cup' races, and the Tornado, the most most successful 'B' class, the middle wing has been replaced by spars and a trampoline-type net on which the crew sit.

Thus in some ways, the Polynesian type of craft and the Prout-pioneered rigid cat have inter-married and we are getting the best of both worlds in cat design.

The principles of cat design are found in light displacement, extreme beam which gives lateral stability, and great speed potential resulting from a very small wetted surface area. The hull shape seems quite important and the rounded or 'U'-shape which Prouts have used on their Shearwaters and also on Snowgoose, one of their most successful large racing cats, seems to be a winner.

One or two designers who have apparently not understood the principles of catamaran design have built large caravan-type deck houses on to the wings. This, in my view, makes the boats quite unsafe for serious cruising. Besides giving great areas of windage, it raises the centre of gravity of the boat. Most of these boats are heavily laden, and because of this they survive.

An organization which has had a lot to do with recent multihull development is the Amateur Yacht Research Society (A.Y.R.S.). It is very largely due to the individual initiative of their members that real progress has been made in the development of multihulled boats. Any intending multihull sailor would do well to join. They have produced a number of books on a variety of subjects. Of particular note is *Cruising Catamarans*. Their address is:

Amateur Yacht Research Society,
Hermitage,
Newbury,
Berkshire.

Trimarans

Theoretically the trimaran, i.e. a boat with one large central living hull and two smaller outer hulls, is the safest and fastest craft afloat, as has been shown by the 1972 Single-Handed Transatlantic Race winner, *Pen Duick IV*. But although much development has taken place, the trimaran has not yet become as widely used as the catamaran.

Safety-wise, its three hulls should be superb, but the problems which have held back development, have often been associated with the methods of connecting the three hulls.

A catamaran becomes safer when loaded (up to a point), but with a trimaran the opposite is true and it cannot carry too much weight. This has been an important restriction, but these problems have been and are being overcome, and 'tris' might well become the cruising boat of the future.

Some of the most 'way-out' designs in recent years have been trimarans; like the 'swing wing' type, a tri having outer hulls which hinge inwards when in harbour. Few British builders have regarded tris as a sound investment, and most of the well-known classes have come from America or Australia, designed by Arthur Piver and Hedley

Nichols, both, alas, lost at sea, a circumstance which has also had a rather adverse effect on trimaran popularity.

The 1972 Observer Single-Handed Transatlantic Race must have confirmed the trimaran as the race-winning type that it is: out of the first six places, tris were placed first, third and fifth.

Rigs

The tendency of modern racing dinghies to go for large headsails and high aspect ratio mainsails is logical when one notes that most races are won or lost on the windward leg.

So, traditionally, racing dinghy rigs are bermudian sloops with mainsails as tall as the rules allow and overlapping genoas replacing smaller jibs.

In restricted classes there is sometimes room for experiment with sail plans, but on the whole, and certainly in the case of one-designs, it is in the interests of the class to keep changes to a minimum.

It is only with new classes that we can expect to see radical rigs appearing, and really the modern dinghy rig has reached such a state of near-perfection that we are hardly likely to see any dramatic developments, except perhaps in masts and rigging technology.

Turbulence caused by masts, vangs, shrouds and the like detracts from the efficiency of the best cut sails, and it is perhaps in the un-stayed mast that future development will take place. Wing masts, revolving masts and unstayed masts are all ripe fields for research. Possibly the introduction of carbon fibres with their great strength-weight ratio will revolutionize spar making in the not-too-distant future, although at present the cost of a carbon-fibre spar would be prohibitive.

It might be thought that the development of single-handed long-distance sailing would have affected small boat rigs, but this is hardly so. Single-handed sailing in cruising yachts is a far cry from a typical racing dinghy or cruising day boat. The only offshoot of any importance has been in the wider use of self-steering gears and the general awareness that it is possible to make boats sail themselves if they are well-balanced. It is rare, however, to see self-steering fitted to boats under twenty-five feet in length.

The future

I think traditional monohulls will continue to find a steady market for many years to come, but the shapes will develop, particularly in the family-sized cruiser/racer. The old idea that a cruising boat does not need to be fast, only seaworthy, is dying with the 'Old Gaffers'. Modern cruisers have to be both fast *and* seaworthy to enable people to make the most of their time afloat.

Centreplates and lifting keels may well come into favour in bigger boats; they have obvious advantages over fixed keels and deep draught boats.

In the future there will be record sales of boats each year as many people look for relaxation afloat.

I think that the multihulled classes both of dinghies and yachts will gain popularity, and there will be more boats built for specific purposes such as single-handed sailing, world speed records and so on.

The era of speed sailing is just beginning. As the list of 'final challenges' diminishes, speed will become the new challenge. There will, of course, always be those (the vast majority) who get pleasure from simply 'messing about in boats', to whom leisurely cruising will appeal; but there are a growing number of people, who not only want to win races but who also want to set up new speed records. This is now the challenge; boats will have to be designed to go very fast.

Racing

Most people start racing by crewing for others. In this way tactics and rules can be picked up gradually. There are many helmsmen needing competent crews at sailing clubs throughout the country.

Racing is organized on four levels:

1. Club racing;
2. Open Meetings;
3. National Class Championships;
4. World Class Championships.

In the large classes, the national championships will be preceded by area or regional championships.

The keenest and most equal racing is in one-design classes. Full details of all classes can be obtained from the R.Y.A. in booklets G.13 (price 18p) and Y.R. 2 (price 17½p), the latter dealing with the Portsmouth Yardstick. Another useful booklet is G.14 (price 18p). This gives a geographical list of clubs and the classes that they race. All these booklets are free to members.

If there is no class racing for your particular class of boat at a club, there may be handicap racing. This is a poor substitute for class racing, but necessary nevertheless.

Racing rules are international and are made by the International Yacht Racing Union (I.Y.R.U.), while our national authority, the Royal Yachting Association (R.Y.A.) may make certain national changes where this is allowed in the rules. Clubs, too, are allowed to modify certain specified rules.

All well-known classes of boats which race have been given a rating called the Portsmouth Yardstick so that in handicap races different types or classes of boat can compete against each other. In order to convert 'elapsed time' to a 'corrected time', under the Portsmouth Yardstick one must possess a copy of the *Langstone Handicapping Tables*. These are obtainable only from:

> Mr. S. Zillwood Milledge,
> 77, Northway,
> London, N.W.11 6PD
>
> at 65p including U.K. postage

Racing is a fascinating part of the sport and, by the nature of the thing, is fairly complicated. Another R.Y.A. booklet, Y.R.3, *Yacht Racing Management* (price 25p) will help the newcomer to understand how it is organized, while Y.R.1 (37½p) contains the International Racing Rules.

Generally a club race is governed by the I.Y.R.U. rules and is in the hands of a Race Committee who appoint an Officer-of-the-Day to supervise the race. He will have assistants, all volunteer club members, to hoist flags, fire guns, record results, handle the safety boats and place racing marks in position. Well-run races will often have printed sailing instructions, but in club racing these may simply be displayed on a blackboard.

At ten minutes before the start, a warning gun will be fired and a class flag broken out at the flag mast. At five minutes, the preparatory flag (P) is broken out, and from then on until the end of the race all competitors must obey the racing rules.

After the starting gun, when both flags are dropped, the race may include one or more laps of a course. Fig. 47 shows a typical club racing course and also an olympic course.

Many other flags are used to give information about postponements, cancellations, reverse course, shortened course, etc., and the

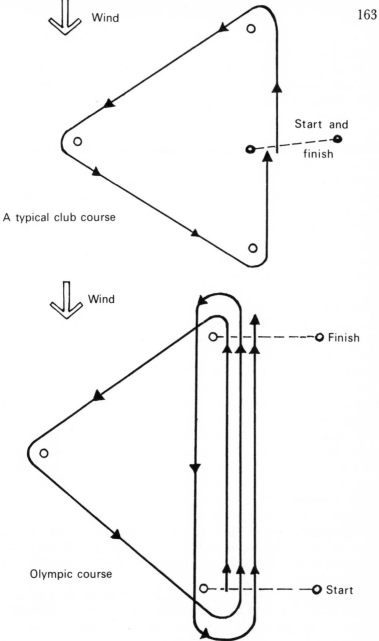

Wind

Start and
finish

A typical club course

Wind

Finish

Start

Olympic course

Fig. 47. Typical Club and Olympic courses

rules are numerous and complicated. It usually takes about a season of racing to learn the rules.

At the end of a race, if there have been any rule infringements, the race committee or a protests committee will meet to hear protests and give judgement. Competitors have the right to appeal to the R.Y.A. and ultimately to the I.Y.R.U. if not satisfied with the decision of a race committee.

Before a class boat can race, it normally has to possess a certificate of measurement. This ensures that it conforms to the class rules about construction, weight, sail area and so on. Never be tempted to buy a boat without a class certificate if you intend racing it. It may not measure and could be a liability.

The R.Y.A. have official measurers listed in booklet Y.R.6 (price 13p) for international and national classes. For other classes, sailing club official measurers will normally oblige. There is a charge for measuring a boat, which varies from class to class.

Cruising

By cruising I am thinking again in terms of small boats at first and shall try to follow a logical progression from dinghies to the larger yachts. This small section is intended only to point the way to the proficient small boat helmsman who wishes to move on to cruising. There are several excellent books on the subject, particularly Eric Hiscock's *Cruising Under Sail*, a very complete work by a man of great deep-sea experience.

Dinghy cruising is essentially a matter of being prepared for the worst. Once used to his boat, an enthusiast would be well advised to try a few short trips first in a semi-sheltered area. The Solent is ideal for this purpose, as are many of the east-coast rivers or Falmouth and Poole harbours.

Some dinghies, such as the Wayfarer, have canvas awnings which can be purchased from the manufacturers. Two people can spend quite a comfortable night in a Wayfarer with a little preparation; it would, however, be advisable to have had some camping experience ashore first.

The Dinghy Cruising Association is a useful contact for anyone intent on this type of cruising. Some of its members are very ingenious in the gadgetry that they have developed for cooking, eating and sleeping in confined spaces.

A little further up the scale comes the small family cruiser of about

18 ft to 22 ft. The 'Debutante', with several Atlantic crossings to her name, is a good example of this type of boat. They are just large enough to accommodate two berths (some have three and even four) but can still be towed behind a car on a medium-sized trailer so have all the advantages of a dinghy plus a little more comfort and luxury.

In choosing a boat of this size I would try to avoid those having only bilge keels. A centre ballast keel plus a centreplate is best, having self-righting qualities and windward performance plus the adaptability of a shallow-draught cruiser. Both the Seafarer and Kestrel are good seaworthy boats meeting this requirement at the smallest end of the range.

The difference between a twenty footer and a twenty-five footer is quite surprising. Within 25 ft four people can be comfortably accommodated. But some boats of around 25 ft are cramped, so look carefully if you have this much money to spend. A Folkboat, for instance, while having graceful lines and an excellent performance, is very cramped for cruising, and one would be better choosing one of the excellent Westerly range of cruisers: the 'Tiger', for instance, handles well, moves fast and is very roomy. But it *is* more expensive.

Before buying, first consider where you are likely to do most of your sailing. The east coast with its shoal areas rules out deep-keeled boats but most other areas have harbours where a keel boat can be moored, and a keel boat will generally have better sea-keeping qualities and sailing performance.

Where cost is concerned, fibreglass will be more expensive than wood initially, but maintenance will be much less and it will even out over a period of about five years.

Very large craft will be quite a liability. They will cost more to buy (though not necessarily if bought secondhand), be more expensive to maintain and moor, will probably require a larger crew and are not nearly so suitable for the D.I.Y. man to handle.

On the other hand, there are a few bargains to be found in yachts over 40 ft for exactly the above reasons; and a secondhand boat may well be a good buy if built by a reputable builder. It is essential to have a survey when buying secondhand; there are many pitfalls for the unsuspecting amateur.

Multihulls should not be ruled out for cruising. For family cruising in particular, they have many advantages over monohulls. They do not heel, have large, safe deck areas, and secondhand they tend to be much cheaper than a mono of the same size. At sea they behave well once the different techniques of handling have been understood. Their stability and speed means that the crew arrives in harbour much fresher than they would in a monohull. To be able to sit down to meals which actually stay on the table, even in a gale, is something which I, personally, enjoy very much!

Cruising requires a much more general experience of sailing than does racing. Wider issues of safety and pilotage have to be learnt, and it is sensible to 'serve an apprenticeship' as crew member on someone else's boat before investing in one of your own.

Many organizations cater for the beginner in cruising. One of the best is the Island Cruising Club, based at Salcombe in Devon. This Club owns several large cruising yachts which are run by the members, and membership entitles one to take part in all types of cruising according to ability and experience.

There are also a number of R.Y.A.-recognized sailing schools which offer cruising courses. Addresses can be obtained from the R.Y.A. The National Sailing Centre also runs coastal cruising courses, based at Cowes.

Eventually it will be necessary to learn some basic navigation, and many local authorities run evening classes in this subject at further education centres and technical colleges. Some clubs, too, run courses and there are also a number of correspondence courses which are advertised in sailing magazines. Most of these are organized during winter months.

One should try to combine theoretical knowledge with practical experience for best results.

There are two qualifications which the cruising yachtsman may find useful. The Yachtmaster's Certificate, which is issued by the Department of Trade and Industry, and the National Coastal Certificate, issued by the R.Y.A.

The Yachtmaster's Certificate is issued in two parts; coastal and ocean. It is almost entirely to do with navigation and pilotage. The syllabus does not include any practical work afloat, which is a pity.

The National Coastal Certificate, on the other hand, is a well-balanced syllabus, and while it is not as advanced as the Yachtmaster's it is more likely to serve the needs of the average 'weekend' yachtsman who wishes only to be able to navigate his boat safely around the coastal waters of the U.K. The syllabus for this certificate can be found in Appendix II p. 192.

In addition to the Island Cruising Club already mentioned, a

number of organizations cater for young people who wish to go cruising and for those under twenty-one one of the following may have a
course for you:

> *The Captain Scott*, a sail training schooner of 380 tons, run by the
> Loch Eil Trust.
> The Sail Training Association run two schooners, the *Sir Winston
> Churchill* and the *Malcolm Miller*.
> The Sea Cadet Corps and the Girls Nautical Training Corps
> have recently launched a brig called *Royalist*.
> The Ocean Youth Club have several large craft and are now
> regionalizing so that there will be opportunities for cruising in
> all areas of England.
> The London Sailing Project likewise run several large boats.
> Crew are mainly limited to boys from the London area.

Full details of all these organizations are given in R.Y.A. booklet
G.11 (price 10p).

The R.Y.A. also issue an Offshore Logbook which leads to an
Offshore Certificate. For those with deep-sea experience, this is a
useful way of keeping a record of personal sea-going experiences.

As all the booklets mentioned in this chapter are free to members
of the R.Y.A., it would probably pay those newcomers to the sport
who intend to stick with sailing to become full members. That is a
rather mercenary reason for joining our National Authority; it is also
desirable that the governing body of our sport should have as much
support as possible so that it can safeguard our interests from a position of strength in membership and finance, so I hope readers will
feel that it is worth joining for these reasons too.

In this book I have tried to take the newcomer to sailing through
all aspects of the sport, and it will be apparent that there is a great
deal left unsaid. Sailing is a vastly interesting pastime and there is
always something new to be learnt. It is really a way of life, and once
you, dear reader, 'get the bug' I think that you will find it a very
consuming thing. Sailing gives great enjoyment to many people from
the 'ditch-crawler' to the 'Round-the-Horn-man'. I am sure that you
will not be an exception.

Good Sailing!

APPENDIX I

INTERNATIONAL REGULATIONS FOR THE PREVENTION OF COLLISION AT SEA

PART A
PRELIMINARY AND DEFINITIONS

Rule 1

(*a*) These Rules shall be followed by all vessels and seaplanes upon the high seas and in all waters connected therewith navigable by seagoing vessels, except as provided in Rule 30. Where, as a result of their special construction, it is not possible for seaplanes to comply fully with the provisions of Rules specifying the carrying of lights and shapes, these provisions shall be followed as closely as circumstances permit.

(*b*) The Rules concerning lights shall be complied with in all weathers from sunset to sunrise, and during such times no other lights shall be exhibited, except such lights as cannot be mistaken for the prescribed lights or do not impair their visibility or distinctive character, or interfere with the keeping of a proper look-out. The lights prescribed by these Rules may also be exhibited from sunrise to sunset in restricted visibility and in all other circumstances when it is deemed necessary.

(*c*) In the following Rules, except where the context otherwise requires:
  (i) the word 'vessel' includes every description of water craft, other than a seaplane on the water, used or capable of being used as a means of transportation on water;
  (ii) the word 'seaplane' includes a flying boat and any other aircraft designed to manoeuvre on the water;
  (iii) the term 'power-driven vessel' means any vessel propelled by machinery;
  (iv) every power-driven vessel which is under sail and not under power is to be considered a sailing vessel, and every vessel under power, whether under sail or not, is to be considered a power-driven vessel;
  (v) a vessel or seaplane on the water is 'under way' when she is not at anchor, or made fast to the shore, or aground;
  (vi) the term 'height above the hull' means height above the uppermost continuous deck;
  (vii) the length and breadth of a vessel shall be her length overall and largest breadth;
  (viii) the length and span of a seaplane shall be its maximum length and span as shown in its certificate of airworthiness, or as determined by measurement in the absence of such certificate;
  (ix) vessels shall be deemed to be in sight of one another only when one can be observed visually from the other;

(x) the word 'visible', when applied to lights, means visible on a dark night with a clear atmosphere;

(xi) the term 'short blast' means a blast of about one second's duration;

(xii) the term 'prolonged blast' means a blast of from four to six seconds' duration;

(xiii) the word 'whistle' means any appliance capable of producing the prescribed short and prolonged blasts;

(xiv) the term 'engaged in fishing' means fishing with nets, lines or trawls but does not include fishing with trolling lines.

PART B – LIGHTS AND SHAPES

Rule 2

(*a*) A power-driven vessel when under way shall carry:

(i) On or in front of the foremast, or if a vessel without a foremast then in the forepart of the vessel, a white light so constructed as to show an unbroken light over an arc of the horizon of 225 degrees (20 points of the compass), so fixed as to show the light $112\frac{1}{2}$ degrees (10 points) on each side of the vessel, that is, from right ahead to $22\frac{1}{2}$ degrees (2 points) abaft the beam on either side, and of such a character as to be visible at a distance of at least 5 miles.

(ii) Either forward or abaft the white light prescribed in sub-section (i) a second white light similar in construction and character to that light. Vessels of less than 150 feet in length shall not be required to carry this second white light but may do so.

(iii) These two white lights shall be so placed in a line with and over the keel that one shall be at least 15 feet higher than the other and in such a position that the forward light shall always be shown lower than the after one. The horizontal distance between the two white lights shall be at least three times the vertical distance. The lower of these two white lights or, if only one is carried, then that light shall be placed at a height above the hull of not less than 20 feet, and, if the breadth of the vessel exceeds 20 feet, then at a height above the hull not less than such breadth, so however that the light need not be placed at a greater height above the hull than 40 feet. In all circumstances the light or lights, as the case may be, shall be so placed as to be clear of and above all other lights and obstructing superstructures.

(iv) On the starboard side a green light so constructed as to show an unbroken light over an arch of the horizon of $112\frac{1}{2}$ degrees (10 points of the compass), so fixed as to show the light from right ahead to $22\frac{1}{2}$ degrees (2 points) abaft the beam on the starboard side, and of such a character as to be visible at a distance of at least 2 miles.

(v) On the port side a red light so constructed as to show an unbroken light over an arc of the horizon of $112\frac{1}{2}$ degrees (10 points of the compass), so fixed as to show the light from right ahead to $22\frac{1}{2}$ degrees (2 points) abaft the beam on the port side and of such a character as to be visible at a distance of at least 2 miles.

(vi) The said green and red sidelights shall be fitted with inboard screens projecting at least 3 feet forward from the light, so as to prevent these lights from being seen across the bows.

(*b*) A seaplane under way on the water shall carry:

(i) In the forepart amidships where it can best be seen a white light, so constructed as to show an unbroken light over an arc of the horizon of 220 degrees of the compass, so fixed as to show the light 110 degrees on each side of the seaplane, namely, from right ahead to 20 degrees abaft the beam on either side, and of such a character as to be visible at a distance of at least 3 miles.

(ii) On the right or starboard wing tip a green light, so constructed as to show an unbroken light over an arc of the horizon of 110 degrees of the compass, so fixed as to show the light from right ahead to 20 degrees abaft the beam on the starboard side, and of such a character as to be visible at a distance of at least 2 miles.

(iii) On the left or port wing tip a red light, so constructed as to show an unbroken light over an arc of the horizon of 110 degrees of the compass, so fixed as to show the light from right ahead to 20 degrees abaft the beam on the port side, and of such a character as to be visible at a distance of at least 2 miles.

Rule 3

(*a*) A power-driven vessel when towing or pushing another vessel or seaplane shall, in addition to her sidelights, carry two white lights in a vertical line one over the other, not less than 6 feet apart, and when towing and the length of the tow, measuring from the stern of the towing vessel to the stern of the last vessel towed, exceeds 600 feet, shall carry three white lights in a vertical line one over the other, so that the upper and lower lights shall be the same distance from, and not less than 6 feet above or below, the middle light. Each of these lights shall be of the same construction and character and one of them shall be carried in the same position as the white light prescribed in Rule 2(*a*)(i). None of these lights shall be carried at a height of less than 14 feet above the hull. In a vessel with a single mast, such lights may be carried on the mast.

(*b*) The towing vessel shall also show either the stern light prescribed in Rule 10 or in lieu of that light a small white light abaft the funnel or aftermast for the tow to steer by, but such light shall not be visible forward of the beam.

(*c*) Between sunrise and sunset a power-driven vessel engaged in towing, if the length of tow exceeds 600 feet, shall carry, where it can best be seen, a black diamond shape at least 2 feet in diameter.

(*d*) A seaplane on the water, when towing one or more seaplanes or vessels, shall carry the lights prescribed in Rule 2(*b*)(i), (ii) and (iii); and, in addition, she shall carry a second white light of the same construction and character as the white light prescribed in Rule 2(*b*)(i), and in a vertical line at least 6 feet above or below such light.

Rule 4

(*a*) A vessel which is not under command shall carry, where they can best be seen, and, if a power-driven vessel, in lieu of the lights prescribed in Rule 2(*a*)(i) and (ii), two red lights in a vertical line one over the other not less than 6 feet apart, and of such a character as to be visible all round the horizon at a distance of at least 2 miles. By day, she shall carry in a vertical line one over the other not less than 6 feet apart, where they can best be seen, two black balls or shapes each not less than 2 feet in diameter.

(*b*) A seaplane on the water which is not under command may carry, where they can best be seen, and in lieu of the light prescribed in Rule 2(*b*)(i), two red lights in a vertical line, one over the other, not less than 3 feet apart, and of such a character as to be visible all round the horizon at a distance of at least 2 miles, and may by day carry in a vertical line one over the other not less than 3 feet apart, where they can best be seen, two black balls or shapes, each not less than 2 feet in diameter.

(*c*) A vessel engaged in laying or in picking up a submarine cable or navigation mark, or a vessel engaged in surveying or underwater operations, or a vessel engaged in replenishment at sea, or in the launching or recovery of aircraft when from the nature of her work she is unable to get out of the way of approaching vessels, shall carry, in lieu of the lights prescribed in Rule 2(*a*)(i) and (ii), or Rule 7(*a*)(i), three lights in a vertical line one over the other so that the upper and lower lights shall be the same distance from, and not less than 6 feet above or below, the middle light. The highest and lowest of these lights shall be red, and the middle light shall be white, and they shall be of such a character as to be visible all round the horizon at a distance of at least 2 miles. By day, she shall carry in a vertical line one over the other not less than 6 feet apart, where they can best be seen, three shapes each not less than 2 feet in diameter, of which the highest and lowest shall be globular in shape and red in colour, and the middle one diamond in shape and white.

(*d*) (i) A vessel engaged in minesweeping operations shall carry at the fore truck a green light, and at the end or ends of the fore yard on the side or sides on which danger exists, another such light or lights. These lights shall be carried in addition to the light prescribed in Rule 2(*a*)(i) or Rule 7(*a*)(i), as appropriate, and shall be of such a character as to be visible all round the horizon at a distance of at least 2 miles. By day she shall carry black balls, not less than 2 feet in diameter, in the same position as the green lights.

(ii) The showing of these lights or balls indicates that it is dangerous for other vessels to approach closer than 3,000 feet astern of the mine-sweeper or 1,500 feet on the side or sides on which danger exists.

(*e*) The vessels and seaplanes referred to in this Rule, when not making way through the water, shall show neither the coloured sidelights nor the stern light, but when making way they shall show them.

(*f*) The lights and shapes prescribed in this Rule are to be taken by other vessels and seaplanes as signals that the vessel or seaplane showing them is not under command and cannot therefore get out of the way.

(*g*) These signals are not signals of vessels in distress and requiring assistance. Such signals are contained in Rule 31.

Rule 5

(*a*) A sailing vessel under way and any vessel or seaplane being towed shall carry the same lights as are prescribed in Rule 2 for a power-driven vessel or a seaplane under way, respectively, with the exception of the white lights prescribed therein, which they shall never carry. They shall also carry stern lights as prescribed in Rule 10, provided that vessels towed, except the last vessel of a tow, may carry, in lieu of such stern light, a small white light as prescribed in Rule 3(*b*).

(*b*) In addition to the lights prescribed in section (*a*), a sailing vessel may carry on the top of the foremast two lights in a vertical line one over the other, sufficiently separated so as to be clearly distinguished. The upper light shall be red and the lower light shall be green. Both lights shall be constructed and fixed as prescribed in Rule 2(*a*)(i) and shall be visible at a distance of at least 2 miles.

(*c*) A vessel being pushed ahead shall carry, at the forward end, on the starboard side a green light and on the port side a red light, which shall have the same characteristics as the lights prescribed in Rule 2(*a*)(iv) and (v) and shall be screened as provided in Rule 2(*a*) (vi), provided that any number of vessels pushed ahead in a group shall be lighted as one vessel.

(*d*) Between sunrise and sunset a vessel being towed, if the length of the tow exceeds 600 feet, shall carry where it can best be seen a black diamond shape at least 2 feet in diameter.

Rule 6

(*a*) When it is not possible on account of bad weather or other sufficient cause to fix the green and red sidelights, these lights shall be kept at hand lighted and ready for immediate use, and shall, on the approach of or to other vessels, be exhibited on their respective sides in sufficient time to prevent collision, in such manner as to make them most visible, and so that the green light shall not be seen on the port side nor the red light on the starboard side, nor, if practicable, more than 22½ degrees (2 points) abaft the beam on their respective sides.

(*b*) To make the use of these portable lights more certain and easy, the lanterns containing them shall each be painted outside with the colour of the lights they respectively contain, and shall be provided with proper screens.

Rule 7

Power-driven vessels of less than 65 feet in length, vessels under oars or sails of less than 40 feet in length, and rowing boats, when under way shall not be required to carry the lights prescribed in Rules 2, 3 and 5, but if they do not carry them they shall be provided with the following lights:

(*a*) Power-driven vessels of less than 65 feet in length, except as provided in sections (*b*) and (*c*), shall carry:

  (i) In the forepart of the vessel, where it can best be seen, and at a height above the gunwale of not less than 9 feet, a white light constructed and fixed as prescribed in Rule 2(*a*)(i) and of such a character as to be visible at a distance of at least 3 miles.

  (ii) Green and red sidelights constructed and fixed as prescribed in Rule 2(*a*)(iv) and (v), and of such a character as to be visible at a distance of at least 1 mile, or a combined lantern showing a green light and a red light from right ahead to 22½ degrees (2 points) abaft the beam on their respective sides. Such lantern shall be carried not less than 3 feet below the white light.

(*b*) Power-driven vessels of less than 65 feet in length when towing or pushing another vessel shall carry:

  (i) In addition to the sidelights or the combined lantern prescribed in section (*a*) (ii) two white lights in a vertical line, one over the other not less than 4 feet apart. Each of these lights shall be of the same construction and character as the white light prescribed in section (*a*)(i) and one of them shall be carried in the same position. In a vessel with a single mast such lights may be carried on the mast.

  (ii) Either a stern light as prescribed in Rule 10 or in lieu of that light a small white light abaft the funnel or aftermast for the tow to steer by, but such light shall not be visible forward of the beam.

(*c*) Power-driven vessels of less than 40 feet in length may carry the white light at a less height than 9 feet above the gunwale but it shall be carried not less than 3 feet above the sidelights or the combined lantern prescribed in section (*a*)(ii).

(*d*) Vessels of less than 40 feet in length, under oars or sails, except as provided in section (*f*), shall, if they do not carry the sidelights, carry, where it can best be seen, a lantern showing a green light on one side and a red light on the other, of such a character as to be visible at a distance of at least 1 mile, and so fixed that the green light shall not be seen on the port side, nor the red light on the starboard side. Where it is not possible to fix this light, it shall be kept ready for immediate use and shall be exhibited in sufficient time to prevent collision and so that the green light shall not be seen on the port side nor the red light on the starboard side.

(*e*) The vessels referred to in this Rule when being towed shall carry the sidelights or the combined lantern prescribed in sections (*a*) or (*d*) of this Rule, as appropriate, and a stern light as prescribed in Rule 10, or, except the last vessel of the tow, a small white light as prescribed in section (*b*)(ii). When being pushed ahead they shall carry at the forward end the sidelights or combined lantern prescribed in sections (*a*) or (*d*) of this Rule, as appropriate, provided that any number of vessels referred to in this Rule when pushed ahead in a group shall be lighted as one vessel under this Rule unless the overall length of the group exceeds 65 feet when the provisions of Rule 5(*c*) shall apply.

(*f*) Small rowing boats, whether under oars or sail, shall only be required to have ready at hand an electric torch or a lighted lantern, showing a white light, which shall be exhibited in sufficient time to prevent collision.

(*g*) The vessels and boats referred to in this Rule shall not be required to carry the lights or shapes prescribed in Rules 4(*a*) and 11(*e*) and the size of their day signals may be less than is prescribed in Rules 4(*c*) and 11(*c*).

Rule 8

(*a*) A power-driven pilot-vessel when engaged on pilotage duty and under way:

(i) Shall carry a white light at the masthead at a height of not less than 20 feet above the hull, visible all round the horizon at a distance of at least 3 miles and at a distance of 8 feet below it a red light similar in construction and character. If such a vessel is of less than 65 feet in length she may carry the white light at a height of not less than 9 feet above the gunwale and the red light at a distance of 4 feet below the white light.

(ii) Shall carry the sidelights or lanterns prescribed in Rule 2(*a*)(iv) and (v) or Rule 7(*a*)(ii) or (*d*), as appropriate, and the stern light prescribed in Rule 10.

(iii) Shall show one or more flare-up lights at intervals not exceeding 10 minutes. An intermittent white light visible all round the horizon may be used in lieu of flare-up lights.

(*b*) A sailing pilot-vessel when engaged on pilotage duty and under way:

(i) Shall carry a white light at the masthead visible all round the horizon at a distance of at least 3 miles.

(ii) Shall be provided with the sidelights or lantern prescribed in Rules 5(*a*) or 7(*d*), as appropriate, and shall, on the near approach of or to other vessels, have such lights ready for use, and shall show them at short intervals to indicate the direction in which she is heading, but the green light shall not be shown on the port side nor the red light on the starboard side. She shall also carry the stern light prescribed in Rule 10.

(iii) Shall show one or more flare-up lights at intervals not exceeding 10 minutes.

(*c*) A pilot-vessel when engaged on pilotage duty and not under way shall carry the lights and show the flares prescribed in sections (*a*)(i) and (iii) or (*b*)(i) and (iii), as appropriate, and if at anchor shall also carry the anchor lights prescribed in Rule 11.

(*d*) A pilot-vessel when not engaged on pilotage duty shall show the lights or shapes for a similar vessel of her length.

Rule 9

(*a*) Fishing vessels when not engaged in fishing shall show the lights or shapes for similar vessels of their length.

(*b*) Vessels engaged in fishing, when under way or at anchor, shall show only the lights and shapes prescribed in this Rule, which lights and shapes shall be visible at a distance of at least 2 miles.

(*c*) (i) Vessels when engaged in trawling, by which is meant the dragging of a dredge net or other apparatus through the water, shall carry two lights in a vertical line, one over the other, not less than 4 feet nor more than 12 feet apart. The upper of these lights shall be green and the lower light white and each shall be visible all round the horizon. The lower of these two lights shall be carried at a height above the sidelights not less than twice the distance between the two vertical lights.

(ii) Such vessels may in addition carry a white light similar in construction to the white light prescribed in Rule 2(*a*)(i) but such light shall be carried lower than and abaft the all-round green and white lights.

(*d*) Vessels when engaged in fishing, except vessels engaged in trawling, shall carry the lights as prescribed in section (*c*)(i) except that the upper of the two vertical lights shall be red. Such vessels if of less than 40 feet in length may carry the red light at a height of not less than 9 feet above the gunwale and the white light not less than 3 feet below the red light.

(*e*) Vessels referred to in sections (*c*) and (*d*), when making way through the water, shall carry the sidelights or lanterns prescribed in Rule 2(*a*)(iv) and (v) or Rule 7(*a*)(ii) or (*d*), as appropriate, and the stern light prescribed in Rule 10. When not making way through the water they shall show neither the sidelights nor the stern light.

(*f*) Vessels referred to in section (*d*) with outlying gear extending more than 500 feet horizontally into the seaway shall carry an additional all-round white light at a horizontal distance of not less than 6 feet nor more than 20 feet away from the vertical lights in the direction of the outlying gear. This additional white light shall be placed at a height not exceeding that of the white light prescribed in section (*c*)(i) and not lower than the sidelights.

(*g*) In addition to the lights which they are required by this Rule to carry, vessels engaged in fishing may, if necessary in order to attract the attention of an approaching vessel, use a flare-up light, or may direct the beam of their searchlight in the direction of a danger threatening the approaching vessel, in such a way as not to embarrass other vessels. They may also use working lights but fishermen shall take into account that specially bright or insufficiently screened working lights may impair the visibility and distinctive character of the lights prescribed in this Rule.

(*h*) By day vessels when engaged in fishing shall indicate their occupation by displaying where it can best be seen a black shape consisting of two cones each not less than 2 feet in diameter with their points together one above the other. Such vessels if of less than 65 feet in length may substitute a basket for such black shape. If their outlying gear extends more than 500 feet horizontally into the seaway vessels engaged in fishing shall display in addition one black conical shape, point upwards, in the direction of the outlying gear.

Rule 10

(*a*) Except where otherwise provided in these Rules, a vessel when under way shall carry at her stern a white light, so constructed that it shall show an unbroken light over an arc of the horizon of 135 degrees (12 points of the compass), so fixed as to show the light $67\frac{1}{2}$ degrees (6 points) from right aft on each side of the vessel, and of such a character as to be visible at a distance of at least 2 miles.

(*b*) In a small vessel, if it is not possible on account of bad weather or other sufficient cause for this light to be fixed, an electric torch or a lighted lantern showing a white light shall be kept at hand ready for use and shall, on the approach of an overtaking vessel, be shown in sufficient time to prevent collision.

(*c*) A seaplane on the water when under way shall carry on her tail a white light, so constructed as to show an unbroken light over an arc of the horizon of 140 degrees of the compass, so fixed as to show the light 70 degrees from right aft on each side of the seaplane, and of such a character as to be visible at a distance of at least 2 miles.

Rule 11

(*a*) A vessel of less than 150 feet in length, when at anchor, shall carry in the forepart of the vessel, where it can best be seen, a white light visible all round the horizon at a distance of at least 2 miles. Such a vessel may also carry a second white light in the position prescribed in section (*b*) of this Rule but shall not be required to do so. The second white light, if carried, shall be visible at a distance of at least 2 miles and so placed as to be as far as possible visible all round the horizon.

(*b*) A vessel of 150 feet or more in length, when at anchor, shall carry near the stem of the vessel, at a height of not less than 20 feet above the hull, one such light, and at or near the stern of the vessel and at such a height that it shall be not less than 15 feet lower than the forward light, another such light. Both these lights shall be visible at a distance of at least 3 miles and so placed as to be as far as possible visible all round the horizon.

(*c*) Between sunrise and sunset every vessel when at anchor shall carry in the forepart of the vessel, where it can best be seen, one black ball not less than 2 feet in diameter.

(*d*) A vessel engaged in laying or in picking up a submarine cable or navigation mark, or a vessel engaged in surveying or underwater operations, when at anchor, shall carry the lights or shapes prescribed in Rule 4(*c*) in addition to those prescribed in the appropriate preceding sections of this Rule.

(*e*) A vessel aground shall carry the light or lights prescribed in sections (*a*) or (*b*) and the two red lights prescribed in Rule 4(*a*). By day she shall carry, where they can best be seen, three black balls, each not less than 2 feet in diameter, placed in a vertical line one over the other, not less than 6 feet apart.

(*f*) A seaplane on the water under 150 feet in length, when at anchor, shall carry, where it can best be seen, a white light, visible all round the horizon at a distance of at least 2 miles.

(*g*) A seaplane on the water 150 feet or upwards in length, when at anchor, shall carry, where they can best be seen, a white light forward and a white light aft, both lights visible all round the horizon at a distance of at least 3 miles; and, in addition, if the seaplane is more than 150 feet in span, a white light on each side to indicate the maximum span, and visible, so far as practicable, all round the horizon at a distance of 1 mile.

(*h*) A seaplane aground shall carry an anchor light or lights as prescribed in sections (*f*) and (*g*), and in addition may carry two red lights in a vertical line, at least 3 feet apart, so placed as to be visible all round the horizon.

Rule 12

Every vessel or seaplane on the water may, if necessary in order to attract attention, in addition to the lights which she is by these Rules required to carry, show a flare-up light or use a detonating or other efficient sound signal that cannot be mistaken for any signal authorised elsewhere under these Rules.

Rule 13

(*a*) Nothing in these Rules shall interfere with the operation of any special rules made by the Government of any nation with respect to additional station and signal lights for ships of war, for vessels sailing under convoy, for fishing vessels engaged in fishing as a fleet or for seaplanes on the water.

(*b*) Whenever the Government concerned shall have determined that a naval or other military vessel or waterborne seaplane of special construction or purpose cannot comply fully with the provisions of any of these Rules with respect to the number, position, range or arc of visibility of lights or shapes, without interfering with the military function of the vessel or seaplane, such vessel or seaplane shall comply with such other provisions in regard to the number, position, range or arc of visibility of lights or shapes as her Government shall have determined to be the closest possible compliance with these Rules in respect of that vessel or seaplane.

Rule 14

A vessel proceeding under sail, when also being propelled by machinery, shall carry in the daytime forward, where it can best be seen, one black conical shape, point downwards, not less than 2 feet in diameter at its base.

PART C – SOUND SIGNALS AND CONDUCT IN RESTRICTED VISIBILITY

Preliminary

1. *The possession of information obtained from radar does not relieve any vessel of the obligation of conforming strictly with the Rules and, in particular, the obligations contained in Rules 15 and 16.*

2. *The Annex to the Rules contains recommendations intended to assist in the use of radar as an aid to avoiding collision in restricted visibility.*

Rule 15

(a) A power-driven vessel of 40 feet or more in length shall be provided with an efficient whistle, sounded by steam or by some substitute for steam, so placed that the sound may not be intercepted by any obstruction, and with an efficient fog horn to be sounded by mechanical means, and also with an efficient bell. A sailing vessel of 40 feet or more in length shall be provided with a similar fog horn and bell.

(b) All signals prescribed in this Rule for vessels under way shall be given:

  (i) by power-driven vessels on the whistle;

  (ii) by sailing vessels on the fog horn;

  (iii) by vessels towed on the whistle or fog horn.

(c) In fog, mist, falling snow, heavy rainstorms, or any other condition similarly restricting visibility, whether by day or night, the signals prescribed in this Rule shall be used as follows:

  (i) A power-driven vessel making way through the water shall sound at intervals of not more than 2 minutes a prolonged blast.

  (ii) A power-driven vessel under way, but stopped and making no way through the water, shall sound at intervals of not more than 2 minutes two prolonged blasts, with an interval of about 1 second between them.

  (iii) A sailing vessel under way shall sound, at intervals of not more than 1 minute, when on the starboard tack one blast, when on the port tack two blasts in succession, and when with the wind abaft the beam three blasts in succession.

  (iv) A vessel when at anchor shall at intervals of not more than 1 minute ring the bell rapidly for about 5 seconds. In vessels of more than 350 feet in length the bell shall be sounded in the forepart of the vessel, and in addition there shall be sounded in the after part of the vessel, at intervals of not more than 1 minute for about 5 seconds, a gong or other instrument the tone and sounding of which cannot be confused with that of the bell. Every vessel at anchor may in addition, in accordance with Rule 12, sound three blasts in succession, namely, one short, one prolonged, and one short blast, to give warning of her position and of the possibility of collision to an approaching vessel.

  (v) A vessel when towing, a vessel engaged in laying or in picking up a submarine cable or navigation mark, and a vessel under way which is unable to get out of the way of an approaching vessel through being not under command or unable to manoeuvre as required by these Rules shall, instead of the signals prescribed in sub-sections (i), (ii) and (iii) sound, at intervals of not more than 1 minute, three blasts in succession, namely, one prolonged blast followed by two short blasts.

  (vi) A vessel towed, or, if more than one vessel is towed, only the last vessel of the tow, if manned, shall, at intervals of not more than 1 minute, sound four blasts in succession, namely, one prolonged blast followed by three short blasts. When practicable, this signal shall be made immediately after the signal made by the towing vessel.

(vii) A vessel aground shall give the bell signal and, if required, the gong signal, prescribed in sub-section (iv) and shall, in addition, give 3 separate and distinct strokes on the bell immediately before and after such rapid ringing of the bell.

(viii) A vessel engaged in fishing when under way or at anchor shall at intervals of not more than 1 minute sound the signal prescribed in sub-section (v). A vessel when fishing with trolling lines and under way shall sound the signals prescribed in sub-sections (i), (ii) or (iii) as may be appropriate.

(ix) A vessel of less than 40 feet in length, a rowing boat, or a seaplane on the water, shall not be obliged to give the above-mentioned signals but if she does not, she shall make some other efficient sound signal at intervals of not more than 1 minute.

(x) A power-driven pilot-vessel when engaged on pilotage duty may, in addition to the signals prescribed in sub-sections (i), (ii) and (iv), sound an identity signal consisting of 4 short blasts.

Rule 16

(a) Every vessel, or seaplane when taxi-ing on the water, shall, in fog, mist, falling snow, heavy rainstorms or any other condition similarly restricting visibility, go at a moderate speed, having careful regard to the existing circumstances and conditions.

(b) A power-driven vessel hearing, apparently forward of her beam, the fog-signal of a vessel the position of which is not ascertained, shall, so far as the circumstances of the case admit, stop her engines, and then navigate with caution until danger of collision is over.

(c) A power-driven vessel which detects the presence of another vessel forward of her beam before hearing her fog signal or sighting her visually may take early and substantial action to avoid a close quarters situation but, if this cannot be avoided, she shall, so far as the circumstances of the case admit, stop her engines in proper time to avoid collision and then navigate with caution until danger of collision is over.

PART D–STEERING AND SAILING RULES

Preliminary

1. *In obeying and construing these Rules, any action taken should be positive, in ample time, and with due regard to the observance of good seamanship.*

2. *Risk of collision can, when circumstances permit, be ascertained by carefully watching the compass bearing of an approaching vessel. If the bearing does not appreciably change, such risk should be deemed to exist.*

3. *Mariners should bear in mind that seaplanes in the act of landing or taking off, or operating under adverse weather conditions, may be unable to change their intended action at the last moment.*

4. *Rules 17 to 24 apply only to vessels in sight of one another.*

Rule 17

(a) When two sailing vessels are approaching one another, so as to involve risk of collision, one of them shall keep out of the way of the other as follows:

(i) When each has the wind on a different side, the vessel which has the wind on the port side shall keep out of the way of the other.

(ii) When both have the wind on the same side, the vessel which is to windward shall keep out of the way of the vessel which is to leeward.

(b) For the purposes of this Rule the windward side shall be deemed to be the side opposite to that on which the mainsail is carried or, in the case of a square-rigged vessel, the side opposite to that on which the largest fore-and-aft sail is carried.

Rule 18

(a) When two power-driven vessels are meeting end on, or nearly end on, so as to involve risk of collision, each shall alter her course to starboard, so that each may pass on the port side of the other. This Rule only applies to cases where vessels are meeting end on, or nearly end on, in such a manner as to involve risk of collision, and does not apply to two vessels which must, if both keep on their respective course, pass clear of each other. The only cases to which it does apply are when each of two vessels is end on, or nearly end on, to the other; in other words, to cases in which, by day, each vessel sees the masts of the other in a line, or nearly in a line, with her own; and by night, to cases in which each vessel is in such a position as to see both the sidelights of the other. It does not apply, by day, to cases in which a vessel sees another ahead crossing her own course; or, by night, to cases where the red light of one vessel is opposed to the red light of the other or where the green light of one vessel is opposed to the green light of the other or where a red light without a green light or a green light without a red light is seen ahead, or where both green and red lights are seen anywhere but ahead.

(b) For the purposes of this Rule and Rules 19 to 29 inclusive, except Rule 20(c) and Rule 28, a seaplane on the water shall be deemed to be a vessel, and the expression 'power driven vessel' shall be construed accordingly.

Rule 19

When two power-driven vessels are crossing, so as to involve risk of collision, the vessel which has the other on her own starboard side shall keep out of the way of the other.

Rule 20

(a) When a power-driven vessel and a sailing vessel are proceeding in such directions as to involve risk of collision, except as provided for in Rules 24 and 26, the power-driven vessel shall keep out of the way of the sailing vessel.

(b) **This Rule shall not give to a sailing vessel the right to hamper, in a narrow channel, the safe passage of a power-driven vessel which can navigate only inside such channel.**

(c) A seaplane on the water shall, in general, keep well clear of all vessels and avoid impeding their navigation. In circumstances, however, where risk of collision exists, she shall comply with these Rules.

Rule 21

Where by any of these Rules one of two vessels is to keep out of the way, the other shall keep her course and speed. When, from any cause, the latter vessel finds herself so close that collision cannot be avoided by the action of the giving-way vessel alone, she also shall take such action as will best aid to avert collision (see Rules 27 and 29).

Rule 22

Every vessel which is directed by these Rules to keep out of the way of another vessel shall, so far as possible, take positive early action to comply with this obligation, and shall, if the circumstances of the case admit, avoid crossing ahead of the other.

Rule 23

Every power-driven vessel which is directed by these Rules to keep out of the way of another vessel shall, on approaching her, if necessary, slacken her speed or stop or reverse.

Rule 24

(a) Notwithstanding anything contained in these Rules, every vessel overtaking any other shall keep out of the way of the overtaken vessel.

(b) Every vessel coming up with another vessel from any direction more than $22\frac{1}{2}$

degrees (2 points) abaft her beam, *i.e.* in such a position, with reference to the vessel which she is overtaking, that at night she would be unable to see either of that vessel's sidelights, shall be deemed to be an overtaking vessel; and no subsequent alteration of the bearing between the two vessels shall make the overtaking vessel a crossing vessel within the meaning of these Rules, or relieve her of the duty of keeping clear of the overtaken vessel until she is finally past and clear.

(*c*) If the overtaking vessel cannot determine with certainty whether she is forward of or abaft this direction from the other vessel, she shall assume that she is an overtaking vessel and keep out of the way.

Rule 25

(*a*) In a narrow channel every power-driven vessel when proceeding along the course of the channel shall, when it is safe and practicable, keep to that side of the fairway or mid-channel which lies on the starboard side of such vessel.

(*b*) Whenever a power-driven vessel is nearing a bend in a channel where a vessel approaching from the other direction cannot be seen, such power-driven vessel, when she shall have arrived within one-half ($\frac{1}{2}$) mile of the bend, shall give a signal by one prolonged blast on her whistle which signal shall be answered by a similar blast given by any approaching power-driven vessel that may be within hearing around the bend. Regardless of whether an approaching vessel on the farther side of the bend is heard, such bend shall be rounded with alertness and caution.

(*c*) In a narrow channel a power-driven vessel of less than 65 feet in length shall not hamper the safe passage of a vessel which can navigate only inside such channel.

Rule 26

All vessels not engaged in fishing, except vessels to which the provisions of Rule 4 apply, shall, when under way, keep out of the way of vessels engaged in fishing. This Rule shall not give to any vessel engaged in fishing the right of obstructing a fairway used by vessels other than fishing vessels.

Rule 27

In obeying and construing these Rules due regard shall be had to all dangers of navigation and collision, and to any special circumstances, including the limitations of the craft involved, which may render a departure from the above Rules necessary in order to avoid immediate danger.

PART E–SOUND SIGNALS FOR VESSELS IN SIGHT OF ONE ANOTHER

Rule 28

(*a*) When vessels are in sight of one another, a power-driven vessel under way, in taking any course authorised or required by these Rules, shall indicate that course by the following signals on her whistle, namely:

> One short blast to mean 'I am altering my course to starboard'.
> Two short blasts to mean 'I am altering my course to port'.
> Three short blasts to mean 'My engines are going astern'.

(*b*) Whenever a power-driven vessel which, under these Rules, is to keep her course and speed, is in sight of another vessel and is in doubt whether sufficient action is being taken by the other vessel to avert collision, she may indicate such doubt by giving at least five short and rapid blasts on the whistle. The giving of such a signal shall not relieve a vessel of her obligations under Rules 27 and 29 or any other Rule, or of her duty to indicate any action taken under these Rules by giving the appropriate sound signals laid down in this Rule.

(*c*) Any whistle signal mentioned in this Rule may be further indicated by a visual signal consisting of a white light visible all round the horizon at a distance of at least 5 miles, and so devised that it will operate simultaneously and in conjunction with the whistle-sounding mechanism and remain lighted and visible during the same period as the sound signal.

(*d*) Nothing in these Rules shall interfere with the operation of any special rules made by the Government of any nation with respect to the use of additional whistle signals between ships of war or vessels sailing under convoy.

PART F–MISCELLANEOUS

Rule 29

Nothing in these Rules shall exonerate any vessel, or the owner, master or crew thereof, from the consequences of any neglect to carry lights or signals, or of any neglect to keep a proper look-out, or of the neglect of any precaution which may be required by the ordinary practice of seamen, or by the special circumstances of the case.

Rule 30

Reservation of Rules for Harbours and Inland Navigation

Nothing in these Rules shall interfere with the operation of a special rule duly made by local authority relative to the navigation of any harbour, river, lake, or inland water, including a reserved seaplane area.

Rule 31

Distress Signals

(*a*) When a vessel or seaplane on the water is in distress and requires assistance from other vessels or from the shore, the following shall be the signals to be used or displayed by her, either together or separately, namely:

   (i) A gun or other explosive signal fired at intervals of about a minute.

   (ii) A continuous sounding with any fog-signalling apparatus.

   (iii) Rockets or shells, throwing red stars fired one at a time at short intervals.

   (iv) A signal made by radiotelegraphy or by any other signalling method consisting of the group . . . — — — . . . in the Morse Code.

   (v) A signal sent by radiotelephony consisting of the spoken word 'Mayday'.

   (vi) The International Code Signal of distress indicated by N.C.

   (vii) A signal consisting of a square flag having above or below it a ball or anything resembling a ball.

   (viii) Flames on the vessel (as from a burning tar barrel, oil barrel, etc.).

   (ix) A rocket parachute flare or a hand flare showing a red light.

   (x) A smoke signal giving off a volume of orange-coloured smoke.

   (xi) Slowly and repeatedly raising and lowering arms outstretched to each side.

   NOTE.—*Vessels in distress may use the radiotelegraph alarm signal or the radiotelephone alarm signal to secure attention to distress calls and messages. The radiotelegraph alarm signal, which is designed to actuate the radiotelegraph auto alarms of vessels so fitted, consists of a series of twelve dashes, sent in 1 minute, the duration of each dash being 4 seconds, and the duration of the interval between 2 consecutive dashes being 1 second. The radiotelephone alarm signal consists of 2 tones transmitted alternately over periods of from 30 seconds to 1 minute.*

(*b*) The use of any of the foregoing signals, except for the purpose of indicating that a vessel or seaplane is in distress, and the use of any signals which may be confused with any of the above signals, is prohibited.

RECOMMENDATIONS ON THE USE OF RADAR INFORMATION AS AN AID TO AVOIDING COLLISIONS AT SEA

(1) Assumptions made on scanty information may be dangerous and should be avoided.

(2) A vessel navigating with the aid of radar in restricted visibility must, in compliance with Rule 16(a), go at a moderate speed. Information obtained from the use of radar is one of the circumstances to be taken into account when determining moderate speed. In this regard it must be recognized that small vessels, small icebergs and similar floating objects may not be detected by radar. Radar indications of one or more vessels in the vicinity may mean that 'moderate speed' should be slower than a mariner without radar might consider moderate in the circumstances.

(3) When navigating in restricted visibility the radar range and bearing alone do not constitute ascertainment of the position of the other vessel under Rule 16(b) sufficiently to relieve a vessel of the duty to stop her engines and navigate with caution when a fog signal is heard forward of the beam.

(4) When action has been taken under Rule 16(c) to avoid a close quarters situation, it is essential to make sure that such action is having the desired effect. Alterations of course or speed or both are matters as to which the mariner must be guided by the circumstances of the case.

(5) Alteration of course alone may be the most effective action to avoid close quarters provided that:

(a) There is sufficient sea room.

(b) It is made in good time.

(c) It is substantial. A succession of small alterations of course should be avoided.

(d) It does not result in a close quarters situation with other vessels.

(6) The duration of an alteration of course is a matter in which the mariner must be guided by the circumstances of the case. An alteration to starboard, particularly when vessels are approaching apparently on opposite or nearly opposite courses, is generally preferable to an alteration to port.

(7) An alteration of speed, either alone or in conjunction with an alteration of course, should be substantial. A number of small alterations of speed should be avoided.

(8) If a close quarters situation is imminent, the most prudent action may be to take all way off the vessel.

APPENDIX II

SYLLABI OF ROYAL YACHTING ASSOCIATION PROFICIENCY CERTIFICATES

Detailed syllabus of the R.Y.A. **National Elementary Day-Boat Certificate**

A – PRACTICAL

1. Handling of boats under oars

pulling	thole pins	removing rowlocks
oars	sculling notch/rowlock	stowing oars
rowlocks	coming alongside	making boat fast
crutches	after use	

2. Handling sailing boats ashore

types of trolleys and trailers	care in support
economy of effort	securing to trolley

3. How to select and make sail according to conditions, including reefing

mainsails	reef points
working jibs	furling
reefing principles	cleating of halliards
when to reef	kicking strap arrangements
roller reefing	

4. Sailing a course (*solo-conditions permitting)

(a) getting under way from beach, hard and mooring
(b) picking up moorings, beaching, coming alongside
(c) knowledge of points of sailing and basic manoeuvres

running	pinching
broad reach	luffing
reach	bearing away
closehauled	gybing
tacking	

5. Righting a capsized dinghy

stay with boat – don't panic	head to wind
get immediate control	lower sails (only in difficulty)
disposition of crew members	bail out
leverage on plate	cleating of halliards
aids to climbing aboard	

* Solo: without instructor (not alone)

B – THEORY (onshore teaching)

1. Basic knowledge of boat parts and their uses

centreboard	mast step	leech of sail
daggerboard	halliard	luff of sail
rudder	shrouds	foot of sail
pintle and gudgeon	fore stay	tack of sail
tiller	boom	clew of sail
mainsail	mainsheet	roach of sail
foresail/jib	jib sheet	shackle
mast/heel/truck	head of sail	jib hank

2. Practical ability to tie bends and hitches

figure of eight knot	bowline
reef knot	fisherman's bend
sheet bend	clovehitch
double sheet bend	round turn and two half hitches

3. Recovery of man overboard

methods: gybe *or* tack

in over side	single handed sailing
practice	aids to climbing aboard
keep man in sight	

4. Safety afloat in respect of personal and boat buoyancy

buoyancy aids	built-in boat buoyancy
life jackets	solid boat buoyancy
B.S.S. 3595 ('69)	buoyancy bags
when to wear	buoyancy checks/repairs
types of lifejacket	fixing of buoyancy

disposition of buoyancy – too much, too little

5. Elementary first aid and lifesaving

likely accidents	effects of sea water on wounds
mouth to mouth resuscitation	sea sickness
first aid kit	exposure

6. Distress and safety signals

types
flares, types and use of
flags or shapes?

7. Winds, tides and currents and their effect on sailing dinghies

tidal sequence
tide tables and tidal stream atlas
ebb and flow
visible indications of tide
wind effect on high and low water
spring and neap tides
speed of boats relative to sailing with a current and against
wind and tide together
wind against tide
shallow water effects

C – TIDAL

1. Sailed a given course on tidal waters
Accompanied by an Instructor in the vicinity of moored boats and other obstructions.
To include: launching, getting away; all points of sailing: tacking, gybing, coming
ashore or alongside.

Detailed syllabus of the R.Y.A. **National Intermediate Day-Boat Certificate**

A – PRACTICAL

**1. Sailed to best advantage a given course
(without an instructor on board)**
get under way
sailed closehauled efficiently and tack
reach and plane
run and sail by the lee
gybe efficiently
sail figure of eight course
sail circular course
use of centreboard, sheets and crew weight (balance and trim)

2. Sailed off a lee shore
methods (a) crew holding head to wind in water
         (b) rowing or padding off
         (c) sailing boat off, heeled
pushing to get way on
hoisting sail
through surf
possible use of fixed rope to haul out on

3. Heaving to
basic methods   effect of current
explanations of reasons why   position of centreboard

4. Anchoring
types (a) fishermans   (b) C.Q.R.
       (c) Danforth   (d) others
advantages and disadvantages of each   depths and lengths ratios
stowing problems   tripping devices – buoying
knots used   choice of anchorage
rope, chain or both

5. Making fast to ordinary and jambing cleats, belaying pins, posts, etc.
hemp rope   ⎫   figure of eight turns
synthetic ropes ⎬ cleats   coiling spare rope
locking turn   ⎪   knots to use
slippery hitch   ⎭   rise and fall of tide – lengths
positioning of boat before making fast
lee side/weather side: of jetty, etc.

6. Reefing afloat and under way

sequence of operations
reef points, where tied
care, faults, reasons
roller reefing
kicking straps – types which allow reefing and replacements
square on gooseneck – strains and care needed
handling the main and shaped booms
care of battens when reefing
heaving to – methods (*a*) dinghies
                   (*b*) larger day boats, keelboats, etc.
when to reef

7. Handling under tow

methods (*a*) alongside
           (*b*) astern singly
           (*c*) astern two or more
rules   (*a*) weight distribution
           (*b*) centreboard up
           (*c*) make fast tow to firm fixing point, e.g., mast, thwart,
               ring bolt, etc.
               steering
               comparative length of tow to towed boat
               need to free sails and/or drop sails
               safe towing speeds

B – THEORY (onshore teaching)

1. Basic knowledge of sea terms

fore and aft	bear away	make fast
amidships	luff	bend on
weather	in irons	broaching
windward	in stays	wearing ship
leeward	pinch	aground
abaft	under way	leeway
abeam	weighing anchor	reef
ahead	mooring	sternway, etc.
astern	belay	

2. Simple meteorology

high barometer
low barometer
falling, steady, rising – meanings
wind directions and their relationship to weather patterns
cloud formations and their relationship to weather patterns
visibility – fog
Beaufort wind scale
wind effect on high and low water

3. Practical ability to make simple splices and whippings

short splice	common whipping
back splice	sailmakers whipping
eye splice	palm and needle whipping
	west country whipping

4. Basic rules of the road and courtesy and customs of the sea
sail and power
power – meeting, head on
sail – crossing (starboard tack rule)
sail and power – overtaking (overtaking boat rule)
sail – meeting head on
weather boat (sail)
lee boat (sail)
sail and power in confined waters
racing and cruising flags/burgees

5. Resuscitation and first aid
R.L.S.S./R.Y.A. Certificate

C – TIDAL

1. Basic knowledge of use of tidal stream atlas

2. Rate of tidal rise and fall

3. The compass:
variation, deviation, steering a given course, handbearing compass, taking bearings to fix position of craft

4. Practical sailing manoeuvres
including coming to a mooring and man overboard. Heaving to.

Detailed syllabus of the R.Y.A. **National Advanced Day-Boat Certificate**

A – PRACTICAL

1. Holds R.Y.A. National Elementary and Intermediate Day-Boat Certificates (or has been examined *practically* on syllabuses by Principal of Recognized Teaching Establishment).

2. Handling a rescue boat

engines	escort positions
anchors	picking up a man overboard
towing	mooring
warps	coming alongside
righting an inverted boat	making fast
effects of tides/currents	windage
fire risk and fighting	safety drills

3. Sailed to best advantage a given course
Sailed before the examiner to best advantage a given course in tidal/non-tidal waters including a run, reach and beat in conditions of not less than Force 3 with an inexperienced crew and hove-to during this course.
Conducted a practical capsize and recovery before the Examiner with an inexperienced crew in conditions of not less than Force 3.

B – THEORY (onshore reaching)

1. Basic knowledge of boat parts and their uses

keel	mast/heel/truck	mainsail
centreboard	mast step	foresail/jib
daggerboard	hounds	genoa
rudder	shrouds	spinnaker
pintle and gudgeon	fore stay	head of sail
tiller	runners	leech of sail
tiller extension	cross trees	luff of sail
breasthook	back stay	foot of sail
hog	bowsprit	tack of sail
king plank	bumpkin	clew of sail
gunwhale	bobstay	roach of sail
coaming	pulpit	belly of sail
fairleads	transom	thimble
snap hooks	blocks	cringle
main sheet	piston hanks	reef points
jib sheets	kicking strap	lacings
horse	whisker pole	earings
belaying pins	jambing cleats	battens/pockets
painter	cleats	seams
boom	toe straps	burgee
knees	stem	thwart

2. Boat maintenance

running checks	correct support of hull, mast, boom, etc
annual refits	boat covers
rubbing down	sea water; effect on wood, etc.
re-varnishing/painting	fresh waters; effect on wood, etc.
advantages of a G.R.P. hull	anti-fouling

storage methods   (a) during season
               (b) winter

Storing dinghies and equipment

in/out season	effects of sun, rain, frost, etc., on paintwork/varnishwork
types	G.R.P.
indoor – outdoor	bungs – drain – limber holes
chocking	outboards
other supports	rigging
masts and booms	limited space – vertical storage
sails	

3. General safety rules

personal	swimming ability	the boat	suitability
	fitness		condition/and of gear
	B.S.I. approved equipment		buoyancy
	buoyancy		equipment
	local information		
	know the boat		
	value of knotting		
	safety harnesses		

4. Compass work

orienteering

5. **First aid**
   resuscitation (mouth to mouth and other methods) and hypothermia

6. **The characteristics of different rigs**

cat/una	gaff
sloop	gunter
cutter	bermudan
yawl	square sails
ketch	lug-sails
schooner	fore and aft rig

7. **Knowledge of simple boat repairing**
   hull – dents, scratches, use of G.R.P.
   spars – cracks, shakes
   rigging – breakages, talurit splicing; (swaged)
   sails – tears, seams, use of palm and needle
   holing – scarfing and use of G.R.P. patches
   marine glues, marine ply
   other suitable woods, mahogany, ash, elm

8. **Theory and practical experience of racing**

race procedure	signals
racing rules	fair sailing
tactics	club/class organization
types of racing craft	Portsmouth Yardstick
international and national	Langstone Handicapping Tables
governing bodies	measurement

C – TIDAL

1. **Tides, winds and currents**
   Tides
   springs and neaps
   tidal information
   wind and tide together – range – rise and fall
   wind against tide – shoal water effects
   tide races – effects on boys, etc.
   varying strength of tide – twelfths
   tide tables
   standard and secondary ports – Dover
   tidal streams atlas
   tide rode – meaning of
   use tides to advantage

   Winds and currents
   wind direction and their relationships to weather patterns
   Beaufort wind scale
   wind effect on high and low water
   currents, causes and effects of
   strengths of currents
   speed of boat – with current – against current
   use of charts for information
   safe wind strengths for dinghy sailing
   centre/edge of current/strengths

2. Charts and compasses navigation and pilotage

Charts and compasses

Admiralty charts	compass deviation
other charts	compass variation
symbols and abbreviations (No. 5011)	compass rose
scales	types of compass
correction of charts	compass adjusting
chart datum and soundings	swinging the ship
range of tides	correction card
Mercator projection	three types of north
latitude and longitude	use of hand bearing compass
laying off a course	compass bearings
dead reckoning	night use of compass
care of charts	grid compass – advantages of

Rules of the road

International regulations for preventing collisions at sea

Part A – definitions

Part B – lights and shapes

Part C – sound signals – fog

Part D – steering and sailing rules
        starboard tack rule
        windward boat rule
        power to sail
        power to sail (exceptions)
        overtaking boat rule

Part E – B.O.T. sound signals
        1 short blast
        2 short blasts
        3 short blasts
        4 short blasts plus 2 short blasts
        4 short blasts plus 1 short blast
        5 short blasts
        Morse letter D

Part F – miscellaneous
        distress signals
Local harbour byelaws
courtesy practices

Buoyage systems

types   (*a*) Cardinal – international
                  how it works
       (*b*) Lateral – British water
           starboard hand buoys, shape, colour, numbers
           port hand buoys, shape, colour, numbers
           middle ground buoys, shape, colour, numbers
           isolated danger marks, shape, colour, numbers
           landfall marks, shape, colour
           wreck buoys, shape, colour
           two types may be used together: transition marks
           special buoys – e.g., R.N.

3. Safety at sea, distress signals, and organizations concerned

safety rules when sailing: lee shores
coastguards/E.T.D./E.T.A.
reefing
forecasts
heaving to
charts, use of

distress: equipment
signals
fog

The organizations connected with saving life at sea

Coastguards	Ro.S.P.A.	Police
R.N.L.I.	R.A.F.	Venturers
Club Rescue	Local boatmen	

4. Courtesy and customs of the sea

aid in distress
dressing ship
salutes
racing flags, shape, when used, retiring boats
flags of flag officers: in place of burgee
burgees: when/where flown
        yacht club member
        shape, colour
ensigns: red: for all British yachts
           compulsory in foreign ports
           where flown
           sunrise to sunset
     white: R.N. and Royal Yacht Squadron only
special ensigns: special warrant required
the law: only controls *ensigns*, otherwise a matter of etiquette

5. Handling under sail

to perform required defined manoeuvres, e.g., recovery drill for man overboard

6. Handling under power

to perform required defined manoeuvres

ROYAL YACHTING ASSOCIATION
NATIONAL COASTAL CERTIFICATE

Certificate No.

This is to certify that

....

has been examined for practical knowledge and has had a course of training/had at least two years practical experience and is competent up to a standard of Grade .... except those items deleted overleaf.

He/She is also considered capable of taking charge of ....

(type of boat) on sheltered/coastal tidal waters in winds up to force ....

He/She has had .... hours accompanied tuition and was in charge of the boat for .... hours. He/She is capable of being in command of a vessel of this type for short coastal trips/for passage making out of sight of land.

Signed ....

Position held ....

Establishment ....

Date ....

GRADE 1

* 1. A thorough knowledge of the points of sailing and manoeuvres.
* 2. Practical ability to tie the basic bends and hitches.
  3. Knowledge of simple sea terms.
  4. Knowledge of names and use of parts of the boat.
* 5. How to select and make sail according to weather conditions, including reefing.
* 6. Picking up moorings and anchoring with one and two anchors.
* 7. Multiple moorings springs warps, etc.
* 8. Recovering man overboard and drill and other rules of safety.
* 9. Use of harness, life lines, personal buoyancy.
  10. Holds G.P.O. R/T Licence/can operate R/T in emergency.
*11. Heaving to.
*12. Buoyage systems and elementary ship recognition.
*13. Ability to read and lay off a course from Admiralty charts.
*14. Can steer a compass course in open water under supervision.
*15. Ability to use and handle inflation-type and conventional dinghy.
*16. Knowledge of basic 'Rules of the Road' and courtesy and customs of the sea.
*17. Understanding of weather forecasts.
*18. Precautions and action to take in heavy weather.
*19. Fire precautions and action to take.
*20. Understands compass bearings.
*21. Can teach another crew member deck work, take a watch and keep a deck log.
*22. Understands towing techniques and 'weighing' of tow.
*23. Simple meteorology, winds, tides, currents and their effects.
  24. Can swim 50 yards in sailing clothes.
  25. Has passed A.S.A. personal survival test or equivalent.

GRADE 2

Grade 1, plus:

  26. Making basic splices and whippings.
*27. Logs, log reading and log keeping.
*28. Taking of soundings with lead line and familiarity with depth sounders.
*29. Rules and methods of Fog Navigation.

(*indicates compulsory items)

*30. Mouth-to-mouth resuscitation.
*31. Use of distress signals and navigation lights.
*32. Emergency repair of gear and rigging.
*33. A sound knowledge of 'Rules of the Road'.
*34. Understands correct use of flags, burgees and ensigns.
 35. Can make signals by light in Morse at about 6 words a minute.
*36. Knows Customs regulations for yachts.
*37. Knows urgent and important single letter signals of the International Code (1969).
*38. Elementary knowledge of simple inboard and outboard engines.
*39. Care and use of barometer.
*40. Navigation. Taking of: cross bearings/running fixes/vertical fixes, bearing and distance/D.F. bearings/leading and clearing marks, and radio beacon system.
*41. Use of: tide tables, tidal atlas, and Nautical Almanac.
*42. Compass deviation and variation.

Detailed syllabus of R.Y.A. **Coastal Certificate**

GRADE 1

1. A thorough knowledge of the points of sailing and manoeuvres

(a) running	(g) tacking
(b) broad reach	(h) sailing 'by the lee'
(c) reach	(i) pinching
(d) fine reach	(j) luffing
(e) closehauled	(k) bearing away
(f) fetch	(l) gybing

Practical and theoretical instruction including sailing a figure of eight and circular course.

2. Practical ability to tie the basic bends and hitches

figure of eight knot	fishermans bend
reef knot	clovehitch
sheetbend	rolling hitch
double sheet bend	round turn and two half hitches
bowline	

3. Knowledge of simple sea terms

fore and aft	bear away	make fast
amidships	luff	bend on
weather	in irons	broaching
windward	in stays	wearing ship
leeward	pinch	aground
abaft	under way	sailing full and bye
abeam	weighing anchor	leeway
ahead	mooring	reef
astern	belay	sternway, etc.

(*indicates compulsory items)

4. Knowledge of names and use of parts of the boat

keel	mast/heel/truck	mainsail
centreboard	mast step	foresail/jib
daggerboard	hounds	genoa
rudder	shrouds	spinnaker
pintle and gudgeon	fore stay	head of sail
tiller	runners	leech of sail
tiller extension	cross trees	luff of sail
knees	back stay	foot of sail
breasthook	bowsprit	tack of sail
hog	bumpkin	clew of sail
king plank	bobstay	roach of sail
gunwhale	pulpit	belly of sail
coaming	transom	thimble
fairleads	blocks	cringle
snap hooks	piston hanks	reef points
main sheet	kicking strap	lacings
jib sheets	whisker pole	earings
horse	jambing cleats	battens/pockets
belaying pins	cleats	seams
painter	toe straps	burgee
boom	stem	thwart, etc.

5. How to select and make sail according to weather conditions, including reefing

mainsails	reefing principles *(a)* racing
working jibs	*(b)* cruising
genoas	goosewinged headsails
spinnakers	roller reefing
trysails	reef points
rigs: comparisons	furling
dinghies and ballasted boats	heaving to while reefing, when to reef

6. Picking up moorings and anchoring with one and two anchors

mooring:	anchoring:
no wind	wind rode
no tide	tide rode
wind and tide together	weight of anchor/s
wind against tide	chain
cross winds	types of warp
congested areas	types of anchor: fishermans, C.Q.R., Danforth, umbrella, admiralty pattern
swinging	
fore and aft	length of warp
	height of tide
	names: bower and kedge
	use of kedge
	two anchors: fore and aft
	two anchors: on the bow
	which one first?

7. Multiple moorings, springs, warps, etc.

varying mooring conditions call for different techniques:
alongside jetties, pontoons, etc.

alongside other yachts
on swinging mooring
on fore and aft mooring
on piles, fore and aft
function of springs
use of springs
types of warps
thickness of warps

8. Recovering man overboard and drill and other rules of safety

methods (a) gybe round
        (b) tack and bear away } depending on conditions of wind
in over side   singlehanded sailing
in over stern   aids to climbing aboard
practice – buoy or man?   singlehanded; need to carry aids
keep man in sight   lifebelts: lit and unlit
use of safety harness

9. Use of harness, lifelines, personal buoyancy

Necessary for singlehanded cruising and/or rough weather
harness: types available   lifelines: material
      bowline on bight   fixing points
      fitting of   positioning
personal buoyancy: buoyancy aids: disadvantages of lifejackets B.S. 3595

10. Holds G.P.O. R/T licence/can operate R/T in emergency

distress signals in R/T
SOS in morse
'Mayday' spoken
International code signal of distress

11. Heaving to

methods
explanations of reasons why
effect of current
position of centreboard
keel boats – need for trial and error practice
balance of sails and helm

12. Buoyage systems and elementary ship recognition

1. Cardinal system – international
                 how it works
2. Lateral system – British waters
      starboard hand buoys, shape, colour, number
      port hand buoys, shape, colour, number
      middle ground buoys, shape, colour
      isolated danger marks
      landfall marks
      wreck buoys
two systems may be used together
transition marks
special buoys: e.g. R.N.

ship recognition: power
    liners, tankers, ferries, coasters, dredgers, lightships, pilot vessels, lifeboats,
    I.R.B.'s R.N. types
silhouettes of ships as aids to recognition
visible navigation lights in relation to ships course

13. Ability to read and lay off a course from Admiralty charts

parallel rules, dividers, other	scales
instruments	method of laying off à course
compass rose: true, compass direction	distance log
symbols and abbreviations;	dead reckoning
chart 5011	latitude and longitude

14. Can steer a compass course in open water under supervision

stress need for practice in all conditions
daytime
night time: binnacle light
use of grid compass: ex-services types

15. Ability to use and handle inflation type and conventional dinghy

under oars	rowlocks	coming alongside
under paddles	crutches	after use
sculling	thole pins	stowing oars/rowlocks
outboard	launching	making fast to jetty, etc.
anchoring	beaching	how to leave the dinghy
varying weather conditions	weight distribution	

16. Knowledge of basic 'rules of the road' and courtesy and customs of the sea

sail and power
power: crossing
power meeting, head on
sail: crossing (starboard tack rule)
sail overtaking (overtaking boat rule)
sail meeting head on
sail weather boat (keep clear)
sail lee boat (right of way, maintain course)
sail and power in confined waters
flag etiquette
racing and cruising flags/burges

17. Understanding of weather forecasts

B.B.C. forecasts: weather and shipping
sea areas
forecast terminology
local weather stations: civil, R.A.F., meteorological
visual gale warnings/storm cones

18. Precautions and action to take in heavy weather

reefing: roller, furling, reef points (mainsail)
            wykeham-martin and roller (headsails)
sea anchors: length of warp, types, makeshift sea anchor
running before the wind: jib only, trailing warps
bare poles: centre of gravity to be kept low

lee shores: dangers
use of 'preventers'
lifejackets and boat buoyancy: need to check before sailing
equipment must be suitable for worst conditions
distress equipment and signals
coastguards: notify whenever possible E.T.D. and E.T.A.
on shore: watch for distressed vessels: report producedure '999'
oil: on troubled waters
dropping of mast: practice desirable
need for accurate weather forecasts
seek shelter: weather shores

19. Fire precautions and action to take

causes: calor, petrol, fumes/exhaust, cooking
precautions: well fixed fittings
                positioning of combustibles
                positioning of extinguishers
                backfire traps
                gas detectors
                a tidy boat
                use of correct materials in danger areas
action: isolate fire
                use extinguisher/method appropriate to type of fire
                use safety raft if available
                head boat so that fire is to leeward
                distribute lifejackets, etc.
                shut off all fuel cocks, etc.
                don't panic
                jump off!

20. Understands compass bearings

compass rose   practice in bearings of objects
circular notation   hand bearing compasses
bearings from the boat   compass error
bearings of the boat

21. Can teach another crew member deck work, take a watch, and keep a deck log

winches, hoisting sails, coiling, making fast, belaying, anchor work, anchor leads, mooring warp leads, deck safety, lookout, deck log layout

22. Understands towing techniques and 'weighting' of tow

length and weight of warp
position of attachment of warp in boat   (a) astern
                                      (b) alongside
towing in smooth water
towing in rough water
where tow is wind affected
where tow is tide affected
speeds
type of craft suitable for towing
weighting: position of weight
purpose of weight
'the tail wagging the dog' effect
signals when towing

23. Simple meteorology, winds, tides, currents and their effects

high barometer, low barometer, falling, steady, rising, meanings
wind directions and their relationships to weather patterns
cloud formations and their relationships to weather patterns
visibility: fog
Beaufort wind scale
wind effect on high and low water
spring and neap tides
currents: causes and effects of
currents strengths of
speed of boats relative to sailing with a current and against
use of charts for information
wind and tide together
wind against tide
tide races
shallow water effects
use of tidal streams atlas
meteorological symbols
local variations: hills, high buildings
enclosed water
open sea
effect of currents on buoys etc.
chart datum
varying strength of tide: twelfths
tide tables
standard and secondary ports: Dover

24. Can swim 50 yards in sailing clothes

25. Has passed A.S.A. personal survival test or equivalent

GRADE 2

Grade 1 plus:

26. Making basic splices and whippings

short splice
back splice
eye splice

common whipping
sailmakers whipping
palm and needle whipping
west country whipping

27. Logs, log reading and log keeping

use of
type of entry: course, speed, changes in course/speed, other craft sighted, weather,
visibility, wind force, temperature, pressure, times of mooring, anchoring, making sail, etc. current set and drift, log (distance) reading
legal evidence in court
hourly intervals at sea
deck officers duty to keep log

28. Taking of soundings with lead line and familiarity with depth sounders
methods and techniques
sounding calls and meanings
'loading' the lead
use of safety harness whilst sounding
depth sounders: theory: two scales
                  adjustment (*a*) for depth
                             (*b*) shoals of fish etc.
                  types available

29. Rules and methods of fog navigation
rules: anchor in safe water
       radar reflector
       sound signals
       main channels: other ships
       lee shores

30. Elementary first aid and lifesaving
likely accidents   effects of sea water on wounds
mouth-to-mouth resuscitation   sea sickness
first aid kit   exposure

31. Use of distress signals and navigation lights
types: flares
       code flags NC
       R/T: Mayday and SOS
       raising and lowering arms
       Rule 31, International regs
navigation lights: see rules 4, 6, 7 International regulations
torch only necessary for dinghies/day boats/keelboats
recognition of other boats by their lights

32. Repair of gear and rigging
jury rigging
sails: tears, seams, stitching, use of palm and needle
ropes: splicing
wire: talurit
woodwork
buoyancy bags
hull: dents, scratches, G.R.P., holes – scarfing
spars: cracks and shakes
fittings: replace metal where cracked

33. A sound knowledge of rules of the road
International regulations for preventing collisions at sea
Part A – definitions
Part B – lights and shapes
Part C – sound signals – fog
Part D – steering and sailing rules
            starboard tack rule
            windward boat rule
            power to sail
            power to sail – exceptions
            overtaking boat rule

Part E – B.O.T. sound signals:
    1 short blast
    2 short blasts
    3 short blasts
    5 short blasts
    Morse letter D
Part F – miscellaneous
    distress signals
local harbour byelaws
courtesy practices
essential need to avoid collision

34. Understand correct use of flags, burgees and ensigns
flag etiquette
racing flag: shape, when used, retiring boats
flags of flag officers: in place of burgee
burgees: where/when flown
    yacht club member
    shape, colour
ensigns: red – for all British yachts
      compulsory in foreign ports
      where flown
      sunrise to sunset
    white: R.N. and Royal Yacht Squadron only
    special ensigns: special warrant required
the law: only controls *ensigns*, otherwise controlled by etiquette

35. Can make signals by light in morse
see new International Code 1 April 1969
international: therefore can be used anywhere
single letter signals: meanings
procedure signals: meanings
use of procedure (*a*) call sign
              (*b*) identity of sender
              (*c*) break sign
              (*d*) test of message
              (*e*) ending sign

36. Knows customs regulations for yachts
ships papers
Q flag: certificate of pratique
over 40 tons: duty free stores automatically
under 40 tons: apply to Customs and Excise
French pamphlet: issued in English by
   French Gov. Tourist Office, 66 Haymarket, London, S.W.1.
foreign cruising: consult R.Y.A., A.A., R.A.C.
Dutch pamphlet: obtainable from
   Netherland Nat. Tourist Office, 38 Hyde Park Gate, London S.W.7

37. Knows urgent and important single letter signals of the International Code
N.B. These changed 1 April 1969. See section 35 above

38. Elementary knowledge of simple inboard and outboard engines

inboard petrol/diesel:	starting, stopping
	fuel system, stop cocks, taps
	cooling system
	plugs
	possible faults
	filters
	decompressors
	injectors
outboard: as above plus:	attachment to boat
	safety line, locks, etc.
	carrying position
	use of
	possible faults
driving hints:	revving
	useful speeds
	care of engine

39. Care and use of barometer

how a barometer works
mean sea level adjustments
care of barometer
reliability: general pressure tendencies
falling barometer
rising barometer
steady barometer
Buys Ballots law: N. hemisphere – back to wind – pressure low on left
wind gauges – home made variety
anemometers – importance of height

40. Navigation, taking of: cross bearings/running fixes/vertical fixes, bearing and distance/D.F. bearings/leading and clearing marks

cross bearings:	importance of wide angle (90 degs.) hand bearing compass
running fixes:	method
vertical fixes:	sextant types
	method
	importance of height of eye
	tables for finding distance off (Reeds)

$$\text{distance off} = \frac{0.565 \times \text{ht. of object (ft)}}{\text{sextant angle (minutes)}}$$

D.F. bearings:	positions of beacons
	methods of use: fixes, homing
	R.D.F. sets: use of
	radio beacon charts
	call signs
	null point
	consol system
leading marks:	types, principle
	channels
	day/night
clearing marks:	types
	dangers

Emphasize position is always fixed nearest to danger

41. Use of: tide tables, tidal atlas, and nautical almanac
tide tables: standard ports
               secondary ports
               neap and spring tides
               equinoctial tides
               range of tide
               B.S.T.
tidal streams atlas: strength and direction at neaps/springs at a given time
                      use in conjunction with charts
                      route planning
nautical almanac: Reeds & Browns
                   contents
                   how to find sections
                   current copy essential

42. Compass deviation and variation
deviation: the *boat*'s effect on compass (ferrous)
variation: the *earth*'s effect on compass (magnetic field)
compass adjusters and their work
swinging the ship
compass correction card
variation: 'error west, compass best'
            'error east, compass least'
            allowance to be made – compass to true and vice versa

R.Y.A. reference booklets (available FREE to FULL and LIFE members), which provide more detailed information for this certificate:
R.Y.A. Book 'Flags and Signals' (30p)
R.Y.A. Booklet G2 Regulations for the Prevention of Collisions at Sea
R.Y.A. Booklet YR1 Yacht Racing
R.Y.A. Booklet G5 Weather Forecasts
R.Y.A. Book 'Foreign Cruising' (30p)
R.Y.A. Booklet G2 I.R.P.Ċ.S.

ROYAL YACHTING ASSOCIATION

NATIONAL MOTOR LAUNCH AND POWERBOAT CERTIFICATE

Certificate No.

Delete words not applicable
This is to certify that

....

has been examined for practical knowledge and has had a course of training/had at least two years practical experience/and is competent up to a standard of Grade .... except those items deleted overleaf.
He/She is also considered capable of handling:
  A single/twin engine displacement motorboat
  B displacement day-boat/motor dinghy
  C sports runabout with a maximum speed of under/over 30 knots
  D single/twin engine powerboat (planing)

on inland/sheltered/coastal waters in winds up to force .... on tidal/non-tidal waters.
He/She has had .... hours accompanied tuition during which he/she was in charge of the boat for .... hours.
He/She is considered to be capable of being in command in a vessel of type .... in .... conditions.

Signed ....

Position held ....

Establishment ....

Date ....

GRADE 1

* 1. Basic principles relating to displacement and planing craft.
  2. Practical ability to tie simple bends and hitches.
  3. Knowledge of basic sea terms.
  4. Basic knowledge of parts of the boat, equipment and usage.
* 5. Training in basic functions of inboard and outboard motors, starting procedures and necessary check lists.
* 6. Getting under way from moorings, piers and anchorages.
* 7. Picking up anchorages and moorings, coming alongside under all usual conditions.
* 8. Anchoring with one or two anchors and anchor dragging.
* 9. Appreciation of fire risks in relation to fuel, gas and electrical systems.
*10. Knowledge of methods of fire prevention and action in case of fire.
*11. Rules of personal and boat safety including equipment.
  12. Recovery of man overboard and heaving to.
*13. Rules of the Road and buoyage system.
  14. Simple theory covering propulsion, hull speeds, tidal effects, sea conditions and windage on powerboats.
  15. Use and handling of small inflatable and conventional dinghies.
*16. Courtesy and customs of the sea.
  17. Able to swim 50 yards in sailing clothes.
  18. Has passed A.S.A. personal survival test or equivalent.
  19. Navigation of rivers – negotiating locks, flood stream, tide reaches.
  20. Canal navigation in general, including the operation of locks and lift and swing bridges, negotiating tunnels, aqueducts, etc.
  21. Laying off and steering compass courses.

(*indicates compulsory items)

GRADE 2

Grade 1, plus:
*22. Handling in strong tides or currents.
 23. Make simple splices and whippings.
*24. Anchoring and heaving to in strong seas (use of sea anchor).
*25. Coastal pilotage and chart reading at high speed.
*26. Fog navigation and use of distress signals, navigation lights and electronic aids.
 27. Towing of one or more boats.
*28. Multiple moorings, springs, warps, etc.
 29. Preparation of course cards including fuel estimations.
 30. Knowledge of engine faults, fuel systems, cooling systems and electrical circuits.
*31. Mouth-to-mouth resuscitation and elementary First Aid.

Detailed syllabus of the R.Y.A. National Motor Launch and Powerboat Certificate

GRADE 1

1. Basic principles relating to displacement and planing craft
displacement craft: righting moment, self righting, keel weight
centre of gravity, lateral resistance
heavy displacement, ballast ratio
light displacement hulls
speed and water line length
length and beam: stability and safety
planing craft: shape and principle of planing hull
planing speeds
water conditions
engine and propeller positions

2. Practical ability to tie simple bends and hitches
figure of eight knot	fisherman's bend
reef knot	clovehitch
sheet bend	rolling hitch
double sheet bend	round turn and two half hitches
bowline	

3. Knowledge of basic sea terms
fore and aft	pinch
amidships	under way
weather	weighing anchor
windward	mooring
leeward	belay
abaft	make fast
abeam	bend on
ahead	broaching
astern	wearing ship
bear away	aground
luff	leeway
in irons	reef
in stays	sternway, etc.

(*indicates compulsory items)

4. Basic knowledge of parts of the boat, equipment and uses

anchors	fog horn	quarter
	fairleads	quarter knees
bows	fire extinguishers	
boat hook		rudder
bilges	gear control	
bilge pump	gudgeon	stringers
battery	gunwhale	shaft
breasthook		skeg
block	hog	stem
belaying pins		stem post
	keel	stern
couplings	knees	sea anchor
cuddy	kedge	samson post
compass		
coaming cleats	limber holes	thrust bearing
	lifebuoys	towing post
		throttle
dodger	navigation lights	
dog house		tool kits
deadwood	oars	tiller
distress flares		transom
	propeller	thwart
engine	pintle	
	painter	wheel
fenders	pulpit	wheel house
frames	pushpit	warps

5. Training in the basic functions of inboard and outboard motors, starting procedures, and necessary check lists

propulsion:
types available
servicing
minor repairs
petrol/diesel: advantages of each

starting procedures: check lists:
when cold   boat equipment
when hot   safety equipment
power start
manual start   starting check: valves, cocks, taps, etc.
water coolled   mooring checks
air cooled

6. Getting under way from moorings, piers and anchorages

lee side, weather side   use of fenders
swinging mooring, fore and aft   use of current
  mooring   use of wind
moored by the bow   breaking out anchor, buoying anchor
moored alongside   stowage of anchors (clean)
use of springs   other craft: congestion

7. Picking up ancho rages and moorings, coming alongside under unusual conditions

anchorages:
wind rode
tide rode
weight of anchor
chain or warp
types of anchors
length of warp/chain
use of kedge

moorings:
no wind, no tide
wind and tide together
wind against tide
cross winds
congested areas
swinging
fore and aft

alongside:
windward, leeward
use of fenders
use of springs
height of tide
by the bow: alongside
letting go from the boat:
  (with crew/singlehanded)

general:
when to cut engines
use of gears
single propeller
twin propeller
approach: need for caution (slow)
stern power (inability to manoeuvre satisfactorily)

8. Anchoring with one or two anchors and anchor dragging
see section 7 above
two anchors: fore and aft, and on the bow
reasons for dragging: bottom unsuitable, insufficient warp, steep
                      bottom, fouled anchor
anchor watch
anchor check: shore transits

9. Appreciation of fire risks in relation to fuel gas and electrical systems
causes: calor, petrol, fumes/exhaust, cooking
        need for care in fitting engines, cookers, exhaust systems
        fuel tanks, etc.
        how fire is caused
        fire statistics

10. Knowledge of methods of fire prevention and action in case of fire
(*a*) anti-fire drills
    storage of fuel, gas, etc.
    isolation of fuel, gas, etc. when not in use
    position of fire fighting appliances
    well fixed fittings
    backfire traps
    gas detectors
    a tidy boat
    use of correct materials in danger areas of boat
(*b*) action to take in case of fire
    isolation of fire
    use extinguishers/method appropriate to type of fire
    use safety raft if available
    head boat so that fire is to leeward
    distribute lifejackets, etc.
    shut off all fuel cocks, taps, etc.
    don't panic
    jump off!

11. Rules of personal and boat safety including equipment

personal:
buoyancy aids
lifejackets
B.S.S. 3595
types of lifejacket
when to wear
swimming ability
fitness
know the boat
value of knotting
value of local knowledge
suitable protective clothing
safety harnesses
exposure statistics

distress equipment:
flares
radio
lifebelts
liferafts B.O.T. rules
inflatables

boat:
the right boat for the job
safe speeds in harbours, etc.
type of hull
danger of propeller when collecting persons
    from water
need for good tool kit
need for spare parts
built in boat buoyancy: checks
solid fixed boat buoyancy: checks
buoyancy bags check
repairs and initial fixing of boat buoyancy
disposition of buoyancy: too much – too little

12. Recovery of man overboard and heaving to

man overboard:
in over side ⎫
in over stern ⎭ dangers
keep in sight whilst in water
use of safety harness
single handed recovery
aids to climbing aboard
keep rescued man away from propeller
approach and use of engine
heaving to: basic methods
            effect of current
            effect of wind

13. Rules of the road and buoyage systems

International regulations for preventing collisions at sea:
Part A – definitions
Part B – lights and shapes
Part C – sound signals – fog
Part D – steering and sailing rules
starboard tack rule, windward boat rule, power to sail, sail to power, power to sail
exceptions, overtaking boat rule
Part E – B.O.T. sound signals
  1 short blast
  2 short blasts
  3 short blasts
  5 short blasts
  Morse letter D
Part F – miscellaneous
  distress signals
  local harbour byelaws

courtesy practices
essential need to avoid collision
Buoyage systems:
Cardinal system
Lateral System British waters:
starboard hand buoys
port hand buoys
middle ground buoys
isolated danger marks
landfall marks
wreck buoys
two systems may be used together
transition marks
special buoys, e.g. R.N.

14. Simple theory covering propulsion, hull speeds, tidal effects, sea conditions and windage on powerboats
propulsion: propellers – right handed and left
                       clearance from hull
                       positioning
square root water line length $\times$ $1\frac{1}{2}$: relation to speed
in the water, on the water
shape of hull
tidal effects: foul tide: speed
turning in a foul tide
sea conditions: short seas
               wind against tide
               steep seas
windage: effects on heavy displacement boats
               effects on light displacement boats
               effects on masts, etc.
               effects on super structure
               effects on fast planing hulls

15. Use of and handling of small inflatable and conventional dinghies
under oars
under paddles
sculling
outboard motor
anchoring
varying weather conditions
methods of kedging with a dinghy
rowlocks
crutches
thole pins
launching
beaching
coming alongside
after use
stowing oars/rowlocks
making fast to jetty, etc.
how to leave the dinghy
weight distribution
use of davits
towing and stowage

16. Courtesy and customs of the sea
aid in distress
dressing ship
salutes
racing flags, shape, when used, retiring boats
flags of flag officers: in place of burgee

burgees: when/where flown
        yacht club member
        shape, colour
ensigns: red: for all British yachts
               compulsory in foreign ports
               where flown
               sunrise to sunset
        white: R.N. and Royal Yacht Squadron only
        special ensigns: special warrant required
the law: only controls *ensigns*, otherwise a matter of etiquette

17. Able to swim 50 yards in sailing clothing

18. Has passed A.S.A. personal survival test or equivalent

19. Navigation of rivers – negotiating locks, flood stream, tide reaches
speed limits and byelaws, riparian owners
currents: on bends
        deep water
        weakest on edges of river
lock gate routine
lock safety rules
attended and unattended locks
flood stream: dangers
             speed over the ground
tide reaches: range of tide
            effect of tide

20. Canal navigation in general, including the operation of locks and lift and swingbridges, negotiating tunnels, aqueducts, etc.
speed limits and byelaws
passing places

21. Laying off and steering compass courses
parallel rules, dividers, other instruments
compass rose, true and compass direction
symbols and abbreviations, Chart No. 5011
scales
method of laying off a course
dead reckoning
distance log
latitude and longitude
types of compass: grid and handbearing/multipurpose types

GRADE 2
Grade 1 plus:

22. Handling in strong tides or currents
centre/edge of current
turning
use of throttle
using the current under way
using the current to turn
using the current to moor/come alongside
wind rode, tide rode: meanings
use tides where possible

23. Make simple splices and whippings

short splice	common whipping
back splice	sailmakers whipping
eye splice	palm and needle whipping
	west country whipping

24. Anchoring and heaving to in strong seas (use of sea anchor)

anchoring: types (*a*) fishermans, (*b*) C.Q.R., (*c*) Danforth, (*d*) others
        advantages and disadvantages of each type
        stowage problems
        knots used
        rope, chain or both
        depths and lengths ratios
        tripping devices: buoying
        choice of anchorage
        weight of anchor to boat ratio
        safety precautions in strong seas: e.g. lifeline
heaving to: method: sea, anchor, drogue
        principle: head to wind
        effect of current
        length of sea anchor warp
        type of sea anchor warp
        how long it takes

25. Coastal pilotage and chart reading at high speed

buoyage recognition
symbols and abbreviations (Chart 5011)
see section 13 above
depths
hazards
tidal information

26. Fog navigation and use of distress signals, navigation lights and electronic aids

fog: anchor in safe water
    radar reflector
    sound signals
    main channels: other ships
    lee shores
distress signals: types
    flares
    code flags NC
    R/T: Mayday and SOS
    raising and lowering arms
    rule 31, International regs.
navigation lights: see rules 4, 6, 7 International regs.
        torch only necessary for dinghies, etc.
        recognition of other boats by their lights
electronic aids: depth sounder: scales
                     types
                     re-echoes

radar: small boats may not show: reflector
           care in use
           experience necessary
R.D.F.   use of
           types
           null meter
           bearings and homing
auto-pilot: not for small boats
ship to shore: G.P.O. requirements
                 costs

27. Towing of one or more boats

length and weight of warp
position of attachment in boat being towed (*a*) astern, (*b*) alongside
towing in smooth water
towing in rough water
where tow is wind affected
where tow is tide affected
speeds
type of craft suitable/unsuitable for towing
signals and instructions to towed boats:
advice to dinghies: lower sails – centreboard up – weight amidships or towards stern –
                 steer straight course – how to make fast towing warps – need to
                 take account of total length of tow in multiple tows – avoidance
                 of well-used routes

28. Multiple moorings, springs, warps, etc.

varying mooring conditions call for different techniques
alongside jetties, pontoons, etc.
alongside other yachts
on swinging mooring
on fore and aft mooring
on piles, fore and aft
function of springs
use of springs
types of warps
thickness/weight of warps

29. Preparation of course cards, including fuel estimates

need for over estimates
tidal streams and relation to fuel consumption
bad weather and relation to fuel consumption
need to avoid main shipping channels/areas where possible

30. Knowledge of engine faults, fuel systems, cooling systems and electrical circuits

engine faults: plugs, lack of fuel, oil levels, damp, etc.
fuel systems: petrol/diesel: blocked pipes, dirt, air (diesel), bleeding (diesel),
                    need for filters/clean fuel
cooling systems: air and water: advantages and disadvantages water cooling in
                    winter
                    need for free passage of air/water
electrical circuits: damp, contacts, batteries/storage

31. Mouth-to-mouth resuscitation and elementary first aid
likely accidents
first aid kit
effects of sea water on wounds
sea sickness
exposure
Haynes resuscitation trainer
other methods of lifesaving – see R.L.S.S. handbook

GLOSSARY OF SAILING TERMS

Abaft	Behind, to the rear of.
Abeam	Adjacent to the beam of a boat.
Aft	Rear of the boat.
Ahead	In front of.
Amidships	The middle of a boat.
Anchor	Heavy metal object used to secure boat to the ground.
Apparent wind	The wind caused by the movement of the boat.
Astern	Behind the boat.
Backing the jib	Hauling the jib onto the windward side of the boat.
Battens	Flat pieces of wood used to stiffen a sail.
Beam	The widest part of the boat.
Beam reach	When the wind is blowing on the beam, i.e. at right angles to the boat.
Bear away	Turn away from the direction that the wind is blowing from.
Beating to windward	Sailing closehauled and zig-zagging to get to windward.
Bermudan	A rig with all triangular sails.
Bight	A loop of rope.
Bilges	The bottom parts of a hull under the floorboards.
Block	A device with pulley wheels, used on sheets to achieve reduction.

Boom	A spar, usually attached to the foot of a sail.
Bottlescrew	A metal fitting used on shrouds and stays for tightening up.
Bow	The forward parts of a boat, on either side; e.g. port bow.
Breastrope	A rope used for tying to a quay, jetty, etc., which is fixed at right angles to the boat.
Broad reach	When the wind is blowing over a quarter.
Bulk head	A strengthening section fitted across the boat.
Bung	A stopper.
Burgee	A triangular flag.
Carvel	A method of construction where planks are laid side by side along the boat, producing a smooth exterior surface.
Cat-rig	Rig having only one sail, una-rig.
Caulking	Filling in between planks on a carvel-built boat.
Centreboard	A pivoting plate fixed in the centre of a hull.
Chine	The junction of two parts of a hull, producing an angle.
Chinese gybe	A gybe, usually unintentional, when the top of the sail crosses first and makes a sharp 'S' shape in the leech of the sail.
Cleat	A device for securing a rope by jambing or wrapping.
Clevis pin	Pin used on shrouds and stays to secure it to other fittings.
Clew	Bottom rearmost corner of a sail.
Clew outhaul	A piece of line on a mainsail, used for hauling the clew out along the boom.
Clinker	A method of construction where planks slightly overlap each other for extra strength.
Closehauled	Sailing as close as possible to the wind, usually about 45°.

Close reach   Sailing with the wind ahead of the beam but not closehauled.

C.L.R.   Centre of lateral resistance, the point around which the boat pivots when sails are in use.

Coaming   A raised part of the deck or vertical board which prevents water entering the boat.

Cockpit   The interior part of a dinghy in which one sits or the sunken steering area in a larger boat.

C. of E.   Centre of effort, of the sails.

Coffee-grinder   A large sheet winch, operated by two people with two handles. Usually only found on large racing yachts.

Cringle   A eyelet in a sail.

Cunningham eye   An eyelet in the luff of a mainsail near the foot which is used to tighten the sail in strong winds.

Cutter   A boat with more than one headsail.

Daggerboard   A non-hinging board which is pushed vertically down through its case in the centre of a dinghy to give lateral resistance.

Deck   A covering on top of a hull which keeps water out.

Double chine   A design of boat having two chines.

E.T.A.   Estimated time of arrival.

E.T.D.   Estimated time of departure.

Fairlead   A fitting which a rope is led through, usually on deck.

Fathom   A measurement of six feet.

Foot   The bottom edge of a sail.

Fore-and-aft   The imaginary line running down the centre of a boat; also a type of rig with sails set along the centreline of the boat.

Foredeck — Deck in the forward part of a boat.

Foresail — The fore-and-aft sail set on the aft side of a schooner's foremast; the jib on a dinghy is also sometimes referred to as a foresail.

Forestay — A wire leading from the front of the boat to the mast.

Freeboard — Distance from the water surface to the deck of a boat.

Full and bye — Sailing a few degrees from closehauled so that all sails are well filled.

Gaff — A type of rig having a spar running along the top of four-sided sails.

Genoa — A large headsail with a long low foot.

Going about — Tacking; changing from one tack to another, with the wind ahead of the boat.

Gooseneck — The fitting connecting a boom to a mast.

Goosewing — Sailing with some sails on opposite sides to others.

G.R.P. — Glass reinforced plastic.

Gudgeon — A fitting on the rudder or transom which helps connect each to the other.

Gunter — A type of rig with a four-sided mainsail but giving a similar shape to a triangular sail.

Gunwhale — The top, outer rim of a hull.

Gybe — To change from one tack to another with the wind astern.

Gybe-oh — Command given on gybing.

Halliard — A rope used to hoist sails.

Hard chine — A single chine.

Head, of boat — Front of boat.

Head, of sail — Top corner of a triangular sail or top side of a four-sided sail.

Headed	To be turned away by a wind shift from the direction one wants to go, usually when close-hauled.
Headsail	A sail in front of the mast.
Heave to	To stop the boat by letting the sails flap, or by backing the jib and putting the helm down.
Helm	Steering gear.
Helm down	Putting the helm over to the leeward side of the boat.
Helmsman	The steersman.
Helm up	Putting the helm over to the windward side of the boat.
Hull	The main shell of a boat.
In irons or in stays	Unable to steer on to a tack, having moved into a head to wind position, often drifting backwards.
Jib	The small sail on a dinghy in front of the mast; on a cutter, the foremost headsail.
Jib stick	A pole used to hold a jib in the goosewinged position when running.
Jigger	Tiller extension.
Jury rig	A makeshift rig.
Keel	The lower, central, outermost spine of a boat's hull, sometimes added to the hull by way of ballast.
Ketch	A rig having a main and mizzen mast with the latter forward of the steering post.
Kicking strap	A wire or rope running from the foot of a mast to the underside of a boom.
King plank	The central plank on a foredeck.

L.A.T.	Lowest astronomical tide.
Leech	The aft side of a sail.
Leeboard	A board fixed vertically to the side of a boat to prevent the boat making excessive leeway.
Lee helm	When pressure is felt on the tiller which would turn the boat to leeward if the tiller were let go.
Lee-oh	Command given on going about.
Lee shore	A shore with the wind blowing on to it.
Lee side	The sheltered side, side which the wind is not blowing onto.
Leeward	As lee side.
Leeway	To move to leeward.
Letting fly	To release sheets and let sails flap.
Luff	To turn a boat towards the wind; also front edge of a sail.
Lug-sail	A four-sided sail, the head of which is fixed to a yard and projects ahead of the mast.
Lying ahull	Leaving a boat to find its own position in relation to the waves.
Mainsail	A large sail set on the mainmast.
Mainsheet	Rope controlling a mainsail.
Mast	A spar on which sails are hoisted.
Miss stays	To miss tacking.
Mizzen	Sail or mast fixed near to the stern of the boat.
No-go-zone	An angle of approximately 90° into which it is not possible for a boat to sail.
Painter	A rope attached to the front of a dinghy to tie it up with.
Peak	The top back corner of a square sail.

Pintle   A metal fitting attached to transom and rudder and connecting one to the other; fit into gudgeons.

Planing   Sailing fast on the surface of the water rather than in it.

Port   Left-hand side of a boat when facing forwards.

Port tack   When the mainsail is on the starboard side, i.e. the wind blowing over the port side of the boat.

Pram dinghy   Small dinghy with a cut-off front, having no stem.

Quarters   The back portion of a boat on either side, e.g. starboard quarter.

Reaching   A point of sailing when the wind comes approximately at right angles to the boat.
See also **Close, Beam** and **Broad reaching.**

Ready about   Shouted in preparation for going about.

Reef   To reduce sail area.

Rib   A cross member of the hull.

Rig   The layout of a boat's mast and sails.

Rigging   Wire and rope supporting masts and controlling sails.

Rowlocks   Swivelling fittings which oars fit into when rowing.

Rudder   The hinged steering gear in the water attached to the back of a boat.

Running   Sailing with the wind behind the boat.

R.Y.A.   Royal Yachting Association.

Sailing by the lee Sailing on a run with the wind blowing on the lee side.

Sailing off the wind	Sailing, not closehauled.
Sailing on the wind	Sailing closehauled.
Samson post	A mooring post on the foredeck.
Schooner	A fore-and-aft rigged craft having two or more masts, the mainmast being as tall as or taller than the foremast.
Sculling	A method of propelling a boat through the water by sweeping in a figure-of-eight movement with an oar over the stern.
Sea-anchor	A canvas funnel used to reduce the speed of a boat to the minimum in strong winds.
Self-balers	Apertures which can be opened in the bottom of a hull to allow water to be sucked out.
Shackle	A metal fitting used to attach two pieces of rigging or rigging to sails.
Shackle key	A key for unscrewing shackle pins.
Sheet	A rope by which sails can be tightened up.
Sheeting in	Tightening sails by hauling on a sheet.
Shroud	A wire fixed from the side of the boat to the mast.
Side bench	A seat running fore and aft along the side of a cockpit.
Sloop	Boat having one headsail and a mainsail.
Slot	The gap between two overlapping sails.
Snugging down	Tidying up a boat in preparation for leaving it.
Spar	A pole, mast, boom or gaff.
Spinnaker	A headsail, set right forward and held out with a boom.
Spinnaker pole	A spinnaker boom.
Splice	To work rope back through itself, e.g. to form an eye.
Springs	Ropes tied diagonally from boat to shore to secure a craft.

Sprit	A spar set diagonally on a square sail from tack to peak.
Square rig	A rig having square sails set across the boat.
Stalling, of sail	When a sail shakes and loses power.
Standing part, of rope	The part nearest to the point of attachment, furthest from the free end.
Stand by to gybe	Command given preparatory to gybing.
Standing rigging	The rigging which supports the mast, i.e. forestay, shrouds.
Starboard	Right-hand side of boat when facing forwards.
Starboard tack	When the mainsail is on the port side, i.e. the wind is blowing over the starboard side of the boat.
Stay	A wire rope supporting the mast or other spar in a fore-and-aft direction.
Staysail	A triangular sail set on a stay.
Stem	The front central member of a hull.
Stem dinghy	A dinghy having a stem as opposed to a pram shape.
Stem head	The top of the stem.
Stern	Back of a boat.
Stow	Put away.
Stringer	Strengthening pieces running along the inside of a hull fore-and-aft.
Tack, of sail	Front lower corner.
Tacking	Going about; changing from one tack to another.
Throat	Forward upper corner of a gaff sail.
Thwart	A seat fixed across a boat.
Tide rode	Facing into a tidal stream, i.e. when moored or anchored.
Tiller	A wood or metal bar, secured to the rudder, by which a boat is steered.

Tiller extension   An extension to a tiller which enables a helms-man to lean out and balance a racing dinghy.

Toe straps   Webbing straps secured to the floor of a dinghy.

Transom   The back vertical cross section of a boat.

Transom flaps   Hinged flaps in a transom which are opened to allow water to drain out.

Trisail   Triangular storm sail, set in place of a mainsail in heavy weather.

True wind   The actual wind, unaffected by the movement of a boat.

Una-rig   A single-sailed rig, cat-rig.

Warp   A rope.

Weather helm   When pressure is felt on the tiller which would turn the boat to windward if the tiller were let go.

Weather shore   The sheltered shore, the shore which the wind is not blowing on to.

Weather side, of boat   The windward side.

Whipping   A method of sealing a rope end with twine so that it does not unlay.

Whisker pole   Jibstick, used for booming out the jib when goosewinged.

Winch   A mechanical device used to obtain increased power when hauling on a rope.

Wind rode   Facing into the wind and not the tidal stream, i.e. when moored or anchored.

Windward   The side the wind is blowing on to or the side of a boat opposite to that on which the mainsail is carried.

Yankee   A large high-cut jib sail.

Yawl   A rig having a main and a mizzen mast with the latter aft of the steering post.

Index